Why Don't They Give Them Guns?

The Great American Indian Myth

by Stephen E. Feraca

UNIVERSITY
PRESS OF
AMERICA

Lanham • New York • London

Copyright © 1990 by

University Press of America,® Inc.

4720 Boston Way
Lanham, MD 20706

3 Henrietta Street
London WC2E 8LU England

British Cataloging in Publication Information Available

Library of Congress Cataloging-in-Publication Data

Feraca, Stephen E., 1934–
Why don't they give them guns? : the great American Indian myth /
Stephen E. Feraca.
p.   cm.
Includes bibliographical references.
1. Indians of North America—Government relations.   2. Indians of
North America—Attitudes.   3. Indians of North America—Public
opinion.   4. Public opinion—United States.   5. United States. Bureau
of Indian Affairs.   I. Title.
E93.F35   1989   323.1'197073—dc20   89–39411 CIP

ISBN 0–8191–7624–9 (alk. paper)
ISBN 0–8191–7625–7 (pbk. : alk. paper)

oclc 20294379

The paper used in this publication meets the minimum requirements of American
National Standard for Information Sciences—Permanence of Paper for Printed Library
Materials, ANSI Z39.48–1984.   ∞

For the descendants and relatives of
Mary Fast Horse, Winyan Wastewin (1888-1970)

Eunice White Face (L) and
Mary Fast Horse, circa 1927

"My sister-in-law always lived the Sioux way and
that is why she is dressed like this (in traditional
regalia). She loved both the Indians and the Whites
and even adopted a Whiteman as her son. His last
name I cannot pronounce, but his first name is
Stephen." (Translation of remarks of an aged Oglala
Sioux gentleman at the wake of Mrs. Mary Fast Horse
held at Wounded Knee on Pine Ridge Reservation,
South Dakota, October 1970).

iii

TABLE OF CONTENTS

This book was begun more than a decade ago when I was about half-way through my career in the Bureau of Indian Affairs. The manuscript was buried and unearthed, several times, while I struggled with what was really the impossible notion of seeking publication while still employed by that agency. It became only too evident that given the circumstances I could not ethically discuss what I had in mind. Notes continued to accumulate, however, as the Indian scene changed perceptibly or remained much the same. At one point, during what can only be called a desperate moment, I actually secured written authorization from the BIA to pursue publication, I having gratuitously offered to refrain from the treatment of policy. This might have produced an interesting work but of little value in appreciating the dynamics of the historic and continuing situation. Having retired in February 1985 under the provisions of the "Honkey Out Act," which phenomenon is discussed in these pages, I became free to retrieve what had already been written, to revise just a little of it and add much, and to speak of the policies, the attitudes, the ignorance, the knowledge and the aspirations of those in authority who affect so much of Indian life. I also found myself much less constrained in reflecting the views of the proverbial man in the street that are often hardly distinct from many of those who live and work with Indian people, or from the expressions of Indians themselves.

This is not a book about the Bureau of Indian Affairs, and the writer has no inclination to join the formidable ranks of those who persist in whipping the BIA like a dead horse.[1] These same

---

[1] The Office, later Bureau, of Indian Affairs was placed under the War Department in 1824 and in 1849 was transferred to the Department of the Interior where it remains. Often known as the Indian Service, it traces its origins to the Indian

persons and groups, whether Indian or otherwise, seem usually oblivious to the fact that the concepts and practices of the Bureau almost invariably coincide with those of the dominant society. In this context I pause to affirm that throughout these pages White society is often spoken of as the dominant society simply because it is just that, and surely where Indians are concerned. If I weaken and employ the term "larger society," considered to be at least more polite in some circles, the reference is still to Whitemen. Further, I insist on capitalizing White (and Black) if Indian is to be so written. Nothing is to be read into this usage except that to do otherwise would violate the themes of this book.

This is not a history of Indian-European or Indian-American political relations. It also does not belong to the genre, revived and so popular for more than a decade, that is all too often concerned with the more bloody circumstances of culture

---

[1] *(con't.) Superintendencies maintained by the Continental Congress and modeled after the British system. It is, in fact, the oldest American bureaucracy. Histories of and commentaries on the BIA include: Laurence Schmeckebier, "The Office of Indian Affairs," Johns Hopkins Press, Baltimore, Maryland (1927); Lewis Meriam, "The Problem of Indian Administration," Johns Hopkins (1928); William Zimmerman, "The Role of the Bureau of Indian Affairs Since 1933," Annals of the American Academy of Political and Social Sciences, 311, Philadelphia, Pennsylvania (1957); Paul Stuart, "The Indian Office, 1865-1900," University Microfilm International Research Press, Ann Arbor, Michigan (1979); Alvin M. Josephy, Jr., "Red Power," American Heritage Press, New York, New York (1971); and Edgar Cahn, "Our Brother's Keeper," World Publishing, New York, New York (1969). For a general history of Federal-Indian relations see Francis Paul Prucha, "The Great Father: The United States Government and the American Indian," University of Nebraska Press, Lincoln (1984).*

conflict. I am among those who have read so much of
these works that I must at times remind myself that
the story of a given tribe cannot be chronicled
solely in terms of a series of military triumphs and
disasters. In contrast with the bow and arrow,
Winchester and Hotchkiss gun series that can
continue to delight me and so many others, woefully
little exists about more mundane and more important
and often more tragic matters. I refer to such
aspects as trading with Indians, proselytizing them,
marrying them or not bothering to marry them,
schooling them, administering their lives and
persisting in feeding them a lot of nonsense. The
reader will find, therefore, in the present effort
an avoidance of the cant usually associated with
Indian-White hostilities or the breast-beating that
accompanies the usually gross misapprehensions
concerning the acquisition of Indian land. In these
pages will be found, however, some mention of
intertribal strife and the taking or occupying of
what were sometimes vast territories by one tribe
from others. At times both the possessors and the
dispossessed seek redress from the United States
government. Rarely is it recognized that the lands
in question were often only recently acquired by a
claimant tribe that was then confronted by an even
more persistent, greedy, and powerful arrival
originating in Europe. Indians and the dominant
society both seem to be convinced that these kinds
of real estate transactions have been unknown in
other parts of the globe.

     If this work is not history (and surely it is
not anthropology), and if it is not some form of
apologia, then since it treats of American Indians
what is it? It is a survey of and commentary on the
unique combination of national guilt and what is
contempt for Indians and things Indian pervading the
attitudes of individuals at all social and economic
levels of American society. As a participant
observer of the Indian scene beginning at an early
age I have experienced in a great variety of
contexts the effects of this sense of guilt, but
some time ago I arrived at the realization of the
extent of the damage being done to each succeeding
generation of Indians. I also realized that myself
and the rest of us are all innocent of any historic

wrongdoing. In my own case my ancestors arrived too late and settled in the wrong place to acquire any land that had been recently held by Indians; and they surely would have experienced great difficulty in finding any Indians to molest. In New York City and environs the colonial Dutch and English had early on taken good care of such matters. But there are plenty of Indians to molest and much of the continuing harm is attributable to representatives of the dominant society, including many highly acculturated Indians, whose credentials in any other context are impeccable. They are educated, sophisticated and energetic people who have often at great personal sacrifice done what they sincerely believed ought to be done to better the quality of Indian life, and so redeem themselves and their society. A good many of the succeeding pages describe these people who continue to be afflicted with a form of blindness when confronted with Indian situations. They exhibit a strange breakdown of professionalism in the consideration of Indian cultural and political history, contemporary life and, in particular, severe social and economic needs and approaches to those needs. Consequently, land, jobs, schools, potable water, housing, health clinics and a host of other tangibles continue to be masked in artificial, peculiarly "Indian" features.

The basic problems, the sociopsychological, are hardly perceived to exist, this being quite understandable in consideration of the persistence of the Noble Savage myth, to say nothing of plain, ordinary ignorance about Indian societies. The extraordinary numbers of individuals who regard Indian people to be superhuman (and therefore other than human) cannot be expected to look far beyond approaches to visible Indian poverty that are designed to restore an idyllic existence. The mentality nourished by Rousseau and many other unfettered thinkers defies any reasonable gauge. It is found everywhere and applied to North American indigenes with a fervor hardly associated with any other "primitives." Europeans are not exempt. A rather politically conservative (in fact, an addmitted fascist) friend remarked to a third party that I ought to feel highly privileged working with Indians because they were untainted with social

evils, being "absolutely clean, like fish." Later
the same day this philosopher expressed his
astonishment in learning of the repression of other
tribes by the Iroquois Confederacy in its sustained
efforts to control Indian-European relations and the
trade for goods no Indian could any longer do
without.

How have these baseless, unreal and often
mindless views affected Indian people in their
efforts to adjust to the world around them? I
indulge myself in the obvious; they have not
helped. Indian perceptions of society, whether
tribal, local or larger than that, their
expectations, self-images, misconceptions and fears
are wholly or partially derived from myths,
stereotypes and cliches that have become their own
property. Of course there are numerous and
important exceptions; there always are, but those
who make the rule are only too visible in Indian
communities. The resulting "hostile dependency" is
the most basic of the extremely unhealthful aspects
of Indian existence found in all parts of the
country and among the most culturally diverse
tribes. The quoted term, embodying the worst
influences of the administered reservation system,
is a very useful one coined by two social scientists
who also made some other, very useless statements.[2]
They, too, exemplify the blind eye possessed by so
many professional observers of Indian life in, for
example, believing an ingratiating tribal informant
who assured them that foodstuffs could not be
personally owned in such a cooperative society. If
trained scientists are possessed of such naivete we
can expect that much less from the masses fed on
Rousseau, Hollywood and the nightly televised news.

My introduction to Indian society, to
pan-Indianism in its many forms, and to the
fantasies and the realities of Indian life came at

---

[2] E. E. Hagen, and Louis C. Shaw, "The Sioux
on the Reservations," Center for International
Studies, M.I.T., Cambridge (1960).

adolescence in New York City. As an omnivorous but very unselective reader of anything about Indians, a lot of it worthless as I later learned, I laid my hands on Roman Catholic mission magazines.[3] This was natural enough as I attended a parochial school and a Catholic high school. These publications often featured articles on the incredibly poor but faithful Indians. There was barely a hint of the existence of any aid but that provided by the good priests and nuns. Duly conned, I in turn conned some close friends into forming a mission aid society to provide clothing and funds. I will say nothing more about these activities except that one of the techniques employed to collect used clothing, and very limited cash donations, was to stage "Indian" shows at primarily Catholic grade schools. The rhetorical question concerning blood quantum that forms the title of the first chapter was overheard when I was thirteen during my first year in high school. The conversation took place in a tiny Indian handicraft store located in a most unlikely, commercially isolated Bronx neighborhood. The individual quoted was unimpeachably Indian, and Sioux, and had for many years billed himself as a grandson of Sitting Bull. As a professional showman he was at least in that respect of interest to us in our zeal to clothe and feed poor Indians. I had gone there to meet him with admiration approaching something religious since I had already begun reading biographical material about his impugned ancestor. (It is entirely accidental, but I think worth notation, that the last official letter I drafted while in the employ of the BIA concerned the arrest and the killing by Indian police of that innocent Hunkpapa Sioux chief. Shortly after my retirement a descendant of the agent who ordered the arrest sent me a beautiful piece of catlinite or red pipestone from Minnesota).

----

[3] The Bureau of Catholic Indian Missions was established in Washington, D.C. in 1879, long after Catholic missionary activity began among United States Indians. It operates today and issues a Newsletter.

Readers will find much in reference to the Sioux in this book; some will undoubtedly say indeed too much. Anticipating the criticism I say now that the mounted, tipi-dwelling, warbonnetted, buffalo-hunting, warrior society of the Western or Teton Sioux is more responsible for the national and international Indian image than any other Indian tribe or group. The names of some of their leaders, including some contemporary militants, and events in their history such as the Little Big Horn, have become household terms that affect the self-identity of Indians as foreign to them as Albanians are to Cantonese. But more important it is the Sioux who have been the guinea pigs of approaches to the "Indian problem" running the gamut of war and peace policies, a kaleidoscope of missionary persuasion and all of the associated techniques, a bewildering variety of education philosophies and land use projects that have been spectacular failures. They have suffered all sorts of other related phenomena that mirror quite a bit of what comprises the Indian world. Their past and current situations are particularly indicative of the confusion surrounding tribal nomenclatures, territorial origins, socioeconomic backgrounds and the contemporary Indian political scene. The very name by which they have supposedly become so well known, including by Europeans who usually render it as "Seeyooks," is not their own as is the case with practically every tribe.

My study and work experiences have in no sense been limited to the Sioux. I have usually enjoyed, and at various times bitterly cursed, employment spanning more than 25 years with the Bureau of Indian Affairs, beginning in 1959. Most of that time I operated within the central office in Washington, D.C., and consequently have been close to the Indian atmosphere in the capital city. Two years during the 1960's were spent with the Seminoles of Florida, officially in the fields of education and community services and unofficially with what should be referred to as the bizarre. Suffice it for the moment to say that virtually everything that other tribes have endured for so long has been visited on that unfortunate people only during the last few decades.

For most of the years in Washington I was
assigned to the processing of Indian claims awards
cases, not the litigation of the claims (but we too
sometimes ended up in court) but after the fact of
the granting of a monetary award. Such judgments
are usually made for lands lost well into the last
century. The initial problem was that of
researching the cases and making recommendations
concerning the ultimate or present-day beneficiaries
of awards that often enough amounted to many
millions. In some instances, two or more entities
would be involved in which circumstances we would
usually have a party over the division of the pie.
In this capacity I became intimately acquainted with
the political affairs of very diverse tribal groups,
the peculiar problems of tribal government, an array
of now old and also very contemporary tribal
enrollment situations, and with legal precedent or
the absence of such. In all this, as with field
work on reservations in South Dakota or Florida, or
on visits to tribes affected by claims awards, a
background in cultural anthropology, or in North
American ethnohistory in particular, was a burden as
much as it was of any value. Such disciplines are
of little help while being confronted by societies
disintegrating before one's eyes, by people who know
nothing of their history and who create tradition
overnight, or who want their money yesterday or who
do not want it at all. Those in the latter category
seem convinced that the "Washington man" sent out to
discuss handling the money is in some manner
responsible for taking land from them that they
themselves never used or occupied. This lamentation
should not convey that my all-consuming interest in
every facet of Indian life, including the
construction of many items of material culture (for
I am among other things an "artifaker"), and above
all greatly enjoying the company of Indian people
were not of incalculable worth in functioning in any
programing capacity.

        Unlike most of the denizens of academia,
those bureaucrats who simply do not associate
socially with their Indian colleagues or clients
(including some Indian bureaucrats), people who are
only bona fide Indians, and White "hobbyists" who
interact only with each other, I have been in what

*half-facetiously can be regarded as an enviable
position. As a big city boy of Italian origin (of
all things) who has never made a secret of his
involvement with Indians and the BIA, I have indeed
gotten it from all sides. I have discussed
replicating stone pipes, the content of treaties,
the abandonment of children, the surrenders (in
plural) of Geronimo and the extent of Indian
alcoholism in Indian bars and bars where an Indian
may have never tread. I have discussed such matters
on commuter buses, on street corners, in tribal
council meetings and in the halls of the American
Museum of Natural History. Very often my listeners
were more than skeptical that any knowledge or
understanding of such things could be possessed by a
product of "Brooklyn." (If Indians are all alike to
most people, New York City to the rest of the
country is equated with the one legendary borough
that is almost as foreign to other New Yorkers as an
Indian reservation).*

*The quotations that are found throughout this
book are reflective of what I have heard about
Indians from the most diverse sources. Some of them
represent obvious knee-jerk reactions or bed-rock
ignorance. Most of those responsible for the
statements I have chosen among countless others to
be worthy of note are friends and acquaintances.
Others are total strangers. The statements they
have made, with few exceptions, have been much the
same and in fact identical to a startling degree for
more than forty years (many can be found in early
American history). These utterances, usually
unsolicited and often annoying, have nevertheless to
me been always instructive, as was one of the
latest. This was made only days before penning the
present lines by the fellow patron of a
watering-hole located walking distance from my
home. Overhearing the owner-operator and me
bantering about my retirement he observed that, "The
trouble with the BIA is that it's full of Whites."
I calmly retorted that, "The damn thing is 80
percent Indian." My Sioux godson, whose phenotype
is as Indian as the composite on the nickel, but of
much younger vintage, quickly confirmed the
figure. The belligerent was not to be mollified so
we felt obligated to admit that the agency was truly*

being run by Whitemen or individuals who were barely
Indian in any sense. Neither of us had the courage
to advise that of the longest term fixtures who had
wielded the most influence one was of German and
Slavic descent and the other Japanese, both sexes
being represented. Most of these contributors, like
this Pavlovian type who has little better to do than
harass me while I'm trying to relax, had no hint,
nor did those who played parts in the anecdotes and
vignettes illustrating the concerns of this book,
that they were being recorded (but mentally or on
scraps of paper, never on tapes or the like).
Others undoubtedly knew or at least had their
suspicions.

There are included among the individuals who
have unknowingly played roles in this book many who
have urged its production. A lot of them probably
hope that it will somehow finally silence me, these
well-wishers being found both within and without the
ranks of former or present BIA employees. I am
indebted also to my wife and children for their
constant encouragement. The former is legally an
Indian in that she is a member of the Minnesota
Chippewa Tribe. My children are not Indians but
merely counted among the millions of White, Hispanic
and Black Americans, like the legions of descendants
of Pocahontas, who happen to have Indian ancestry,
some more and some less. They were not enrolled
with the tribe and are now no longer eligible, not
having the required blood quantum. One was born too
late and I'll have further comment on this topic.
We declined to have the first two then eligible
children enrolled simply because we were loathe to
swell the numbers of non-tribally oriented people
whose names are nevertheless on the official books
of the tribes.

Many years ago a very intelligent woman, an
immigrant who was the mother of a close friend and
who found intriguing my association with Indians,
asked, "What do they talk about, the Indians?" In
contrast with the many, including doctors, lawyers
and educators, who ask if only conversationally
which is the "fiercest" tribe, or the poorest,
or the richest, this question has haunted me and may
be responsible for the true beginnings of this

commentary. In large measure, this book is
concerned with what Indians talk about and with what
other people say about them. Both often speak the
same language and what emerges has formed a most
inconsistent, baseless and progressively harmful
view of a society.

Very pertinent to the writing of this book is
a particular sense of unfulfillment, actually a
sense of obligation to Indian people that I
earnestly hope is conveyed in these pages. Above
all, I remain anxious that these same .people receive
this work kindly and understand that I am urging
that they be treated with respect and as responsible
contributors to the cultural polyglot that is
America.

Reston, Virginia
September 1985

PROLOGUE

"And this is my son, Doctor, just returned from the wilds. He and his bride are spending the week with us." The doctor had an Irish surname, was tall, approaching seventy and distinguished looking (I learned later that he was an "eminent surgeon"). We shook hands briskly. He observed in a commanding voice a little too loud for the church steps on which we were standing, "So this is the young man who's been working on an Indian reservation. Your father has told me all about you. Where are you, in North Dakota?"

The scene was Christmas morning, 1959, in Scarsdale, New York. I had been married the previous month on Pine Ridge Reservation, South Dakota, specifically at Holy Rosary Mission, the site of the last armed conflict of any real scope between Indians and Whites. I could not help reflecting during the overlong nuptial mass (they are always overlong), that my wife was born and raised at Wounded Knee on the same reservation, where a genuine massacre occurred on December 29, 1890, and the following day a large number of justly enraged Sioux had pinned down the Seventh Cavalry near the spot where I was uncomfortably kneeling. The place was then known as Drexel Mission.

Many of the wedding guests were descendants of those "Ghost Dancers" killed at Wounded Knee, of those who fought the following day, or of Sioux who were scouts for the U.S. Army at the time. Some had ancestry in all three categories. All of them, and I, were a far cry from my native Bronx, or from Scarsdale.

I hastily corrected the good doctor. It was South, not North, Dakota and offered that I had been employed with the Pine Ridge Indian Agency for some time. "Whatever made you go way out there?"

The explanation was given in simplistic, almost dishonest, terms. I had spent five summers on the same reservation, beginning in 1954 when I arrived just prior to my twentieth birthday. I had, after all, done most of my field studies in

1

ethnology there. This had to suffice. Under the circumstances, how could one attempt to explain that working and living with Oglala Sioux Indian people could be so gratifying, most of the time.

The eminent doctor was persistent. "What are conditions like out there, anyway?" Very bad, I said, and proceeded with a litany. Next to nothing in employment, broken homes, ongoing deculturation (the last term I think I explained), increased drinking, worsening confusion surrounding questions of tribal political status and relations with the federal and state governments, practically no attention to the special needs of local communities, etc., etc., etc. Yes, Doctor, the people are extremely poor in practically every sense but still a vibrant group.

The doctor predicted his damnation, said that such conditions were "just intolerable" and concluded by facing my father and sputtering that he simply could not understand "what the hell is the matter with the government. Why don't they give them guns so they can at least hunt and get something to eat?"

CHAPTER ONE

"HOW MUCH BLOOD YOU GOT?"

A South Dakota Sioux to a
German Jew in the Bronx.

In any attempt to define Indianness some
cliches should be dealt with at the outset.
Foremost among these are the constantly repeated
assertions that the indigenes of the Americas were
misnamed and that another name for them should be
found. It simply does not occur to those who voice
such sentiments, meaning practically everyone, that
it was Europeans who named India and called the
diverse societies of that huge subcontinent
"Indiani," "Indios," "Indians" or other similar
derivatives. These terms were applied equally to
the inhabitants of the southern tip of India to the
Indus Valley peoples of the north who were first
known to Europeans, at least since Alexander the
Great, and who gave rise to the generic name. The
peoples of India have generally accepted the name
for their relatively new nation and the overall
English appellation for themselves. The separate
existences of Pakistan and Bangladesh are duly
noted, as is the penchant of Indians to engage in
bloody riots whenever any serious attempt is made to
establish Hindi as the national language. Americans
continue to wince at the application of the term to
"our Indians," convinced that in no other instance
has ignorance, political fortune or the adoption of
the name of a minority populace been responsible for
the grouping of extremely different peoples under a
single heading. There was a time when no one in
what became India called himself an Indian. I hope
to be forgiven by those many millions of people and
their government for suggesting that if Whitemen had
not controlled that part of the world and named the
land and the people it is unlikely that there would
be an India today in the form familiar to us. The
list of such evolutions includes England with a name
derived from only one Germanic invader; and Italia,
the whole of that peninsula being in time so spoken

3

of by the Romans after the Italic tribes, southern peoples who were actually brutally oppressed by them. In short, American Indians are not alone.

Anthropologists and others have utterly failed in their efforts, which were not solicited anyway, to clarify or simplify the situation. Indians, thankfully, have never really been known as "Amerindians," or worse, "Amerins." Lately, some sustained efforts have been made, and in some instances officially so as applied to federal programs, to persuade Indians and the dominant society toward the term "Native Americans." The predictable child of this usage, even more unpalatable to me and many concerned others, is simply "Natives." I am aware of what is provided in the dictionaries, but "native" does not distinguish between an indigene (or aborigine) and a native American such as myself. I was, after all, born in this country as were my parents. How then, does a young attorney with an obvious but mixed central European accent, born across the Atlantic of an Oklahoma Indian mother and a European father, acquire native status if I do not? A good deal of the fault in all this lies with the pejorative connotations found in "aborigine" and somewhat less so in "indigene." Far be it from me to suggest that Indians be termed "Aborigines" and subsequently acquire the epithet "Abo" as in Australia, or "Indigenes" which so easily lends itself to something like "Indins" or "Injuns," both lamentably still often heard. Alaskans, however, have been stuck legislatively and in ordinary bureaucratic usage with the label "Alaska Natives." They seem to have little or no difficulty with this even though such distinct peoples as Eskimos of any linguistic classification, Aleuts, Tlingits and a variety of Athapaskans are all so grouped. Whether they are of as much Russian or other non-Indian ancestry or whether they have ever lived in Alaska is immaterial. They have all become "Natives." There are many ways to destroy tribal identity, not the least of them being plain, ordinary carelessness in nomenclature.

Whatever the sociological or historical problems, the term "Indian" as applied to the early inhabitants of the Americas has great strength and is overwhelmingly acceptable to Indians. We will all, including Indians, have to inure ourselves to the fellow passenger seated next to me on an aircraft explaining that his next-door neighbor is not "one of your kind; he's an India Indian," and the one across the aisle who declares that his grandmother "can really talk Indian."

Indians encounter or create many problems in defining and asserting themselves as such. Quite illustrative of these phenomena is one of the most hilarious and simultaneously one of the most offensive episodes in my entire career. It occurred during the administration of President Lyndon Johnson. The air at the time was charged with electricity as the first Indian since President U.S. Grant's tenure of office was about to take the oath as Commissioner of Indian Affairs. A White friend and colleague came into my office literally holding his sides in mirth. "That one down the hall actually got her hair done yesterday," he finally shrilled while doubled-up. The source of his amusement, and then mine, was not actually the "mixed blood" employee with very little in the way of Indian physical features who had visited a beauty salon. We are not so crude as to find that much amusement in anyone's hair style. What we were laughing at was the poor woman's great disappointment and that of many other people in the building. She, and all of us employees excepting a handful of managers, had just learned that she was not, despite all her preparations, welcome at the "swearing." Robert LaFollette Bennett, a member of the Oneida Tribe of Wisconsin and a pure product of BIA society (Haskell Indian School, etc.), had risen from the ranks to the then exalted level of Area Director of Alaska. He was much intent, along with the White House, on being surrounded by Indians while taking the oath. Accordingly, the tribal chairmen, or chiefs or presidents, were invited to attend. As the day fast approached with little response from "Indian country," Bennett and the troops panicked. Whether the problem stemmed from poor planning or uncertainty regarding the financing of this spectacle, or a combination of such factors, I have never learned. I do know that the word went out, officially, to all central office employees of at least one-quarter Indian blood that they, and only they, were invited. No other employees were to attend. I was not the only one good and mad at this directive and said so, loudly. For a day or two my anger was, however, tempered by amusement as individuals protested that they really did possess one-quarter blood because one ancestor or the other was erroneously listed as having less blood than entitled. Others wondered whether to wear Indian regalia (which usually meant turquoise and silver jewelry). Very few, Indian or otherwise, seemed concerned about what kind of impression the White-appearing Indians would make when those in control obviously were seeking a genuine Indian backdrop. One fellow worker who was eligible to attend, being one-quarter blood on official records, realized that he would tax the best of make-up artists in creating in him anything resembling Indian features. He once served as a tribal chairman; a highly professional genealogist was unable to find in his background any Indian ancestry whatsoever.

On the morning of the historic day the lady who had her hair done, the biological Whiteman who had once headed a tribal government and all of the others placed in a holding pattern, including individuals who looked stereotypically Indian, were told that they would not be in attendance. Enough chiefs had indicated that they were on their way to Washington, D.C., some with an extra suitcase containing their feathers. Some of them had neither much Indian blood nor a useful phenotype. Bennett, whose father was White, was administered the oath by the President of the United States in 1966. All of his successors (later, the title became "Assistant Secretary for Indian Affairs") have been Indian to some extent.[1]

---

[1] Biographical sketches of the Commissioners and Assistant Secretaries of Indian Affairs are found in: Robert M. Kvasnicka and Herman J. Viola, "The Commissioners of Indian Affairs, 1824-1977,"

Identifying Indians or defining Indianness
cannot in this country be divorced from the
presumption of blood quantum. It is, however,
fundamental to the understanding of what makes an
Indian, and to what functional degree, to distinguish
among that which is legal, racial, cultural and
sociological. I am persuaded that my spouse's
situation well illustrates how an individual fits or
does not fit these basic classifications. She is a
duly enrolled member of the Minnesota Chippewa
Tribe, more specifically designated as a Removal
Mille Lacs Mississippi Band member affiliated with
the White Earth Reservation, the tribal organization
encompassing five other reservation entities. She
is, therefore, legally an Indian on the basis of
such enrollment. Her father was White. According
to tribal and agency records she possesses
one-sixteenth Chippewa blood derived from a
great-grandmother who was designated as one-half
blood. She looks quite Indian.

But what is an Indian supposed to look like?
Almost simplistically, the answer is that an Indian
looks Mongoloid. Anthropologists and other social
scientists are today most reluctant to think in
terms of race or have abandoned the concept
altogether, preferring to speak of "population
groups" or the like, but such terminology does not
lend itself to the problems at hand. A biologically
full blooded Mohave, or someone who has inherited
such traits regardless of other ancestry, does not
look like a Navajo similarly situated. A San Juan
Pueblo does not resemble a Teton Sioux, and a
Western Apache is easily distinguished from Tlingits
and other Alaskans although related to Athapaskans
of that state and Canada. They all do, however,
have Mongoloid traits and all derive ultimately from
Asia. I am not suggesting that Indians look Chinese

---

[1] (con't.) University of Nebraska Press,
Lincoln (1979); and Smithsonian Institution,
"Handbook of North American Indians, Volume Four,
History of Indian-White Relations," Washington
(1988).

but the wife of an Indian Health Service doctor in South Dakota once observed that some of the local Sioux "look like they ought to be operating hand laundries." She was unaware that such "unspecified" Mongoloid features (another term in disrepute) are common in Indian people throughout the Americas. Indians are not simply people with black or dark straight hair, bronze complexions and the Hollywood variety of prominent or aquiline, usually Mediterranean, facial features including crows feet. They also cannot, if of unmixed ancestry, have blue eyes or kinky hair. If they are not Mongoloid in appearance, quite apart from complexion, then they look like Indians only to some lesser extent. Most Mexicans look Indian, including those who would take gross offense at such classification. With few exceptions, Indians in this country refuse to accept any Hispanics as Indians in any sense. They will, however, more than tolerate all kinds of phenotypes on the silver screen, not differing in this respect from the dominant society, as long as feathers and head bands are visible. There is no better or more recent evidence for this than the enthusiasm with which most Indians greeted the highly touted and utterly unauthentic television production titled "The Mystic Warrior." However, some Indians, including the Sioux anthropologists JoAllyn Archambault and Bea Medicine, denounced and attempted to stop the film. There was only one Indian with a speaking part, but even militant Indian spokesmen deluded themselves into praising this soap opera as a movie with a primarily Indian cast. The exception, whose features were distinctly Indian, was the Creek actor, the late Will Sampson. His role was miniscule.

Much more important than any real or presumed Indian physical features, particularly in view of the fact that Indians themselves often embrace individuals without a single Indian racial trait, are sociological factors. By this I mean whether someone is accepted and recognized by either Indian society or the larger society as an Indian and treated as such. My wife is sociologically Indian as far as both societies are concerned, and she has been denied the use of restaurant toilet facilities and has been hooted at by Whites. Culturally Indian she is not, although acquainted with some traditional and many more relatively recent traits associated with an Indian lifestyle. She played with, attended school with and served in her father's store Oglala Sioux Indians, most of whom were sociological full bloods (a concept discussed later) and many of them probably wholly of Indian ancestry. She has had next to no involvement with the affairs of the White Earth Reservation or the Minnesota Chippewa Tribe. However, she has received three small checks representing her per capita shares of Mississippi Band land claims awards.

Another Chippewa (Ojibwa), Ed High Rock (a pseudonym), is not of the Woodland but of the Plains variety. He generally resides on the Rocky Boy's Reservation of the Chippewa Cree Tribe in Montana where his wife is enrolled. Phenotypically, High Rock represents the stereotype of the equestrian Plains Indian, is a native speaker of the Plains or Bungi dialect of Chippewa, also speaks Plains Cree, and is enrolled nowhere. His family moved so often in Montana, being among the "landless" people of that state, that they never appeared on any of the censuses utilized to establish tribal rolls. He is in every sense but the legal a member of the Chippewa Cree Tribe, an entity that only officially dates from 1916. The tribe, however, bound by its even more recent constitutional enrollment provisions, is unable to admit him. This situation, not unique, is of course totally nontraditional. Formal enrollment concepts and procedures have been adopted by the tribes and I am the first to agree that they are entirely necessary. Provisions can and should be made, though, such as selectively amending tribal constitutions, to relieve the situations of the Ed High Rocks of the Indian world. Such are particularly ironic phenomena in view of the thousands of individuals who are sociologically, culturally and racially White but are tribal members. Further, large numbers of mixed bloods, including those with Indian ancestry contributed by both parents, would be hard pressed to find a forebear with an original Indian name, this condition obtaining even in the last century. Ed High Rock would experience no such difficulty.

Hardly exhausting the varieties of Indianness, I include the cases of two members of the Seminole Nation of Oklahoma. One man, and his wife, is as Negroid in appearance as he is Indian, which is not wholly ignored by his peers. He is one of the principal traditionalists of the tribe and one of the officers of a "stomp ground," which is a center of the ancient, pre-Christian religion containing a ceremonial fire. This man is enrolled as a Seminole "by blood" and is a native speaker of the language as is his entire family who all reside on the ceremonial site. Another enrollee is wholly Negroid phenotypically, but is most probably also of Seminole ancestry which he cannot prove. He derives from the "Freedmen" element, very numerous within the tribe, whose ancestors were not so much slaves of the Seminoles in the Florida homeland, but escaped slaves of Georgians who formed their own towns within the Seminole territory. During the infamous Seminole wars they exhibited a level of courage that was matched only by the Seminoles themselves who had protected them from slave raiders. By an 1866 treaty they were freed and became full members of the tribe, and in 1906 were officially enrolled. If all of the eligible descendants of the Seminole Freedmen actually became enrolled they would probably number at least 5,000 (the enrollment by blood would be more than 9,000). The subject individual, locally considered to be Black, has long represented one of the two Freedmen "bands" within the tribal council of fourteen bands (from the historic tribal towns), speaks the Seminole variety of the Muskogee or Creek language, which is extraordinary for a modern Freedman, but is deemed eligible for no federal Indian services. I am among the few who have long been convinced that the Freedmen who are enrolled tribal members should be eligible for all those federal services or programs that do not require the one-quarter blood minimum. I include Indian preference in employment with the Bureau of Indian Affairs and the Indian Health Service, as odious as I find such preference as concerns anyone at all.

Before leaving these categories I am constrained to include those who are the products of Indian society, particularly that special society of

the BIA and off-reservation boarding schools and
urban Indian communities, but who have no definite
tribal identity. These are the people, whether
enrolled with a tribe or not, who announce that they
are "Pima-Seneca," which is like saying
"Lebanese-Hungarian," or "Otoe-Delaware-Wasco,"
representing an even greater mixture of totally
unrelated tribes. With increasing frequency,
persons in still another category identify with the
reservation or agency name and are unsure about any
specific tribal origin. One of the prize examples
of mixed tribal origins, real or assumed, is that of
a graduate of Indian boarding schools, born in
Oklahoma, who rose to an impressive height in the
BIA. When asked with which tribe he was enrolled
the answer was, "For Bureau purposes I'm a
Wichita." (I employ fictional but illustrative
tribal names). His mother was of Great Lakes
Potawatomi ancestry who had been adopted by a
Mexican captive of the Comanches. This man speaks
his adoptive grandfather's tribal language and is
knowledgeable in the traditions of that tribe. He
proudly displayed two of the bows his grandfather
had used for hunting. He looks quite White and is
in no sense a "Wichita" except, evidently, the
"legal."

All of those described above are Indians, yet
we have seen that not one fully meets all the
criteria in terms of the racial, the sociological,
the cultural and the legal. This is increasingly
the situation throughout the country with some
tribes being comprised of persons who are little
more than legal Indians. In other instances tribes
are formed of individuals who are Indian by all tests
and largely biologically full blooded, or look like
they are. Among the former are the Miamis of
Oklahoma and the Narragansetts of Rhode Island (a
very new addition to the tribal roster) and among
the latter the Utes of Utah and Colorado and the
Western Apaches of Arizona. With the adoption of
blood quantum limitations by tribes as they formally
organized, many older tribal members are now found
among the more acculturated and the less Indian in
appearance. A fine old man residing on Fort Peck
Reservation in Montana said, "I wouldn't have made
it today; I don't have the blood."

While it has long been held that the tribes, whether formally organized or not, are responsible for their own membership criteria, it has also been more recently established that they can blithely ignore sociological factors. In 1978 the United States Supreme Court rendered a decision in the *Martinez* case involving the Santa Clara Pueblo of New Mexico (an astonishing number of Indian controversies reach that court).[2] Julia Martinez, a full blooded Santa Clara and evidently a lifelong resident of the pueblo, had married a Navajo. The pueblo's government refused to enroll their children. This decision was made on the basis of a tribal ordinance providing that the children of male members and non-members be admitted but not the reverse. We are here concerned with definitions of Indianness but it should be remarked in passing that the real problem with the Martinez decision is that it essentially provided that the courts have no jurisdiction over a tribal government and its officers. If a tribal government can deny enrollment to individuals who are participants in the tribal society it can also convey rights to those who are far removed. Only recently a Sioux tribal court admitted to membership a child who cannot possibly approach the one-quarter specific tribal blood required and who was born and resides almost two thousand miles away from the home reservation. It is also a safe bet that the new enrollee will never be associated with any Sioux community. In his magnaminity the tribal judge conveyed United States citizenship on the applicant, whose status in that regard was not open to question anyway.

Ultimately, blood quantum may be characterized as nothing more than the perversion, as applied to racial mixtures, of the ancient and unscientific belief prevalent in the Old World and still very much in vogue, that one inherits blood from all ancestors and that with blood are inherited physical,

---

[2] *Santa Clara Pueblo, et al.,* v. *Julia Martinez, et al.,* 436 U.S. 49 (1978).

mental and cultural attributes (the "blood will tell" cliche). As applied to North American Indians, the concept and terminology are about as old as European contact, "half breed," "full blood," and "pure blood" being household terms long before the era of Westward Expansion. It is to be expected, therefore, that the concept would be incorporated into Indian affairs legislation and regulations. An Act of May 25, 1918, places the limit for special education services to Indians, including day school enrollment, at one-quarter blood. Employment services involve the quarter blood quantum criterion for adult vocational training.

My personal experience has been that BIA personnel, both Indian and non-Indian, are very often imbued with some of the larger society's most ludicrous views of the blood quantum aspect. These range from great surprise at the sophistication of a supposed biological full blood, or the solemn pronouncement that a particular individual could not possibly be a full blood in view of his baldness, to the school teacher on Pine Ridge Reservation who proudly announced that she often exhorted her mixed blood pupils to "show what that quarter or eighth blood can do." Some of these young people had given evidence of a sense of inferiority about their lack of Indian blood or associated physical traits, a common problem encountered in Indian communities.

Typical of the funny remarks made about Indian blood is that of the Washington, D.C. cabdriver who boasted about his Indianness, declaring that he was of one-third blood. The Secretary of the Colorado River Tribes, herself a Mohave who complained about a dissident threatening to form a separate tribe of the Chemehuevi element at Colorado River, asserted that this man had practically no Indian blood and that "he lost that when he cut himself." Not too idly, I have often wondered how many people actually conceive of a measurable quantity of Indian blood either coursing through their veins or, in truly medieval style, being stationary in a specific part of the corpus. Apropos the situation of the Chemehuevis, a really tiny group if spoken of sociologically and

13

culturally, is that a tribe was not formed after all by the gentleman who was the subject of my visitor's ire. It was Congress, in its unwisdom, encouraged by a White BIA official who is a cultural anthropologist, that established a tribal organization in the process of distributing the Chemehuevi land claims award. The actions of all the involved executives and solons, taken after I transferred to a Florida field office, resulted in the creation of a tribe of urban southern California Hispanics, few bona fide Chemehuevis having joined. For the record, I and others had strenuously urged that the Chemehuevi funds and their uninhabited reservation all be comingled with the Colorado River tribal patrimony.

Blood quantum designations were established long after the tribes had intermixed with Europeans and, particularly in the Southeast, also with Africans. Even if the admixture had not begun so early, there still remains the fact that Indian people are not the products of controlled breeding; no society is. But there are plenty of official documents and directives that more than imply that such is the case. One of the more notable of these is a memorandum of July 26, 1965, titled "Determining degree of Indian blood," from the Commissioner of Indian Affairs to field personnel and tribal officials. The paper was actually signed by James E. Officer as Associate Commissioner, himself an anthropologist as was the Commissioner, Philleo Nash. It states in part:

> *In cases where a discrepancy in degree of Indian blood shown on a roll is determined to be the result of a mathematical error in computation, such as one parent being shown as 4/4 degree, the other parent shown as 3/4 degree, and their children listed as 5/8 degree rather than 7/8, changes will be made by the official approving the roll. The changes will be called to the attention of the tribal officials and a list of the changes and the reasons therefor will be attached to the roll.*

This kind of unavoidable nonsense gives rise to Indians identifying themselves with a straight face in terms of fractions. It is still alarming to me to hear an otherwise thoughtful person say with total self-assurance that he is "five-eighths Indian" (or "nine-sixteenths" or "seventeen-thirty-seconds") or something else equally ridiculous and just as meaningless from an ethnic or sociological standpoint. Genetically, such labels are not at all of the value they purport to be. One-half, for example, does not convey that one parent is Indian and the other is not. I have been caught by this one myself and was unable to destroy all of the copies of a paper of mine in which this piece of illogic appeared. The same above-cited memorandum directs that:

> In determining degree of Indian blood possessed by illegitimate children only 1/2 of the degree of Indian blood possessed by the mother may be counted unless paternity has been acknowledged by the purported father or established through the courts. If paternity has been established, the document on which the determination is based should be cited. Statements made by the mother as to the paternity of the child will not be acceptable.

This, I submit, is absurd, but it is acceptable to Indians. Long before the issuance of this missive I discussed the problem with the President of the Oglala Sioux tribal council. I suggested that most of the fathers in such cases were probably Indian and of the same tribe. He scoffed, saying "Oh, no. It can't be; they're Washichu (the general Sioux term for Whites)." I remain unaware of any young male Indians who thereby feel insulted.

The dominant society has been very successful in foisting the fiction of blood quantum on the tribes. Among the more spurious tribal "base rolls," from which contemporary tribal rolls are derived, is that of the Turtle Mountain Band of Chippewas of North Dakota. The members of the Turtle Mountain Band, about 28,000 in number, are

15

overwhelmingly Red River _Metis_, meaning "half" in French and rendered _Michif_ in the Metis jargon of archaic French, Plains Cree and Plains Chippewa. These people formed, through French and Indian intermarriage, a fascinating buffalo-hunting and trading society on the American and Canadian Plains, marginal to the traditional Chippewas and Crees and to the Anglo societies of both countries. They were responsible in the 1860's and 1880's, in their attempts to form a separate nation, for two rebellions in Canada that constitute the only "Indian" wars fought in the Dominion. Only two Cree bands militarily supported the Metis. At least 20,000 of these people actually reside in North Dakota and Montana with thousands more in Canada, especially in Winnipeg, where they are not accorded Indian tribal status. Many others are scattered throughout both countries. In North Dakota, before the turn of the century, Canadian Metis refugees inundated the lands of their traditional Chippewa relatives, causing chiefs Little Shell and Rocky Boy to actually leave the Turtle Mountain Reservation. However, in Manitoba and Saskatchewan the Plains Ojibwa reserves contain truly tribal people and few or no Metis. At Turtle Mountain all of the Metis were originally listed as one-half blood, and all of the traditional people, a small minority, were listed as four-fourths blood. In another sense, if the terms half blood and full blood have any sociological significance, then it might be said that the Turtle Mountain rolls truly reflect the existence of two rather distinct sociological groups. However, consider the situation of a four-fourths Chippewa from a traditional family married to a White and who has half blood children. These children are not Metis.

On the Florida Seminole base roll of 1957 practically every adult is listed as four-fourths despite the plethora of very obvious Caucasoid and Negroid traits. Only in those instances in which the existence of a Black ancestor was remembered is an aged person listed as less than four-fourths. Some ethnologists and bureaucrats, when questioned about romantic groups such as the Seminoles, are loathe to admit of widespread intermixture. A noted anthropologist, now of the Smithsonian, assured a gathering of Columbia University graduate students years ago that the overwhelming majority of Florida Seminoles was unquestionably full blooded on the strength of a study revealing type O blood for almost the entire tribe. My good wife is of German, Irish, French, Dutch, English and Chippewa ancestry. Her possession of type O blood is not to be considered a genetic miracle. In this context it should be noted that the Florida Seminoles are extremely inbred.

Blood quantum can be a very useful device in developing a viable tribal organization. I reference the case of the Prairie Potawatomies of Kansas. It is evident that the tribe's BIA-conceived constitution of 1961 fails to grant recognition to the local community. The great majority of the membership simply is not part of the local community, enrollment being originally desired by these people primarily for the purpose of including themselves in the distribution of a claims award. It is apparent that a blood quantum restriction of one-quarter, which was not included in the 1961 membership provision, would have been a distinct asset to the formation of a representative tribal community.[3] Fanciful as blood quantum designations may be (and some are utterly laughable such as an Aleut friend listing himself as a full blood and all his ancestors as three-quarters), some observers are realistic in recognizing that the quarter-blood limitation is of value in view of extensive intermarriage with non-Indians. Further, it is virtually harmless as very few individuals yet unborn would be participating members of tribal society absent the possession, albeit on paper, of a quarter degree of blood. I have met few Indians who insist on a higher fraction, but a few tribes provide for a half blood limitation. Tribes with no blood quantum criterion nevertheless think and

---

[3] James A. Clifton, "The Prairie People: Continuity and Change in Potawatomi Indian Culture 1665-1965," The Regents Press of Kansas, Lawrence (1977), pp.431-37.

speak in terms of blood. Extensive damage has already been done as far as many tribes are concerned, but for the unborn those tribes without the limitation should be encouraged to adopt it. Legislation is probably necessary, however, unless Congress continues to accept that all the tribes are to be left to their own devices in defining membership. In so doing they continue to create White, Hispanic and Black Indians who today do not resemble the frontier children of White fathers and Indian mothers, the old Freedmen or the Mexican captives of Kiowas or Comanches. In saying this I remain fully cognizant that with each passing day even full bloods, at least as so designated on a tribal roll, are becoming further and further removed from tribal life.

"Full blood" and "mixed blood" can and should have meanings other than biological. In 1937 the Superintendent of the Pine Ridge Agency wrote in a letter to the Commissioner: "The typical person referred to as a mixed blood is well exemplified in the President of the Council. He is proud of his white attitudes. He refers to full blood Indians in his letters and in his speeches as ration Indians, and indicates that they are non-progressive, and non-intelligent." These days, neither the letter itself nor any such sentiment publicly expressed by a tribal leader is conceivable. I hasten to add, though, that I have known and continue to know many mixed bloods who refer to full blood types as "black" (in color), as being "just like niggers" (in behavior), as being "dumb Indians" or as a lot of other unsavory things. Some of these same individuals occupy influential positions as professional Indians.

The terms found in the letter quoted are employed in a sociological rather than a biological context. The anthropologist Gordon Macgregor, who himself served as an Agency Superintendent, coined the terms "sociological" mixed blood and full blood.[4]

_____

4   Gordon H. Macgregor, "Warriors Without

18

*The full blood (sociologically understood) resembles
the traditional but modified reservation Indian
regardless of any admixture with other tribes or
other races, and the mixed blood more closely
resembles the surrounding Whites. All sorts of
gradations are evident in both categories with some
borderline cases being difficult to classify.
Macgregor applied the concept to the Pine Ridge
Sioux but it is reflective of the atmosphere found
in many tribes, particularly on the Plains, in
Oklahoma and in the Plateau area. The concept,
however, is of decreasing usefulness as more and
more young mixed bloods sport long hair (generally,
with exceptions such as Navajos and Pueblos, the
hair styles of both full and mixed bloods were short
prior to the new nativist trends), participate in
Indian social dancing and in such religious
ceremonies as the Sun Dance, and consort with
shamans. Full bloods are very rapidly losing, with
exceptions, the tribal languages, the preference for
an Indian language being at one time one of the
basic criteria in distinguishing between the two
sociological groupings. Among the fully
acculturated mixed bloods have lately emerged some
of the longest haired exponents of what they and the
general public perceive to be tradition. It is, of
course, impossible for a tribe or a federal agency
to officially classify the membership in any
sociological sense. I am personally acquainted with
a significant number of individuals on tribal rolls
as "four-fourths," and who look it, who are
sociological mixed bloods or are quite divorced from
tribal society. Some are urbanized people whose
parents and grandparents were traditional.*

*There are some tribes of primarily
sociological full bloods, phenotypically Indian,
traditionally oriented people who are larger in
numbers than they were during the last century. We
have mentioned the Utes and the Western Apaches. The*

---

4 (con't.) Weapons: A Study of the Pine
Ridge Sioux," University of Chicago Press, Chicago
(1946).

*Navajo Tribe, the largest, belongs in this category,
but there are others such as the Hopis who are
surrounded by Navajos, the Crows of Montana, some
Western Shoshone and Northern Paiute groups in
Nevada, and to a lesser extent the Teton Sioux of
South Dakota. All of these have differing enrollment
criteria and all can be contrasted with the Cherokee
Nation of Oklahoma, once again formally organized
under a constitution that requires for membership
nothing more than an ancestor on a 1906 roll. Long
prior to that date the tribe contained large
elements with but the slightest Cherokee ancestry,
such as Will Rogers, and included numbers of
Delawares and Shawnees, many of them virtually
White, and many Freedmen. If all of those who are
eligible for enrollment actually sought such status
there is little doubt that the membership would
reach 150,000. The Cherokees of Oklahoma would,
therefore, rival the Navajos in numbers but there
the resemblance ends. There are, however, by now
perhaps 15,000 Cherokees designated by one scholar
as "those who take part in the Cherokee way of
life."[5] These are extremely tribally oriented
people, Cherokee speakers generally, who reside in
remote communities in northeastern Oklahoma within
the old Cherokee Nation (there have not been
reservations in Oklahoma since 1907 but there are
tribal lands and individual lands held in trust by
the federal government). These tribesmen, also
called the "hill people," remain generally aloof
from other societies including whatever constitutes
the rest of the Cherokee Nation. They in no way
resemble those White Cherokees who have for so long
controlled the affairs of the tribe and who have
been so visible in the agencies concerned with
Indian programing. There are, to be sure, others
who are the products of Cherokee households, speak
the language fluently, but do not derive from the
hill communities.*

---

[5] *Albert L. Wahrhaftig, "The Cherokee People
Today," Carnegie Corporation Cross-Cultural
Education Project of the University of Chicago,
Tahlequah, Oklahoma (1966).*

An anthropologist, who is a native Oklahoman and long in practice there, was told by me that he was eligible for membership with either the Oklahoma Cherokees or Choctaws after he explained that he had ancestors on the turn of the century rolls of both tribes. This man, who fully identifies as White and is a lifetime student of Indian society, was appalled at the realization that he could become a legal Indian with ease. He is the only person I have ever met who positively refused to take advantage of eligibility for tribal membership, exasperating that tribes were "no longer sociological entities but corporate membership organizations." It is not quite that bad, but it can be worse. I stated in the Preface that my first two children were not enrolled deliberately (if the Preface has not been read it should be, and before proceeding). At the time they were eligible they needed no specific blood quantum. However, before my youngest son arrived the Minnesota Chippewa Tribe required a minimum of one-quarter blood. Historically, for a tribe to distinguish among full siblings was unknown. Sociologically, it is ridiculous and represents one of the worst instances of Indians blindly accepting the tenets and the advice of representatives of the larger society. If I join those who find the quarter blood limitation to be of value I surely do not favor such separations. Had the first two children been enrolled I would have enjoyed challenging the tribe and the Secretary of the Interior in this matter. I would have even more gladly taken up the cause of those in similar circumstances who were actually residing in Chippewa communities. I know of no tribes that make provision for later-born children after adopting a blood quantum criterion. My friend from Oklahoma would undoubtedly also have much to say about the practice of enrolling some children with the mother's tribe and others with the father's, and the same children having no intercourse with either tribe. Corporate membership organizations, indeed; tribes are supposed to be kinship-oriented societies.

Returning to the Cherokees, I wonder how many of the readers of these lines are saying to themselves that they are Cherokee or partly so. The

21

Cherokees hail from the hill country of Georgia and the Carolinas, the much smaller of the two Cherokee tribes being situated in the Smoky Mountains of North Carolina having not migrated west and having avoided forced removal to what became Oklahoma. As a close friend with Cherokee associations said, "'Cherokee' is simply southern Indian," meaning that any southerner who thinks he has Indian ancestry almost invariably picks on the Cherokees. For a very long time, and at enormous expense, the BIA has been plagued by what are known as the "Cherokee letters." These are initiated by an extraordinary number of persons who either claim to be Cherokees or of Cherokee ancestry and often expect a check to be awaiting them. By no means are such letter writers, telephone callers or visitors confined to those from southern states. A very large portion is composed of Blacks. I have hardly known a Black who did not offer in any Indian conversational context that he was part or all Cherokee, or so respond when questioned about Indian ancestry. No friend or acquaintance involved with Indian society with whom I have discussed this phenomenon has ever expressed surprise, their own experiences being similar. I have conducted experiments along these lines for a long period, beginning in New York City where the numbers of Blacks identifying as Cherokees provided Indian people with a constant source of both amusement and annoyance. On one occasion, in Chicago, a fellow anthropology student greeted my assertion about this matter with derision and bet me five dollars that the next Black we met would not so respond. Being as reluctant as I to approach a total stranger, he was trying to renege when I offered a solution, that of questioning an elevator operator in the building where I had been living for some weeks. This man, who was on duty as we were leaving, was a most courteous person who had assisted me while I suffered a staggering case of the flu. I explained to him that my friend was also a student of Indian culture and that I wondered whether he was part Indian. The gentleman won me the money, of course paid out of his sight, by replying with no hesitancy, "My grandmother was a Cherokee. She knew all about the Indian medicine and stuff like that." I should have bet even more heavily on the nature of the response, particularly on the reference to a grandmother. Anthropologists, especially those out of work in a place like Chicago, are to be forgiven such transgressions.

"Louie doesn't want to be referred to as a Mohawk-Sioux anymore. He says that it should be Sioux-Mohawk." So announced the BIA Public Information Officer, with a wide grin, about the late Louis R. Bruce, the brand new Nixon-appointed Commissioner. His mother was an Oglala Sioux and his father was a member of the St. Regis Band of Mohawks located in New York on the international boundary, their Canadian counterparts being literally on top of them. The Oglala Sioux Tribe, one of the potentially largest in the country, has not had an approved, official membership roll since the 1935 Pine Ridge Reservation census, supposedly containing the names of Sioux Indians who "belonged" there or were in residence. Bruce was never in residence on Pine Ridge; his mother was not in residence in 1935, but sure enough his name is included on the census. His desire to reverse the tribal names in his background was prompted by his newly acquired belief that all of the tribes of the Six Nations or Iroquois Confederacy of New York base their membership on strict matrilineality. Since his mother was Sioux, reasoned Bruce, the Sioux should take precedence in his identification. What Mr. Bruce did not know was that the St. Regis Mohawks, their early history as a French Catholic settlement too complex to be discussed here, had early on separated from the Six Nations and in time adopted a patrilineal basis for membership following the European pattern. He was, at least since childhood, enrolled as a St. Regis member.

Mr. Bruce was fortunate in having membership with two tribes, as disparate as they are. The rest of the Iroquois tribes in New York adamantly refuse to enroll anyone whose mother is not of the tribe. The Onondaga Nation recently did so in an extraordinary move, but affecting only one person. A man who is employed by the BIA is in the opposite situation of Mr. Bruce as his mother is Mohawk and his father Seneca. At first blush all of this matrilineality would appear to be a purist's delight, tribes actually maintaining membership traditions free of any European influence. It is no such thing. The Iroquois clan matrons historically filled the places of slain or otherwise lost members through adoption. They could, in fact, adopt anyone. It is improbable that there is an Iroquois anywhere in the United States or Canada who is not descended from a captive Indian, or a member of any one of the remnant groups who sought refuge with one Iroquois tribe or the other, or a captive White.

Strict Iroquois matrilineality, absent the now obsolete practice of clan adoption, is not only nontraditional and at times disfunctional, it smacks of racism in that most of the concerned mothers are White. The fact that so many members descend from captive White women is virtually ignored. Large elements are hardly Indian in any sense but prove matrilineality. Some years ago the BIA produced a public information sheet listing the names of famous Indians. Included, to my great glee and that of many colleagues, was the name of Winston Churchill as a Mohawk. Those responsible for this declaration had learned that Churchill's American mother traced matrilineal descent from a Mohawk woman. Some ardent Iroquois traditionalists in Canada and with the New York Mohawks maintain that those who are not matrilineal are illegally enrolled. They, at least, might have been happy to embrace the Prime Minister. Further concerning the matrilineal system, an aged gentleman on the Brighton Reservation in Florida sadly informed me through an interpreter that he no longer considered himself within the Seminole Tribe as he was the last of the Deer Clan. The tribal constitution contains no mention of clans, one-quarter blood from either or both parents being sufficient for membership. This old man's view of Seminole society was, however, truly traditional. Had I known at the time of the existence of Oklahoma Seminole Deer Clan people I would have been quick to so inform him. The man's paternal grandmother was Black and, like almost all Blacks who remained with the Florida Seminoles, had been classed as a Snake Clan member. His father, called Billie Bowlegs after a famous chief, was highly respected by Indians and non-Indians alike.

Distinguished from tribal enrollees who may

be somewhat or very Black in appearance are those to whom I have referred as the "Nicknamed Peoples."[6] Throughout the Eastern Seaboard, in Appalachia and to some degree westward and in the Gulf States are found many groups, from tiny communities to some numbering in the thousands, of mixed racial composition who generally and increasingly identify as Indians. In very few instances do they have authentic tribal origins or valid tribal names. They are usually nicknamed. There are "Jackson's Whites" and "Brass Ankles," "Moors" and "Redbones," "Wesorts" and "Smilings" and many others. Frank G. Speck, a noted anthropologist, named the Nanticokes of Delaware and the Waccamaws of South Carolina, and was totally in error concerning the latter as their tribal origins remain unknown. Others, like the Haliwas and Lumbees, have fashioned names for themselves. The former, which sounds so beautifully "Indian," derives from an inspired combination of some of the letters that form the names of two adjoining North Carolina counties, Halifax and Warren. "Lumbee," as one irate old man put it, "came out of the river and ought to be put back in there," the reference being to the Lumber in southeastern North Carolina.

Fully aware that I advocate a minority position, I nevertheless cling to the designation Calvin Beale prefers for these groups. He refers to them as Triracial Isolates and in a footnote qualifies: "Excluded from the category described are Indian tribes such as the Narragansett, Shinnecock, or Pamunkey, who absorbed both white and Negro blood, but retained their tribal identity and historical continuity." [7] Some of these groups

---

[6] Stephen E. Feraca, "A Survey of Some Problems of the Federal Relationship to Eastern Indian Groups," unpublished paper delivered before the American Association for the Advancement of Science, Washington, D.C. (1978).

[7] Calvin L. Beale, "American Triracial Isolates: Their Status and Pertinence to Genetic

through the courts, in petitions to the Secretary of the Interior, and through the media, are seeking federal recognition as Indian tribes. Those who have obtained recognition from the State of North Carolina are among the most persistent.

Of all the triracial peoples, only the Lumbees, by far the largest, have been the subject of federal legislation. Known successively as "Croatans," "Indians of Robeson County," "Siouans" and "Cherokee Indians of Robeson County" (which was successfully challenged by the Eastern Band of Cherokees), they finally became "Lumbees" in the 1950's by virtue of state and federal statutes. The federal Lumbee Act of June 7, 1956, repeats the amusing origin myth of these people as plantation owners in Robeson County antedating Europeans, recognizes them as Indians but not as a tribe, and in the same breath denies them special federal Indian privileges or services. The Lumbees continue to press for full federal status. A very vocal faction insists on identity as Hattaras Tuscaroras or the Tuscarora Tribe and filed suit for the loss of Robeson County as their aboriginal territory. The Tuscarora Iroquois of New York and Canada, who are originally from the Carolinas, seem to be unaware of these activities, but they are not from the Robeson area and neither are the ancestors of the Lumbees who probably derive from Virginia and Maryland.

One faction or another in Robeson County has tried to organize around the seven or eight survivors of 22 Robeson County residents who were declared to be of "one-half or more Indian blood" by the BIA in 1938. This declaration was based on a 1936-37 BIA-sponsored pseudo-anthropological study that in retrospect is ludicrous. About 200 individuals were subjected to physical testing, including the examination of blood samples, to ascertain their Indian heritage. Ethnohistorical factors and genealogy were completely ignored. Indeed, immediate

----

[7] (con't.) Research," *Eugenics Quarterly*, Vol. 4, No. 4 (1957), pp. 187-196.

ancestry was dismissed with one brother being rejected as less than one-half Indian and another accepted in terms of the Indian Reorganization Act of 1934 as one-half or more. Rarely has the blood quantum approach suffered such abuse.

There have long been organizations exclusively comprised of Whites who play Indian. Some of these are fraternal groups such as the Ancient Order of Red Men. An official of that organization said to me and an Indian friend in New York City that "an Indian is not a Red Man" and the friend surprisingly produced a membership card to prove otherwise. More recently, these entities are rural, are found in the Southeast, and are becoming much politicized. Predictably, the newly emerging entities usually bill themselves as Cherokee and flaunt comic book style Indian personal names (John "Screaming Eagle" Smith, Alice "Little Fawn" Hoover and Anselm "Strong Oak" McCoy, all fictional but typical). What is actually new about them is that they are forcing fearful, ignorant politicians into forming state Indian commissions in places such as Georgia and Tennessee that do not even have significant triracial populations. If there is anything that frightens a politician it is to be told that he has Indians with whom to contend. Jimmy Carter, while governor of Georgia, recognized one such group, the self-styled "Cairo Creeks." He even proclaimed a reservation for them but the state legislature did not implement this move. The federal government has denied them recognition after examining their petition. Like the triracial communities, these groups make no secret of their interest in seeking federal recognition and special Indian services.

Creating Indians of Whites and Blacks, and Browns such as Mexicans, is hardly new, but historically such individuals had usually become sociologically and culturally tribal. In Oklahoma with the Kiowas, Comanches and Kiowa Apaches the captives, usually Mexicans, were eventually designated full bloods and accordingly allotted portions of the tribal land. With the Northern Cheyennes in Montana, however, are found Whites who make little pretense of being Indian and who were

27

also enrolled with the tribe and given allotments. Some of the descendants of these people, themselves enrolled members, have not married Cheyennes. The anomalies are numerous and found throughout the country with one of the most unjust manifestations developed in Michigan. There the recently recognized Sault Ste. Marie Chippewas have been permitted by a negligent BIA, assuming that the tribal officials would limit themselves, to enroll thousands of scattered individuals of very remote Indian ancestry. These people have no sense of tribalism except the formality of enrollment, or are attracted to the Indian mystique, and anticipate claims awards payments. Among the unrecognized Ottawas of the same state are persons who reside in or derive from historic Indian communities. Many are Ottawa speakers as was a dear friend and colleague, Louise Gilbault Perkins, who was arbitrarily designated as "at least five-eighths" Indian (she looked like a full blood) in order to admit her to Haskell Indian School. She died officially tribeless while the Sault Ste. Marie organization was beginning to enroll every "Chippewa" within reach.

"Everybody wants to be an Indian" is a statement often made and with varying degrees of disgust. The ease with which non-Indians "pass" into segments of Indian society is something that continues to fascinate me. So does the eagerness with which so many Indians, including those who are from very traditional tribal societies, embrace as fellow Indians an interesting assortment of phonies. The worst, or best, example is that of the "prince" in New York City many years ago. This young Black, by accent and otherwise a New Yorker and not even of Latin American origins, did not pose as a Quechua or Aymara of Peru or Bolivia but went all the way to nonexistent Inca royalty. Winnebagoes and others expressed interest in the Indian organization he said he was forming and were introducing him on his own terms. For years Johnny Cash made much of his assumed Cherokee heritage but in a _Playboy_ magazine interview denied any Indian ancestry.[8] The actress-

---

[8] _Playboy_, Chicago (November 1970).

singer Cher claims to be Cherokee but has also admitted to her origins in Armenia. She and Cash have the features that the general public, and many, many Indians, would like to believe best represent the Indian phenotype. Deserving special mention is the woman who, during the Carter Administration, wormed her way right into the White House as a Penobscot from Maine and an expert in Indian education. Questioned by the tribal chairman and other suspicious persons, including myself, she quickly became a Delaware, and subsequently a Mashpee. Her role is analogous to that of Princess Pale Moon who heads what ostensibly is an Indian cultural heritage foundation headquartered in Virginia near Washington, D.C. She claims to be Cherokee and Chippewa but cannot identify with either of the Cherokee tribal organizations or any of the numerous Chippewa tribes found from Michigan westward to Montana, not mentioning those in Canada. More pertinently, Indians do not question her openly (but the State of Virginia and some members of Congress have), support and attend the events her organization sponsors, and address her by her title and her stage name, which has been borne by an array of Indian "princesses" since before my introduction to it while in my teens.

Participating in a Council of Energy Resources Tribes (CERT) fundraising ball held in Washington, D.C., appeared out of the blue as Oklahoma Indians the stars James Garner, Dennis Weaver and others. No Indians, to my knowledge, asked where these people were during the 1950's and 60's that saw a very ill-inspired termination of the federal relationship with the tribes, or during the ugly days of the 70's and early 80's when militancy dealt a severe blow to the local Indian image. Their charisma, whether they are essentially White or not, might have been useful. Some Indians, however, reveled in recounting the cute stories these screen personalities told about their "reservation days." This sort of thing is not confined to Indians. It is part and parcel of some of the realities of the minority syndrome. It is akin to the National Italian American Foundation honoring Henry Fonda as an outstanding Italian American shortly before his death. By his own admission, Henry Fonda's last

Italian ancestor was someone who left Italy for Holland the same year that Columbus first sailed westward.

The last member of the Deer Clan in Florida was deceased before the making of the 1980 national census and I question that he had been counted by any national census. The census of 1980, as applied to the Indian populace of this country, requires so many qualifiers as to render it practically useless. It was based, ethnically and racially, on self-identification. Consequently, a horde with not the slightest connection with any tribe had a field day. Previous censuses have not, however, been free of such problems or could they have been. I received a telephone call from a 1970 census-taker operating within Prince Georges County in Maryland who registered considerable concern about the numbers of respondents who identified as "Apaches" (not rivalling Cherokee in terms of self-assumed Indian identity but in my experience surely the second choice). She elaborated that the subjects were the same kind of people with the same surnames as others she regarded to be non-Indian. Asked for the surnames the reply was that they could not be revealed under census-taking regulations. Playing the game, I mentioned the two most common names found among the Wesorts of southern Maryland, a very large triracial group. It was quickly established that these people were unquestionably not Apache. They are, it should be noted, developing an increasing awareness that their Indian ancestry is probably Piscataway but records remain unavailable. Some days later this conscientious worker called to inform me that her supervisor directed her to accept the tribal, and therefore racial, designations given by any of her respondents.

According to the 1970 census there were 827,108 Indians including 34,378 Aleuts and Eskimos in the United States. With the completion of the 1980 census the figure jumped to 1,421,367 with 201,369 of these in California, by far the highest state in Indian population with most residing in urban areas. This rise cannot, of course, be due to any natural causes; and it is not due to Indians being unreported to any significant degree in the previous census. It is simply the result in large measure of non-tribal people, or out and out non-Indians, identifying as Indians, especially in North Carolina which has a true tribal resident population with the Eastern Cherokees of only a few thousand. North Carolina counts a whopping 64,652. Another factor to be considered in the swelling of the census is that of the many thousands of persons who have received as descendants, but not as tribal members, federal checks for their per capita shares of land claims awards. As one who has processed many of these judgments, I am acutely aware of just how much Indianness has been created in the last 25 years on the strength of applications successfully establishing Indian ancestry, no matter how remote.

An irresistible but by no means novel observation was made by a student whom I accompanied on a buying trip while this chapter was being written. Seeking camouflage equipment in a northern Virginia town, this paramilitary enthusiast, otherwise intelligent and well spoken, noticed two young Indian women with two little girls in the fast food place where we had stopped. I inanely remarked that the little kids sure looked Indian. He responded that it was "too bad that they were all exterminated." Ignoring the redundancy but not the vitality of the the kids who almost tripped us on our way out, I spent about ten minutes trying to educate him. He finally insisted that he was at least correct in reference to the indigenes of Virginia after I explained that the people we saw were probably not Virginians. Of the several small Indian enclaves in Virginia only two deserve to be classed as tribes, the Pamunkey and the Mattaponi. Both have state-supervised reservations. They have not petitioned for federal recognition, to which they are unquestionably entitled, for fear of jeopardizing their relationship with the state.

Notwithstanding the increasing presence of Americans who are Indian in every respect, and given the very disproportionate attention Indians receive in the mass media, the disappearing or disappeared Indian myth persists. It is practically as old as European contact, particularly in the minds and hearts of Anglo Saxons whose missionary fervor was

mostly inspired by the belief that the untutored
pagans would all be lost before receiving Christ. A
more than poignant note is still sounded by many
Indian people who themselves believe that their
tribe and their race will soon be no more. Some
years ago I made an initially derisive Lower Brule
Sioux very happy by encouraging him to think in
terms of his own situation being typical of that of
most Indians. His wife was Indian and Sioux, very
much so, and they had several healthy children. This
man, through a mutual friend, actually conveyed to
me his surprise and gratitude after going home and
thinking for a day or so. An elderly and very
kindly shaman was not so easily comforted. An
Oglala Sioux, he regularly placed a tiny wooden
hoop, to which two wrapped tobacco offerings were
tied, on the altar peculiar to his practice. He
explained that the hoop represented the people and
that the offerings were made because "the Indians
are dying out." This gentleman succumbed to
pneumonia, not having been hospitalized in time
after being treated by an associate shaman. One of
the attending interns seriously asked, "Do they send
them here to die?" It is often very hard to be a
real Indian.

CHAPTER TWO

"AFTER   ALL,   WE   TOOK   THEIR   LAND."

A retired cop in Florida.

The descendant of Charley Osceola (the ancestor of the Florida Osceolas but no relation to the famous war chief) had been asked to come to the education office of the Seminole Agency in Hollywood, Florida, to explain why he had not taken advantage of a pre-college entrance program. Questioned by the Community Services Officer, this high school football star responded that he chose not to attend because the required residence in Tampa would have conflicted with his driver-training program. The athlete was reminded that all of the several candidates for the agency's higher education grants knew that the pre-entrance courses were mandatory and considerable pains had been taken to make the necessary arrangements. (Please don't ask why these kids had been encouraged in the first place as all were ill-prepared and some were functionally illiterate.) He remained sullen and uncommunicative and became more so when the bureaucrat opined that he had no interest in furthering his education and had been uncooperative for the entire school year. It was emphasized that every other candidate was taking the required courses and, further, all had been warned that funding was short. The interview ended with the young Seminole being advised that he would not be recommended for a grant but could appeal to the Agency Superintendent. At that point he rose from his seat and in a rage accused the officer of being concerned solely with saving money. He was told to get out of the office. As the BIA employee turned away he was viciously punched, thrown against a metal filing cabinet and then to the floor. A colleague who witnessed the final stages of this episode through the open doorway screamed at the boy who then fled the building. Days later the victim, his face and scalp lacerated and his left forearm in a cast, visited a retired policeman and his wife. Upon being told the cause of the cuts, bruises and broken arm this extremely conservative individual, an avowed George Wallace supporter, declared that it was a damned shame but "after all, we took their land." I was the employee so attacked, and years later while visiting the Hollywood Reservation I shook hands with the would-be college student. He actually was permitted to attend, after I transferred at my request, and dropped out as quickly as every one of the others who entered that fall.

The manifestations of the national sense of guilt arising from what is perceived by society as the taking or stealing of Indian land are everywhere visible. The rationales of the dominant society and of Indian people are employed to condone the most destructive Indian attitudes and behavior. They are voiced or written on a daily basis and are inseparable from popular concepts of Indian-White warfare. The most baseless of the related myths is that all Indian tribes were forcibly removed from their aboriginal or historic territories to distant and worthless lands. A telephone call from Vice President Spiro Agnew's office is among the most noteworthy of the numberless questions asked of me in this regard. A very pleasant lady explained that Agnew was scheduled to appear on about a dozen reservations, all west of the Mississippi, and was particularly interested in the original homes of the involved tribes. I succeeded in astonishing the caller by advising that all but one of the tribes was situated in an area that was known to them aboriginally or at least throughout the period of contact with American society. She admitted that she had not been informed otherwise but presumed that all on her roster were far from any original homeland. Even in Oklahoma, which became home to so many unrelated tribes, there are the Wichitas, the Kiowas and those Apaches associated with them, Comanches, Southern Cheyennes and Southern Arapahoes, Osages, and a large group of Cherokees who either owned or were quite familiar with various parts of that area.

When the English arrived at Jamestown they found a chief who was actually a king and in fact approached the status of a petty emperor. Known to *history as Powhatan after one of his principal villages, he formed a confederacy of more than thirty tribes, some of them having been conquered by him just prior to the advent of the English. Powhatan exacted tribute from people as distant as the Conoys on the Potomac River in southern Maryland. His favorite daughter, Pocahontas, who married into English nobility through her husband, John Rolfe, is the only Indian woman known to American history truly deserving of the title of princess. Her father lasted longer and controlled more land and people than many European royal figures. After Powhatan's death the uneasy association between these Algonquian people and the colonists rapidly deteriorated. Two wars and Bacon's Rebellion brought them to utter devastation, disease simultaneously playing its part. The remnants were reduced to very small reservations and, ironically enough, were required to pay tribute to the Virginia colonial governor. The tribute was token in the form of arrows but tribute nevertheless. Today, the only "reservated" Virginia Indians, the Pamunkey and Mattaponi tribes, separately pay tribute to the state governor in wild turkeys or deer for his Thanksgiving table.*

During one of my early visits to these tidewater Virginia tribes I met a deputy sheriff from King William, the county containing both reservations, who expressed the highest regard for these people. He also considered them to be "wards of the state" on the basis of all their aboriginal lands except the reservations being taken, and said that they could not vote in local or national elections because they were exempt from the taxation of their reservation land. The conversation, extremely amicable, ended with a complaint from the officer about most of the Pamunkeys not utilizing their land. The meeting is memorable principally because all these and still other typically inconsistent expressions of a representative of the larger society were encompassed in but a few minutes.

Tribal lands on most of the Eastern Seaboard, and most of Texas and southern California, were not lost to the United States of America. They were encroached upon, purchased or taken by European colonial powers that in the process often waged wars or adopted practices that were truly genocidal and made later Indian-American conflicts seem mild in comparison. The situations of the Georgia and Alabama Creeks, the Seminoles of Florida and the destruction of the intertribal movement led by the Shawnee statesman Tecumseh are among the major exceptions involving the United States.

In southern New England, southern New York, and the eastern portions of the Carolinas and Georgia the initially friendly if strained relations between Indians and Europeans collapsed, as in Virginia. Tribes as political powers, who were often fighting each other, were destroyed. Most disappeared, with the survivors confined to missionary colonies or tiny reservations. The English did their part with great vigor, but the record of the Dutch in what became New York City and environs, including Long Island, is particularly brutal. The Mohawks of northern New York, not to be confused with their kinsmen who left the Six Nations Confederacy to settle at French missionary centers along the St. Lawrence River, remained blissfully unaware that in the English view all of their extensive lands had passed to the Crown.[1] Staunch allies of the king, and convinced that the rebels would deprive them of their property and their liberty, they proved a major headache during the American Revolution. At the close of that conflict they fled as a tribe to Ontario, together with portions of the other Iroquois who had supported Great Britain. Their king in his gratitude granted them the Grand River or Six Nations Reserve and a smaller tract nearby.

In southern California, long antedating American acquisition of that territory, the quite numerous and unwarlike simple gathering societies were subjected to the philosophy and the techniques of "reduction" (as translated from Spanish). They led a life of peonage at the Spanish missions, those

---

[1] *Barbara Graymont, "The Iroquois in the American Revolution," Syracuse University Press, Syracuse (1972).*

centers of color and romance where they almost
disappeared, but died baptized and generally
detribalized. After American domination and the
discovery of gold the indigenes of the more northerly
portions of California were slaughtered as
punishment for petty depredations or for being real
Stone Age types and in the way. The accounts of the
deliberate murders of women and children are hardly
surpassed in the history of atrocity.[2] California
contains numerous small reservations or "rancherias,"
some uninhabited, and a real scarcity of indigenous
Indian people representative of a traditional tribal
society. The early inhabitants of Texas, especially
of the south and the coast, made their disappearance
soon after European contact. Mexico, and later the
Republic of Texas, with less than a handful of
exceptions, would not permit any tribes or remnants
to remain. Their determination was especially fierce
as concerned relative newcomers such as Kiowas,
Comanches and Apaches. There are only two
reservations in that enormous state, that of the
Alabamas and Coushattas who originate farther east,
and the little Ysleta del Sur Pueblo tract in El
Paso. The lands are supervised by Texas.

In the popular American consciousness the sins
of the colonial powers have been forgotten or were
never known, as is the rape and slaughter perpetrated
by Americans in much of California. Americans and
Europeans think in terms of the Teton Sioux, the
Cheyennes, and the Comanches and Kiowas, all of the
Great Plains, and of the Apaches and Navajos of the
Southwest. Given that there are always exceptions,
these are precisely the people who had large
reservations and still have extensive lands, tribally
and individually, and are generally comprised of
sociological full bloods. Americans also do not
know that the richest tribe in the country,

---

[2] See for example Robert F. Heizer, "They
Were Only Diggers: A Collection of Articles from
California Newspapers, 1851-1866, on Indian and White
Relations," Ballena Press Publications in Archeology,
Ethnology and History 1, Ramona, California (1974).

individually and corporately, is a very small, much Mexicanized, Cahuilla group with land within the city of Palm Springs, California. There are infants among the Palm Springs people who have enormous lease incomes.

The quality of Indian thinking, often shared by the general public, concerning the loss of land and the subsequent establishment of reservations, can be heard and read within a great variety of contexts. The Eastern Band of Cherokees has for a long period maintained a number of tourist attractions. Among these are some of the more worthwhile and authentic within the Smoky Mountains, an area lamentably scarred by cheap billboards and rows of establishments featuring junk souvenirs. On my first visit to that community a friend and I joined a group of tourists being led through a reconstructed Cherokee village containing a variety of living crafts displays. At the conclusion of the tour we were invited to be seated, and were treated to a brief lecture by the guide and encouraged to ask questions. The guide was a very young man clad in a breech cloth and moccasins not authentically Cherokee. He was informative until a middle-aged man asked if the "Indians" could leave the reservation. We were told that only the Eastern Cherokees could leave their reservation because they had bought it. It was evident that he was believed implicitly. As we had all paid a fair price to be handed this gross falsity, I reminded the guide that he himself had explained that some of the people seen at attractions on the reservation were from other tribes. I asked if the foreign Indians were then all fugitives. The response was a curt "You must be from the Bureau of Indian Affairs." I was on furlough from Fort Dix having just completed basic training. I thought privately, however, that if the BIA people were the only ones around to counter this nonsense they deserved high commendation. I can only shudder at the thought of how frequently in a given tourist season my fellow visitor's question was asked (I have heard it on more occasions than I can possibly remember) and answered in the same vein.

The general view is that reservations represent token compensation for aboriginal or historic land losses, but that these gifts come with many strings attached, among them some sort of restrictions on Indian freedom of movement and utilization of the land. It is true that until the early part of this century passes to leave reservations were issued by many agency superintendents. This practice was essentially limited to Plains tribes and to others with a recent history of warfare such as some of the Apache subdivisions. They were often safe conduct documents employed for the protection of the Indian recipients. Passes have never been required of any Cherokees and they are not the only Indian people to have bought all or part of their reservation lands.

The acreage in North Carolina that became the Qualla Boundary of the Cherokees, to which other land was added, some in non-contiguous tracts, was bought over a period of years by a local philanthropist, William H. Thomas, who also purchased land in his own name using Cherokee funds.[3] The land was eventually recognized by the state as a reservation and then taken in trust by the federal government. The Sac and Fox Tribe of Tama, Iowa, owes its landed existence to the foresight of those chiefs who refused to live in Kansas and took their band's portion of treaty annuities to buy land in their historic area. Bit by bit they created a sizeable enough tract, and on an annual basis the leading men of these primarily Mesquakie or Fox people, resplendent in otter skin headgear and other traditional regalia, would journey to the local court house to proudly pay the land taxes. The tribe,

---

[3] Mattie Russell, "William Holland Thomas: White Chief of the North Carolina Cherokees," Ph.D. dissertation, Duke University, Durham, North Carolina (1956).

Regarding the same Cherokee entity, some of the themes found in the present work are echoed by Fred Bauer, "Land of the North Carolina Cherokees," George Buchanan, Printer, Brevard, North Carolina (1970).

having accepted the Indian Reorganization Act, is now secure in that the reservation is inalienable. Taxes are, however, still paid on a limited basis. It is not inappropriate to remark that the Mesquakies are among the most traditional people in the country. They retain their language and functional patrilineal clans, many ancient religious ceremonies and a strong Native American (Peyote) Church.

The voluntary tax-paying Mesquakies are unique, but other tribes have bought their reservations or bought into reservations through treaty provisions. They were not always coerced by the federal government into so doing. Often the atmosphere became so intolerable that the tribes found themselves anxious to move, this being especially true of those in Kansas. During and just after the Civil War Indians were most unwelcome in that part of the United States. The Delawares provide an interesting study in this respect. The main body of Delawares, the Unamis, having arrived in Kansas after movement from the New York-New Jersey-Delaware area through Pennsylvania and the Ohio country, needed a new home. It was the Cherokee Nation in the Indian Territory (later Oklahoma) that was forced to accept them, the Delawares using their own tribal funds to buy their way in after the Civil War. The Cherokees, being largely supportive of the Confederacy, were being punished to the extent that they also had to provide a haven for the principal group of Shawnees. Later in the century the Delawares, and the Cherokees, were pressured to accept Munsee Delawares who had been guests of the Senecas of New York. The Unami Delaware element was most resentful of this intrusion into their new home and particularly so because their funds were utilized to accommodate these northern kinsmen whom they had forgotten. Accordingly, they sued the federal government and won; and to this day steadfastly maintain that Munsees are not Delawares.

The history of the Cherokee-Delaware-Munsee interrelationships is analogous to that of the Assiniboines and Sioux of Fort Peck Reservation in Montana. The Assiniboines began in Minnesota as a split-off of a Yanktonai Sioux band. As early as

40

the seventeenth century they had joined Chippewas
and Crees and had become implacable enemies of the
Sioux. The personal war record of Sitting Bull,
some of whose band members ended up on Fort Peck,
includes many pictographs of battles with
Assiniboines. The Assiniboines in the United States
abandoned their own country, acknowledged by an 1851
treaty, which extended south from the Missouri River
in eastern Montana. They moved north onto the lands
of the Blackfeet and Prairie Gros Ventres or Atsinas
(distinct from the Gros Ventres or Hidatsas of North
Dakota). The involved Sioux, mainly Yanktonais but
also comprised of Sisseton Santees and Hunkpapa
Tetons, had vacated their own 1851 and 1868 treaty
lands west of the Missouri and still other lands east
of that river. Both Sioux and Assiniboines
congregated at the Milk River Agency, later Fort Peck
Agency, on the Blackfeet-Gros Ventres lands. They
did not until 1888 obtain title to what became the
Fort Peck Reservation that included an eastern tract
not recognized as the exclusive property of any
tribe. The immense Blackfeet Reservation had
previously been greatly diminished. The Sioux
communities are located in the eastern portion of
the reservation and the Assiniboines to the west,
distinctions obtaining despite considerable
intermarriage. To this day each tribe insists that
the other vacate. Neither will believe that they
both encroached upon and at times invaded the
country of the Blackfeet and Gros Ventres. I know;
I tried to explain at a well-attended tribal council
session upon which occasion an Assiniboine member
rose to demand of the Washington man when he was
"going to get the Sioux off our reservation." The
tribal chairman thanked me publicly for reviewing
the history of the arrival of the two tribes on Fort
Peck, advising that for years he had been saying much
the same thing to no avail. He is of both
Assiniboine and Sioux ancestry but officially is
identified as Sioux.

The notion is probably ineradicable that
Indian land loss, supposedly always accompanied by
warfare and forced movement, is responsible for the
severe and indeed often frightening social and
economic, essentially sociopsychological, conditions
found in Indian communities. I regard the prevailing

perception to be of little merit. The picture in Canada, by all accounts, is just as repelling. The worst scenes found in both countries are identical in all pertinent details as evident in Alan Fry's work, he being one of the most candid observers of such aspects of Canadian Indian society.[4] Other than the Metis rebellions alluded to previously, and reiterating that the Metis are not to be regarded as tribal people, there have been no Indian wars engaged in by the Dominion of Canada. There has been nothing whatever resembling any east to west movement or the Oklahoma concentration of tribes as on this side of the international boundary. Canada has, therefore, no background resembling the U.S. Cavalry harassment of Indians, no Sand Creek or Washita massacres of Southern Cheyennes, no Wounded Knees, no Tippecanoes and no "Trails of Tears," yet Canada has plenty of poor, alcoholic, bitter and alienated Indians and Eskimos. The Alaska people--although only one small group, Metlakatla, has full reservation status--have control of vast lands and resources and have not been moved anywhere by the United States. Curiously enough, the Metlakatla people are from British Columbia, this Tsimshian Christian religious community having been led to their present home by their pastor. In Alaska the only Indian-American "warfare" occurred when a U.S. gunboat shelled the Tlingit village of Angoon (the village has been compensated through a claims award); and the only people moved any distance, but by Russians, were some Aleuts. Professional observers of the Alaskan scene report a steady increase in dependence and very visible social deterioration.

Upon analysis, a history of land loss with or without military pressure or actual warfare, and the emergence of reservations within or without aboriginal territory, cannot in themselves account for the problems of Indian society. In this context the state of Montana offers some instructive contrasts. The Rocky Boy's Reservation people had

---

[4] Alan Fry, "How a People Die," Doubleday Canada Limited, Toronto (1970).

led a pariah existence, most of them having fled the
intolerable conditions on what was left of their
North Dakota reservation, until an abandoned
military post was found for them as late as 1916.
They had previously been joined by a group of Plains
Crees who were among the few tribal people involved
in the last Metis rebellion. These people are the
most traditional and vibrant of all the Plains
Chippewas or Ojibwas and yet were homeless for about
thirty years with families or clusters roaming
throughout Montana and adjacent locales in Canada.
The nearby Fort Belknap Reservation organization is
comprised of Assiniboines and Gros Ventres. The
latter are within their aboriginal and
treaty-recognized lands. The Assiniboines, like
their cousins to the east on Fort Peck, were
interlopers but the area had been well known to
them. On Fort Belknap, speakers of either
language, totally unrelated as one is Siouan and the
other Algonquian, are now limited to a few generally
elderly members. The Fort Belknap people had also
reached the point where traditional life was
notoriously absent. Only recently, and without the
language base, has there been a "resurgence." Fort
Peck Assiniboine sociological full bloods, other
than young people, speak the language. The
Assiniboines also conduct language and history
classes. They exhibit a healthy sense of tradition
characterized, among other things, by the revival of
the Sun Dance in what is apparently very authentic
form. They castigate the Sioux for not having
reinstituted their own version of the same Plains
ceremony. Similar contrasts in other parts of the
country are numerous. No wallowing in guilt on the
part of the dominant society about land can offer
much to explain the viccissitudes, the tragedies or
the successes of Indian reservation life.

There has lately emerged a school of thought,
to which I do not subscribe, maintaining that only
through native history, including oral accounts, can
the Indian past be fully understood. These sentiments
are especially strong among young, militant Indians.
However, in pursuing some factors concerning
intertribal territorial and trade wars I do find
some Indian historical documents to be of value.
One of these is included here because, in

addition to other and better reasons, translating and interpreting it, and completing a reproduction (the first of several) preserved my sanity while in traction due to a herniated disk. The original document actually consists of two elongated sheets, U.S. Army deserter report forms. One sheet is of inked drawings, many of them quite attractive and much more realistic than other similar accounts, the only color employed being red which usually indicates blood. Accompanying this is a sheet of often maddeningly cryptic notes corresponding to each pictograph. They are written in Lakota, the tongue of the Teton or Western Sioux. This work was done by Wounded Bear, an Oglala Teton, for the grand sum of a dollar and a half as indicated on the paper of drawings. Properly called a "winter count," many tribes referring to a year as as a "winter" or spring to spring, the period covered runs from 1815-16 to 1896-97.[5]

The Wounded Bear Count is one of some thirty extant Sioux annual calendars. What attracts attention are the exceedingly graphic representations of intertribal warfare and territorial acquisition and losses. The year 1832-33 is memorialized by a battle with the Prairie Gros Ventres, one of the tribes the Sioux drove from the eastern Wyoming-Montana area. The drawing of that event, a big battle as indicated by the line encircling the action, includes scalped and bleeding women and children. The Sioux were among the many tribes who had no compunctions about killing, maiming or capturing women and children, and neither did the Gros Ventres. It should be noted, however, that with Plains societies the highest honors were bestowed on those courageous enough to strike an enemy without actually inflicting any harm, and this included women and children. It is often called "counting coup" from the French term for a blow.

---

[5] Photocopies of the originals and notes and translations have been deposited in the Sioux Indian Museum, Rapid City, South Dakota; and in the Anthropology Archives of the Smithsonian Institution.

Thirty Oglalas were killed in 1844-45 by Shoshones, Wounded Bear showing a scalped and bleeding Sioux and thirty strokes or dashes. Many Shoshones from Nevada had become equestrian nomads. In an amazingly short time they succeeded in occupying a large part of Wyoming and posed a severe threat to the tribes of Montana, including Crows, Assiniboines and Sioux who were all at war with each other. The count, like all other Oglala and Brule Teton records, contains numerous references to warfare with the Pawnees of south central Nebraska. As buffalo became scarce in their own country, primarily due to their burgeoning population and their increasing need for robes to trade, these Southern Tetons began invading the Pawnees at an early period. Wounded Bear and other chroniclers make mention of a formal war expedition to the Pawnee country in 1839-40. In 1852-53 a Pawnee was burned to death and the drawing for the year 1863-64, all the more fetching because of the crude attempt to convey conjugality, is of a Pawnee and his wife killed together. The entry of 1873-74 translates as "one hundred Pawnees were killed," a major disaster for any Indian tribe. The corresponding pictograph is unstinting in the inclusion of slaughtered women and children (see following plate). Only the end of the buffalo in their area and the provision of an American military escort to Oklahoma saved what remained of the Pawnees. The early years in Oklahoma were not kind to them either.

Further concerning territoriality, there is not a single Sioux historical calendar that makes any reference to the Northern Plains treaty of September 17, 1851, as anything but the occasion of a grand distribution of presents, ordinarily a blanket being depicted. For all of the tribes participating at this very important event, held at Fort Laramie in Wyoming, their first reservations were established, although the term "reservation" does not appear in the treaty itself. These were truly immense areas as reflected in many maps, one of the more recent and useful provided by the Indian

*Above: A Pawnee and his wife were killed together.
Below: One hundred Pawnees were killed. Drawn by
the author from a photocopy of the Wounded Bear
calendar (less than actual size).*

Claims Commission as part of its final report.[6] The Sioux area described in the treaty included all of South Dakota west of the Missouri, and large portions of North Dakota, Montana, Wyoming and Nebraska. Every square foot of this territory had been acquired by the Sioux through invasion or encroachment, mostly from the Arikaras and Crows, and even from the Cheyennes and Arapahoes who later were friends and allies. The Teton Sioux have forgotten or deny that the original homeland of all the Sioux divisions was in Minnesota and adjacent areas. The Chippewas took the whole of the northern two-thirds of Minnesota from the Sioux who were, however, beginning to gravitate westward.

There is in few Sioux calendars any specific mention of the taking of the Black Hills from them in 1877. The year 1876-77 is usually devoted to the confiscation of the horses of those at the agencies who were suspected of planning to join the non-agency Tetons who had wiped out Custer. Very few winter counts mention the Battle of the Little Big Horn of 1876; but there is hardly an American to be found, Indian or non-Indian, who is not aware of this event and convinced that the people encamped along that river in Montana were simply defending their lands. Firstly, the great majority of the Tetons was quietly situated at their respective agencies that spring and summer, although a disproportionate number of young men had joined the "hostile" camps in Montana. Secondly, the Tetons associated with Sitting Bull, Crazy Horse and some other Sioux leaders who would not accept the agency dole, and those Northern Cheyennes with them, had invaded the country of the hated Crows. They were happily killing Crow buffalo and would have just as gladly lifted the scalps and the horses of any Crows they found. It is true that they were not expecting an attack from American

---

[6] Indian Claims Commission, "Indian Land Areas Judicially Established 1978," map prepared by U.S. Geological Survey, Washington (1978). 1851 treaty lands include Sioux, Arikara-Mandan-Hidatsa, Assiniboine, Crow, and Cheyenne-Arapaho.

forces, particularly in view of their numbers and after just badly beating General Crook, but they were not hunting or otherwise disporting themselves on their own land. The Arapahoes often declare that they too were instrumental in ending the career of that legendary egomaniac who dearly loved to kill Indians. Five young Arapahoes were present. During the fray one of them accidentally killed a Sioux-- with a lance. How this was accomplished has never been adequately explained. The Arapahoes quickly and quietly got out and returned to their agency, actually a Sioux agency in western Nebraska. The only people legitimately occupying that part of the Big Horn country on that fateful June afternoon were Crow scouts in the employ of the U.S. Army.

To turn to societies quite removed culturally and geographically from the Northern Plains I reference the Navajo-Hopi land dispute. The news media in prime time television and front page coverage have devoted much attention to this problem that has no end in sight. It is still not understood by the public that the Navajos were encroaching on the lands of other tribes, Hopis and other sedentary groups and much simpler hunter-gatherers, long before their overwhelming defeat by the United States and the beginnings of their reservation existence. Their early history in this respect is very similar to that of their relatives, the Apaches. Both of these Athapaskan peoples are relatively new to the Southwest. The various divisions of Apaches, and the Navajos, carved out impressive territories for themselves for which they have been paid by the federal government. Those Navajos personally involved in the dispute with the Hopi farmers are by contrast mainly herdsmen. They have long occupied Hopi reservation lands and have a healthy penchant for overgrazing and thus taking the desert with them. They also rationalize that the Hopis are not using the land. Typical of "Indian" journalese, *Newsweek* magazine stated, "Bands of Navajo resisters vow they will not be removed alive--raising the specter of Indian against Indian in a struggle started by white people

48

almost a continent away."[7] The reference is to Washington, D.C., and no Whites started this ancient intertribal struggle. However, it has been rightly reported that the federal government was extremely lax in not preventing Navajo expansion onto Hopi lands.[8] A much lesser known situation involving Navajos is that their early encroachments and warfare affected some Southern Paiutes. Some of the Southern Paiute lands, and some Southern Paiute groups themselves, were included within the boundaries of the huge Navajo Reservation in an Executive Order annexation of 1900. The Paiutes have retained their identity and their language and are now seeking federal recognition as a separate tribe. It is anticipated that they will also seek restoration of what has been judicially established as that portion of their aboriginal lands included within the Navajo Reservation. The Navajos are not pleased with these developments and have given notice that they will resist any Southern Paiute efforts.

Some years ago a close friend and next-door neighbor invited me to discuss things Indian at his home where he, as president, was hosting a meeting of the local Jewish mens association. Selecting the topics treaties and land I began with a standard set of questions designed to rid the audience of their favorite misconceptions. Things proceeded well, the group being attentive and eager, until one young man said something to the effect that he expected a discussion of contemporary Indian poverty. My reply in terms of insufficient time did not satisfy and still another guest vehemently announced that Indians were poor "because we stole their land." I registered mock surprise at the author of this statement ever stealing anyone's land. He and others

---

7 <u>Newsweek</u>, New York, New York (September 23, 1985), p.78.

8 Jerry Kammer, "The Second Long Walk: The Navajo-Hopi Land Dispute," University of New Mexico Press, Albuquerque (1980, p.b. 1987).

blurted that while they themselves hadn't, American society had taken the whole country. Cautioning the group about colonial and tribal land grabs I also reminded them that they, and I, were only a generation or two removed from Europe and, further, that it was highly improbable that any Eastern European Jews were involved in Indian land transactions. This truly enthusiastic group was then abruptly silenced by a member who forcefully brought up the dispossession of Arabs in Israel. My day was made, and not in any political sense but on the basis of all present requiring themselves to think. The meeting ended with the consensus that both modern nation-states of America and Israel were extraordinary in their attempts, however halting or ill-conceived, to recompense the indigenous landlords.

I am aware that Canadian officials have examined the approaches this country has taken regarding compensation for tribal land; and I think that Israel and Australia have expressed similar interests.[9] We have little to teach them. Even prior to the close of the Second World War, and despite the exemplary record of Indian people in personal sacrifice at home and abroad, Congress began to express its impatience with the continuation of "Indian business." Such impatience, not uncharacteristically, was combined with a concern about compensation for land losses. The passage of the Indian Claims Commission Act of August 13, 1946, represented the most tangible aspect of the mood of the country to "finally pay the Indians off and let them get on their own two feet." Prior to the passage of this act each tribal land claim required special jurisdictional legislation to enable a tribe to sue the United States, this being one of the many items that vexed the members of Congress. The then already old Indians of California and Sioux Black Hills claims were foremost among those annoying the

---

[9] See for example "Indian Claims in Canada: An Essay and Bibliography," with reference also to the United States, Ottawa (1975).

*solons. In establishing an Indian Claims Commission
the same lawmakers, and other people who should have
evidenced some healthy skepticism and a lot more
imagination, reflected instead an astounding
ignorance of Indian history and the normal processes
of law. In attempting to quickly settle and silence
Indian claims no one foresaw that suits would be
filed by small entities that had never in this
century appeared before Congress and were surely not
part of the public consciousness, or by descendants
of tribes extinct as such. As a result about 650
claims were filed. Although half of these have been
dismissed there are still unsettled claims that were
originally filed with the commission. Further,
Congress, inconsistent as always, continues to pass
special jurisdictional acts. The Wichita Tribe
failed to timely file a claim with the commission
for aboriginal lands in Texas, Oklahoma and Kansas.
Under a special jurisdictional act the tribe sued in
the United States Court of Claims and did very well
in achieving a quick compromise settlement. In
March of 1985 Congress appropriated $14 million to
satisfy the award. This is real money. As of that
year an updated tribal roll reached the grand total
of 1,202.*

*Among the grandiose statements made in
support of the commission was that it would complete
its work in ten years. The life of the commission
had to be extended to 1978 when all unfinished
cases, a very large number, were transferred to the
Court of Claims. In 1982 this became the United
States Claims Court where the action continues.
With this passage of time there are few observers
who believe that any tribes or individual Indians
have been or ever will be satisfied. There is
widespread misinformation among Indian people and
their White neighbors about the source of judgment
funds, and in particular the methods employed to
establish the value of land and other goods. An
anthropologist who testified in a number of claims
cases succinctly states, "Even where there is
understanding that awards are based on lost lands,
there is bitterness because often it is not
understood that compensation is based on the
appraised value of land at the time it was ceded and
not on the wealth the land generated for the white*

man since then."[10]

Contrary to practically everyone's expectations it is not generally the publicly and historically better known tribes that have received the most valuable awards, but usually small or almost forgotten entities. The Wichitas have just been mentioned and who has heard of them? The Goshute claims award amounted to $7 million for aboriginal lands in Nevada and Utah. Known as "Desert Utes" they are actually the easternmost bands of the Western Shoshones but their lands have been described separately, partly on the basis of a treaty made with them alone. All Western Shoshone bands or collections of families were typically small and needed huge areas to sustain themselves by seed gathering and small game hunting. The award funds have been shared by two organized tribes, successors to the aggrieved entity that hardly boasted any political organization. These are "The Confederated Tribes of the Goshute Reservation," a pretentious and misleading title adopted when plans were underway under the Indian Reorganization Act to include the other Goshute group, the Skull Valley Tribe. The Goshute proper numbered 321 when the funds were partly distributed and Skull Valley 172. Most of these funds, fortunately, have been invested on the basis of tribally developed plans for a variety of programs. Knowledgeable persons have, however, expressed serious concerns about the ability of either tribe to implement such programs. The Goshutes have never been moved anywhere. They were always small and remote; they so remain.

Congress had been aware of the deep-seated interest of the Pembina Chippewas in pursuing claims but nobody, ethnohistorians included, knew quite who they were, although cognizant that at least some portion of the Turtle Mountain Band was Pembina.

---

[10] Nancy Oestreich Lurie, "The Indian Claims Commission," The Annals of the American Academy of Political and Social Science, Vol. 436, Philadelphia (March 1978), p. 106.

They are the Chippewas mentioned earlier who, on entering the Plains, gave rise to the Metis element but retained a traditional, tribally oriented society and do still. They reached out from their earlier Red River, including Pembina, North Dakota, settlements eventually taking and holding a large territory in north central North Dakota. Warfare between them and the Sioux over these lands was incessant, nothing in this being new as it started in Minnesota over wild rice lakes and fur trapping and deer hunting areas and continued into the buffalo country. The Pembina awards, both the first which was insignificant monetarily and the second which appears substantial, are included here not for the amounts involved but because the Pembinas were never part of the public concern about land losses. The first award was a miserable $237,000 for their lands immediately west of the Red River ceded by treaty in 1863. Despite the strenuous efforts of this writer to divide the award in thirds among the reservation-based groups found to be representative of the historic Pembinas, legal and other minds prevailed. Instead of programing this small amount for the White Earth Pembinas in Minnesota, the Turtle Mountain Band in North Dakota and the Chippewa Cree Tribe in Montana, legislation provided essentially for the creation of a descendant roll. This roll, given the size of the award, is by far the costliest ever made by the BIA. Not a soul, including myself who made all sorts of dire predictions, knew that over 24,000 applications would be submitted and that most of these people, Metis, would be able to trace ancestry to last century annuity rolls consisting of untranslated Chippewa names. Although the original award was invested, which is always the case, the 20,000 eligible applicants were each mailed a check for $43.81. The point is that entirely too many people conceive of land claims in terms of not the tribe being wronged but the individual ancestors of present-day Indians.

By the time we were confronted with the second Pembina award in 1980 (actually two combined awards), we knew much more about the origins and contemporary identities of these people. The award of $52 million was made for the North Dakota aboriginal area ceded by agreement as late as 1905.

We were able to establish that the entire Turtle
Mountain Band is a successor to the Pembina Band.
Previously, the Chippewa Cree Tribe we had found to
be Pembina to the extent of over 80 percent, the
research beginning in 1964 with my interviewing aged
informants on the reservation. The very term
"Pembina" was so little understood, however, and the
documentation on this Rocky Boy element so sketchy,
that their own claims attorney stated in 1962 that
they were not parties in the case but that others of
his clients, all Metis, were.[11] The commission
innocently dismissed the tribe as a plaintiff in
1970. In our office we knew better. To his
enduring credit my close friend and immediate
supervisor, Robert M. Pennington, supported by a
mutual friend and colleague in the Solicitor's
Office of the Department of the Interior, totally
sustained me in my efforts to include these people
in the award. Our recommendations were adopted by
Congress in the form of the Pembina Chippewa Act of
December 31, 1982. Many Turtle Mountain people are
very mad at us. It is an old pastime on that
reservation for one group or the other to label
everyone else as "Canadians." There cannot be a
member of the tribe who does not have an ancestor
born in Canada. So much for the vicissitudes of
finding the proper beneficiaries of claims awards,
and so little; many of the cases we handled could
have each produced a book in themselves.

    If someone wanted to engage in a discussion
about which Indian groups were treated the worst by
the United States, an unrewarding pastime at best,
he would be constrained to include the Pribilof
Islanders. Who? The Pribolovians, the descendants
of those Aleuts who were transported to the islands
of Saint Paul and Saint George in the middle of the

---

[11] Indian Claims Commission, Dockets 113,
246, 191, and 221, unpublished transcript of
hearings of September 18, 1962, pp. 295-6, and Order
of June 30, 1970. Bureau of Indian Affairs,
unpublished "Results of Research Report in 1905
Pembina Chippewa Award," Washington, August 19, 1980.

Bering Sea by the Russians beginning in 1810. Confined far from the Aleutians at sites even more inhospitable than their original homes, they were forced to produce and process sealskins. Much Russianized through intermarriage and conversion to Russian Orthodoxy, many still speak and write Russian. They have nevertheless retained a strong Aleut identity. The oppression of these people was continued by the United States, by both trading companies operating with the full sanction of federal agencies or the agencies themselves. These included, under a series of statutes regulating the fur seal trade, first the Department of the Treasury, then Commerce and Labor, and after 1939 the Interior Department. Faced with the threat of invasion early in the Second World War (not the <u>actual</u> invasion by the Japanese of the Aleutians), they were evacuated and throughout the war many existed in virtual concentration camp conditions. They were fed and otherwise provided for as meagerly as on the Pribilofs, corned beef rations being among the items most acutely remembered. Learning that I had been assigned to the case, an old friend, who had not resided on the islands since the evacuation, telephoned from his office in Fairbanks. Voicing his concern that he, like so many others, was no longer in residence, he asked, "Are you protecting my interests in the corned beef money?" He was assured that our worries were identical to his as no official rolls had been made.

The claims attorneys for the Pribilovians were faced with an extraordinary task. Theirs was not a land claim nor did it properly fall into the category of an accounting claim for funds misused or inadequately protected by the government. The Court of Claims accepted the case as one of lack of fair and honorable dealings through the period 1870-1946. The Pribilovians were awarded $8.5 million. There are residing on or deriving from the islands only 1,041 persons, including my initially worried friend who recently shared in the award.

When two or more entities are recommended by the Secretary as beneficiaries of an award there can be, not surprisingly, an awful lot of trouble. To a great extent the woeful ignorance of Indian people *about their sociopolitical history is to blame. The classic nightmare, which I most reluctantly left uncompleted, is the Seminole award for the Florida lands ceded by treaty in 1823. The Seminoles or Seminolee, from the Spanish cimarrones meaning "wild," were not too appropriately named. They began primarily as Lower Creeks and some portions of other tribes that separated from the older Creek Confederacy towns and established themselves in northern Florida. At the close of the Creek-American war of 1813-14 they were joined by many Upper Creeks who fled to what was then Spanish Florida. As a result of the quickly ensuing first Seminole war with the United States the Seminoles ceded their lands and were given a large but then worthless reservation.*

Originally amounting to $16 million, the very nature of the Seminole award should pose a problem for any historians or archeologists specializing in Florida. The Indian Claims Commission made the award for almost all of Florida down to and including the Keys. The people who became the Seminoles, including the Hitchitis and Mikasukis, had no need to concern themselves with northern or central indigeneous Floridians because they had disappeared, mainly through disease. In 1823, however, the Seminoles were not using or occupying south Florida. In fact, during the second Seminole war of the 1830's, this brought on by their refusal to move to the Indian Territory, United States troops fired on Calusas in the Tampa area. The Calusas, one of the original Florida peoples, resented being confused with the Seminoles and gave a good account of themselves. They then left the pages of history but there are ethnographic hints that at least some were eventually absorbed by those Seminoles who remained in Florida and sought refuge in the south. On occasion, we who were handling the case would amuse ourselves in fantasizing about the possibility of an attorney finding at least some individuals who could establish Calusa identity. Given the tortuous history of the attempts to process the award, too detailed for this account and some of it unprintable, any such *development would have afforded relief.[12] I will only say that I was accused of bias in favor of the Oklahoma Seminoles, a charge demonstrably ridiculous and disbelieved.*

Many questions arose over the division of the funds among the Oklahomans and three Florida entities, the organized Seminole Tribe of Florida being by far the largest in that state. Having worked among the Florida people I knew well before the award was granted that those who had given it any thought were convinced that only their people should or would participate, rationalizing that only they had the fortitude to remain in the ancestral area. Others, especially those on the Tamiami Trail who refuse to join either of the constituted tribal organizations, have always maintained that they will not touch the money. I was also cognizant of the Freedmen question in Oklahoma. With this encouraging background I was assigned to the case and recommended that the funds be first divided on an Oklahoma-Florida basis and then a second division be made among the Florida entities. Given the disparities in modern tribal enrollment criteria between the Florida people and those in Oklahoma, with the latter having no blood quantum limitation, we resolved to employ historic rolls to effect the primary division. The Oklahoma by blood total of their roll of 1906 was adopted and the closest, useful roll to it in Florida, that of 1914. The roll was reconstructed, with the involvement of the Seminole Tribe of Florida, a most exhausting task. The Floridians, amazingly since they derive from a small remnant of the mid-nineteenth century, actually thought that they could equal the number of Oklahomans. The Oklahoma Freedmen were not included, clear precedent having been established that they should not share in awards arising prior to 1866 when they achieved tribal membership. We submitted the

---

[12] *Anyone interested in the tortuous tale can find much of this in my letter of April 7, 1978, and enclosures, to Hon. James Abourezk, Chairman, U.S. Senate Select Committee on Indian Affairs.*

recommendation that the Oklahoma share be precisely 75.404 percent and that of Florida 24.596 percent. Immediately, suits were filed against the Secretary by the Seminole Tribe of Florida, by the Oklahoma Freedmen, and by an individual purporting to represent a large group on the Tamiami Trail who viewed any payment as jeopardizing their rights to a big chunk of south Florida. In time, one of the U.S. Senators from Florida wrote to the Secretary that with investment bringing the award to a certain figure it had become appropriate to give her constituents their just due--50 percent--the logic in her view being inescapable. The Oklahomans are bankrupt and their tribal government was for years in total disarray. The Floridians have high stakes bingo and other lucrative operations and are in no hurry to press their case.

What has happened to all the money that has actually been distributed? Leaving aside the earlier awards made by the commission, and those few made prior to its creation, the year 1973 is selected as a useful focus. Congress, admitting that it was tired of having to pass legislation for the actual disposition of each award, developed an approach in the Act of October 19, 1973, directing the Secretary to submit a plan to Congress within six months of the appropriation of the funds. This deadline proved totally unrealistic. Consequently, the act was amended in 1983 to extend the period to a year. Cases failing to meet the deadline still demand legislation. The 1973 Act further provides, except in extraordinary instances to be justified by the Secretary, that 20 percent of an award be conserved for tribal social and economic programing. Therefore, fully 80 percent could be expended for per capita payments. Throughout Indian country, with notable exceptions such as the Jicarilla Apaches, the Washoes, and the Goshutes previously mentioned, the cry was raised for the full 80 percent and more if possible. With descendant groups the funds are entirely individualized. This was the route taken with the celebrated California award, originally $29.1 million and shared by 70,000 descendants. Neither the BIA nor the Interior Department chiefs ever questioned our small office regarding the programing percentages or the nature of such programing as appeared in any given proposed Secretarial plan or legislation. The congressional committees had earlier scrutinized some proposals but, despite the often enormous amounts involved, since 1973 Congress has only once questioned the Secretary concerning such matters. This occurred when Morris Udall, Chairman of the House Subcommittee on Indian Affairs, requested a justification for the inclusion in a Mescalero Apache plan of an airplane for the tribal chairman's use. The justification was provided; this particular chairman is the most durable and powerful in the country.

The record is so poor that the next Indian generation can be expected to file many suits charging the Secretary with failure in his capacity of trustee to conserve these funds. The 20 percent requirement is not a maximum but a minimum. The funds, as per capita payments, have generally been thrown to the four winds and continue to be so dissipated. From the implementation of the 1973 Act until January 1986, plans and legislation accounted for more than $900 million. Only $200 million were made available for social and economic programing. There are no official BIA reports to be cited and it should be emphasized that the actual effectiveness of programing elements remains unknown but to a few tribal people and field personnel. The Bureau has ignored its own regulations (Part 87 of Title 25, Code of Federal Regulations) requiring annual field reports concerning the implementation of plans and legislation.

Not only are the Indian people generally unaware of the source of the funds, that is, the nature of the claims awards, they often cannot recall just what happened to them. There are many horror stories. Perhaps the experiences of the Yankton Sioux of South Dakota and the Three Affiliated Tribes of North Dakota are the worst. The Yankton Sioux, with the modest current tribal membership of 4,840, went through 80 percent of $20.8 million in the space of a decade. The tribe and the BIA would have real difficulty in accounting for the programing portions of the several plans. The Three Affiliated Tribes of Fort Berthold Reservation is the successor to the once very

populous Mandans, Hidatsas and Arikaras, riverine or
semi-sedentary peoples of the Northern Plains. They
take the cake in spending judgment funds. Some years
ago a field colleague and I met with the tribal
council to discuss the development by them of a
proposal for one of their awards. I encouraged the
members to conserve more of the funds, or all of
them, in contrast to their earlier submittals.
During a recess one of the councilmen took me aside
and quietly informed me that although he agreed fully
it was "impossible on this reservation: they even
have a forty-nine that goes eighty-twenty." The
"forty-nine" is an old and basic pan-Indian dance
with a simple, clockwise step. In this instance the
lyrics, with accompanying drum beat, were sung in
English. On Fort Berthold all claims awards are
simply called "per caps," and one woman announced in
my office that she had placed cloth and tobacco
offerings on a hill, prior to visiting Washington, in
order to insure our support of an 80 percent per cap.
These people, in the same time as the Yanktons, have
eaten up 80 percent of $53.6 million with a
membership of no more than 8,000 persons. Both
tribes are now looking for all available assistance.

There are very large factions within tribes
who vehemently insist that they have never sought
monetary compensation for land and, in fact, that
they were sold out by a few individuals who conspired
with attorneys to file claims. Some of the subject
awards have been handled through Secretarial plans
and the beneficiaries have been determined. Others,
needing legislation, are so controversial, like
Seminole, that some of the respective congressional
delegations have given evidence that they won't go
near them. The "selling of our sacred lands"
rhetoric and the concomitant demand for land
restoration are incipient in some tribes such as
Hopi. For practical purposes, however, it can be
dated as of Richard Nixon's signing into law on
December 15, 1970, in the presence of the Cacique or
supreme religious authority, the bill for the return
of Blue Lake to Taos Pueblo in northern New Mexico.
Another factor basic to this philosophical and
political phenomenon is the marvelous success of the
Maine tribes in achieving monetary compensation and
vast acreage in one legislative swoop with the Act of

October 10, 1980. The most basic element, of course, is the sense of national guilt that the tribes expect to exploit.

Blue Lake is unquestionably a sacred site. It is an ancient Taos shrine and adjacent to the pueblo's lands when usurped not too long ago by the National Park Service. No portion of the site became private. Consequently, its return to the tribe was both justifiable and feasible. The Indian Claims Commission was not empowered to restore land, but the Passamaquoddy and Penobscot peoples of Maine, including some Malecites (Maliseets) of the far north, did not file claims with the commission. They are undoubtedly very happy that they did not. The Secretary of the Interior had the obligation to advise all tribes regarding their rights under the Indian Claims Commission Act. The "state reservation" tribes of New England, Long Island in New York, and Virginia were not so advised, primarily because practically no one in the BIA considered them to be Indians. The Maine people, who are tribally oriented, have affected the thinking of many Indians who previously had never heard of them, Maine being far from what is generally thought of as Indian country, but the Maine situation is actually far removed from that of tribes who have long maintained federal relations. What the Passamaquoddies and their other Wabanaki relatives did was threaten titles to private lands in those parts of the state they perceived to be aboriginally theirs. They stoutly maintained that the federal government permitted the State of Massachusetts, and later Maine that was carved from it, to usurp their lands. The principal legal argument turned on the Indian Trade and Intercourse Act of July 22, 1790, and other early statutes that fixed the federal responsibility for protecting tribal lands from individuals and the states.[13] Some Pequots of Connecticut, adopting the stratagems of the Maine tribes, have achieved similar success with the passage of the Act of

_____

[13] Passamaquoddy Tribe v. Morton, 528 F. 2d 370 (2d Cir. 1975).

October 18, 1983. Unlike the Maine peoples, they are practically devoid of authentic tradition and did not maintain a viable tribal organization.

To illustrate the unrealistic, uninformed and ethnohistorically baseless premises upon which the land restoration efforts are pursued, three other claims awards cases are examined here. One of these, the Black Hills, together with a closely related case, is further analyzed in the following chapter concerning treaties. The smallest monetarily, but indicative of many aspects of the total atmosphere, does not at all concern the loss of land. This is the case in which the awesome amount of $29,930.25 was granted to the Six Nations. As an accounting claim under the treaties of 1792 and 1794 it was established by the commission that the government, at various periods, failed to provide the goods, usually cloth, specified as annuities. The participating New York Iroquois still receive annually their portions in the form of muslin. Long before the appropriation of the award in 1974 the traditionally organized New York tribes asserted through a different set of attorneys that they had never authorized any such suit, and that a settlement would jeopardize their continued title to a good portion of upstate New York. The designation of the case, "Six Nations," added to the confusion as one of the historic founders of the league, the Mohawk Nation, was not in any manner involved. However, the Stockbridge-Munsee Community of Wisconsin is among the beneficiaries, these people deriving in part from the Mohicans (Mahicans) who became affiliated with the Iroquois and who had earlier participated in the cloth annuities. (James Fenimore Cooper did not kill off the Mohicans. They survived, in much diluted form, far from their native Hudson and Housatonic rivers). The processing of the award reached a climax with a Hearing of Record held in Syracuse, New York, on a Secretarial proposal. That hearing, a shambles to begin with, is especially memorable in that the enraged tribal leaders, who thoroughly cowed the Department of the Interior representative and the poor man hired to make a transcript that never was, then discovered a National Guard convoy outside the meeting place. Added to the accusations of the theft of land were cries that the troops had

been sent in. The "hearing" abruptly ended. The
Guard unit had no interest in the problems of the
League of the Longhouse (which has not functioned as
such since before the American Revolution). The
troops were on their way to summer camp.

The constitutionally organized beneficiaries,
that is, the Seneca Nation of New York, the Oneida
Tribe of Wisconsin, and the Stockbridge-Munsee
Community, all quietly accepted their insignificant
shares to be added to existing program accounts.
These are the "sellouts" who are not considered to
be part of the anachronism still called the Six
Nations Confederacy. The Onondagas, Tonawanda
Senecas, Oneidas, Cayugas and Tuscaroras, all of New
York, ignore their respective shares that continue to
be invested for them. They remain convinced that
they are preserving their land even after their suit
for an injunction against the Secretary was dismissed
by the U.S. District Court, District of Columbia, in
1977, the decision upheld by the U.S. Court of
Appeals, and certiorari denied by the Supreme
Court.[14] Their leaders and spokesmen, and their
attorney who heads an Indian legal aid office in
Washington, D.C., have explicitly advised other
tribes that they have won a legal victory. That
attorney, accompanied by an Onondaga who
traditionally held a string of "wampum" as he spoke
(they were plastic beads), made such assertions at a
crowded and highly volatile meeting in Elko, Nevada,
in 1978. They were speaking after the Six Nations
award had been appropriated and the Secretarial plan
had become effective, and after losing the first
round in court. I was present at this meeting. So
were many Western Shoshones.

An excellent way to get yourself despised by
millions of Americans, and have your children
ridiculed by their peers, is to be cast in the role
of a heavy in the CBS television production "Sixty

----

[14] _Six Nations Confederacy v. Andrus, et.
al._, 447 F. Supp. 40 (1977); affirmed 610 F. 2d 996
(1979); certiorari denied 447 U.S. 922 (1980).

Minutes." You might, for good measure, specify that
Mike Wallace host the affair in his inimitable
manner. I was subjected to all of this during my
assignment to the Western Shoshone case. I will
never forgive myself for not filing suit against CBS
although advised that as a "public figure" such
action would have been futile. Public figure,
nonsense. I was a Grade 13 federal employee and a
staff person at that.

Anticipating a large award for their
aboriginal lands in Nevada extending into California,
the Western Shoshone Claims Committee scheduled a
meeting at Elko in May 1973 to begin formulating
plans to identify the beneficiaries and distribute
the funds. I was directed to attend but justly
balked. Although it was well known that the amount
would be for $26 million, the award had not been
made and little research had been done. My pleas
went unheeded and I journeyed to Nevada at least
satisfied that the claims attorneys would be present.
They did not show. The committee, the Agency
Superintendent, and I were alone with a battery of
cameramen and a group consisting of the loudest and
rudest people, given any racial or ethnic cast, whom
I have ever confronted. This group, a distinct
minority among the Western Shoshones, is known by a
variety of names but often called the "traditionals."
They are no more traditional than many others who
have earnestly pursued a monetary settlement for
their lands. They had descended upon the meeting
with a vengeance and hurled insults and accusations
at the committee members and at me particularly as I
attempted to answer questions or counter statements.
These concerned the very nature of the litigation
itself, which is the business of the claims
attorneys, not the handling of the award which is
the responsibility of the BIA. Foolishly, I did not
demand that the camera crew refrain from taping my
voice or filming my classic Greco-Roman profile.
Among the things I told the audience was that "you
lost the land" and said further that this occurred
with the making of the Ruby Valley Treaty of October
1, 1863. The Superintendent supported these
statements. We learned later that the government and
the claims attorneys had stipulated a "gradual
encroachment" concerning the Nevada land with an

aggregate date within 1872. They had not based the land loss on the treaty. I was dead wrong, but to this day not a single Western Shoshone, "traditional" or otherwise, and not one of the successive attorneys for the holdouts has recognized the error. As stated, the research was by no means complete.

The resulting film is titled "Broken Treaty at Battle Mountain." The cited small colony in Nevada is the home of some of the most ardent foes of the award and the most vociferous proponents of land restoration, meaning all of the federal land within the area described in the treaty. Why they do not also claim the very considerable acreage in Nevada that the commission allowed outside the treaty boundaries remains a total mystery. In any event, they are talking about more than a fifth of a state that is primarily comprised of federally owned land. The treaty has not been broken anywhere. It is a mystifying document that cedes no land but at the same time provides for a reservation to be established at the pleasure of the President. Several reservations, albeit small colonies, have been created by Executive Order of the President within the bounded treaty lands. The holdouts will not concede that these are reservations. The sellouts don't care. These details are not covered in this technically excellent film that nevertheless represents a distortion throughout. For example, it places conservation agencies and personnel in the roles of truly venomous characters who are denying these late twentieth century hunter-gatherers their traditional staple foods, notably piñon nuts. No Western Shoshone is any longer dependent on such foodstuffs. The bone-crushing, tear-jerking scenes of piñon trees being chained off the land were in reality filmed in a conservation area no less than two hundred miles from Battle Mountain. The portrayal of the lone BIA functionary made him even more ghoulish than the conservation people. I was cast in the role of a bureaucrat somehow responsible for the loss of the land or at least being contemptuous of their assertion that they had never lost the title. "Sixty Minutes" excerpted this "documentary" on May 4, 1975. I had introduced myself when first speaking at the meeting and I am identified in both the documentary and the excerpt.

Mike Wallace, in his patronizing closing remarks, further mentioned me by name. Days later, at a fraternity alumni gathering in Alexandria, Virginia, one of those present laughingly asked if anyone had seen "that guy from Brooklyn who told those Indians they had no land?" I was sitting next to him. He did not get away with it.

The dissidents delayed by legal tactics the appropriation of the funds until 1979 and continued, as the "Sacred Lands Association," to sabotage every effort made by all other Western Shoshones to have the funds distributed. They, like the Iroquois, wrecked the Hearing of Record held on a proposal developed by the claims committee. The Sacred Lands group coalesced around a suit filed by the United States against the Dann sisters, two Shoshones who refused to pay federal grazing fees on the land they maintained had never been lost and which, of course, was sacred. The Western Shoshones, indeed all Shoshones before some took to the horse, had one of the simplest hunting and gathering societies known to mankind. They had little in the way of ceremonialism and such items as shrines were unknown to their cultural inventory. Predictably, the growing response among Indians to such sober and sterile scholarship is that all land is sacred. At one Elko meeting a Northern (also Eastern) Shoshone visitor said in the crowded hall that the only sacred land they might have provided for them would be found six feet under. He is from Fort Hall, Idaho, where the Shoshones have eagerly accepted substantial awards.

Sacred or not, the Dann sisters' cattle grazed upon the land unmoved by the series of contradictory legal decisions that finally forced the suit into the Supreme Court. In my opinion, the Department of Justice handled the case in such a slovenly manner that the government deserved to lose. The federal attorneys did not even realize that colonies are reservations, a critical element in establishing that the treaty had been fulfilled. The United States won, however, on February 20, 1985, the Supreme Court deciding that once the appropriated award is deposited into a trust account (which is always done immediately) payment is effected and the question of title to tribal land is answered.[15] The decision affects the Six Nations, the Sioux Black Hills case and all others in which payment has been so made. So the matter is over with. But not really. We do not know, for example, how such a factor as gradual encroachment is determined. More difficult to understand is why the BIA continues to negotiate with Western Shoshone factions about adding land to the greatly increased judgment fund. There are perhaps 7,000 interested Shoshones, most of them very Indian in every respect, mostly in Nevada and quite scattered. Many are not residing on reservations, including the colonies, and have little interest in tribal corporate matters, typical of Great Basin Indian societies. They are also not generally ranchers and they do want a full per capita distribution.

During the summer of 1978 Margaret Mead requested my participation in a panel discussion on "Fact and Truth in Film," part of an ethnographic film festival to be held that September at the American Museum of Natural History in New York City. The "Broken Treaty" film was to be viewed and discussed with the producer, Joel Freedman, participating. The Assistant Secretary for Indian Affairs, Forrest Gerard, a Blackfoot, readily sanctioned my attendance. I don't know why Professor Mead was so insistent on my presence. Although terminally ill she needed no assistance in using, to the delight of the audience, a very long, serrated blade on Mr. Freedman. I was almost vindicated but was not then being viewed by millions.

Thirty years ago, and for long afterwards, when you "loaned" a Sioux Indian a buck and a quarter for a six-pak the response usually was *toksha Paha Sapa*. Loosely translated this means "I'll pay you back when I get my Black Hills money." At that time everyone, and I mean everyone, from aged full bloods to mixed bloods whose knowledge of the language was limited to phrases like the above, was salivating

---

[15] *United States v. Dann*, 105 U.S. 1058 (1985).

over prospects of something like $15 million. In 1960, Charles Red Cloud, a venerable Oglala leader and a grandson of the famous Red Cloud, said to Jan Szczepanski, a visiting Polish sociologist and a student of Sioux history, "The Black Hills are still mine because I have never been paid for them." He elaborated, and at times it was necessary for me to translate into English, that the claim would be pursued until payment was made. The visitor was amazed at such tenacity.

Neither Mr. Red Cloud nor anyone else gave much thought to dividing what would have been a relatively small sum in consideration of the many thousands of interested Sioux from several tribes. With the emergence of the militant American Indian movement (AIM), and other nativist proponents of the sacred lands sloganism, the attitudes of many Sioux have very perceptibly changed. Boiled down the story goes something like this: the Sioux came from the Black Hills of South Dakota (and totally ignores the Wyoming portion); their culture, including traditional religion, originates in and is dependent upon the hills; and the hills are sacred containing many shrines or holy places indispensable to the maintenance of Sioux welfare and continuing identity. Embellishments to all this are created with ease. Most of those who hold this philosophy have honestly come to believe it and many other myths and fictions about their cultural and political history. They are encouraged by numerous American and European professionals. Except in South Dakota, students everywhere support them. Indisputably, no Indian entity north of Mexico has received more attention from historians and anthropologists. As good publications about particularly the Teton Sioux will fill a decent-sized home library, the emergence of these assertions is enough to make one cringe. They typify what I like to call "instant tradition." Quite in contrast with the mythology, some of the salient facts are as follows.

As has been said, all Sioux have their origins as Woodland people in Minnesota. Some evidence points to an even earlier home in the Ohio Valley. The Tetons were the first of the Sioux to reach and cross the Missouri River. With the acquisition of the horse they displaced the Black Hills tribes, like the Crows and Kiowas, and pushed them westward or southward, later allowing the Cheyennes and Arapahoes to continue to utilize that area and much more. The hills were part of the Great Sioux Reservation as recognized by the treaties of September 17, 1851, and April 29, 1868, and were "taken," as distinct from "ceded," by an 1877 act in clear violation of the 1868 treaty. Because they were found by the Court of Claims, as upheld by the Supreme Court on June 30, 1980, to have been taken without the consent of the Sioux, five percent interest was added to the land values of 1877.[16] With this addition, computed for the period 1877 to 1980 when the funds were appropriated, the award granted was almost $106 million. For their success in proving a "Fifth Amendment" taking, that is, without the consent required by the 1868 treaty, the claims attorneys are vilified by the tribal governing bodies and many individual tribal members. What is especially resented in arranging this "sale" of the hills is that the attorneys have received their fees and expenses, the fees in Indian claims cases being limited to ten percent. Today, most of the involved Sioux boldly assert that they never sought cash compensation and will never accept same for their sacred lands.

There is no Sioux shrine in the Black Hills. There has never been any such thing there and the area was not even popular for encampments or public ceremonials. There is no evidence that any Sun Dances, for example, were ever held in the hills until recently by those militants who defiantly occupied a site on public lands known as Yellow Thunder Camp. Not a single chief who met with the Black Hills Commission in 1875 made any mention of a sacred character possessed by the hills. They did ultimately demand either $7 million or $70 million, the confusion probably due to a language

---

[16] *United States v. Sioux Nation of Indians*, 448 U.S. 371 (1980).

barrier.[17] Of the same and many more chiefs and
leading men who met with the second commission the
following year only one, a Crow Creek Yanktonai,
referred to a shrine. He complained bitterly about
extensive quarrying by Whites at the sacred pipestone
site in southwestern Minnesota.[18] There is, however,
an ancient Cheyenne shrine at Bear Butte at the
eastern edge of the hills where those people still
conduct religious rites. Much of the site has been
taken in trust by the federal government for the
Northern Cheyenne Tribe of Montana and the
Cheyenne-Arapaho Tribes of Oklahoma. The Sioux have
lately claimed it as their own and have displayed
the courage to include it in a bill for the
restoration of the hills. Amidst the clamor and the
confusion hardly anyone seems to remember that for
many tribes, including enemies of the Sioux and each
other, the hills were of great value as the source
of an item of Plains material culture both
commonplace and basic--lodge or tipi poles.
According to oral tradition these "lodge pole pines"
were often cut, skinned and dried in a climate of
truce.

The BIA has failed to make recommendations on
the identities of the beneficiary tribes (who in my
opinion should be limited to those modern entities
comprised of Teton and Yanktonai Sioux) and the
division of the funds. This is partly due to the
avowed rejection by the Sioux of the award, and
partly because the bureaucrats (again, in my view)
lack the fortitude to advise one of the plaintiffs,
the Santee Sioux of Nebraska, that the tribe should
never have been involved in the litigation even
though it commenced in the 1920's. The Black Hills

---

[17] One of the best accounts of those chaotic
meetings is found in James C. Olson, "Red Cloud and
the Sioux Problem," University of Nebraska Press,
Lincoln (1965).

[18] "Report of the Sioux Commission," United
States Senate, 44th Congress, Second Session,
Executive Documents, No. 9 (1876).

area is nowhere near their Minnesota, eastern
Dakota, Iowa and Wisconsin lands for which they have
been paid and the money spent. They now adopt the
rhetoric of their western cousins as concerns the
hills.

Without the benefit of any advice based on
professional research, the Teton and Yanktonai
tribes, and the Santee Tribe, representing over
60,000 interested people (many of whom want their
money now), had a bill introduced in the Senate on
July 17, 1985. Sponsored by a Democrat from New
Jersey, Bill Bradley, the bill provides for the
restoration of federal lands in the Black Hills to
evidently all Sioux tribes, the "Sioux Nation,"
including those who remained essentially Woodland
societies and never saw the area. Although
unspecified in the bill, the attendant propaganda
usually fixes on the figure 1.3 million acres. And
lo and behold, Section 10 of the bill provides for
the monetary award to be invested by the Sioux
Nation with some of the accrued funds to be
distributed annually to those tribes designated in
the Secretary's "Results of Research Report." This
report was prepared by myself. It remains unsigned
by the Secretary and is therefore officially
nonexistent.

Mr. Bradley, with no constituent Sioux
community, was introduced to some Oglala Sioux and
the Black Hills case during his professional
basketball-playing days. His action is
irresponsible and surely it is so viewed by the
South Dakota congressional delegation. Any
progression of his bill, which reached the hearing
stage, can only be retrogression and serve to
further embitter, confuse and disappoint the Sioux
people. Seemingly, it has not occurred to any
significant numbers of them that with this kind of
money it is possible to negotiate for select locales
in the hills for, let us say, professionally
conceived and executed cultural, educational and
economic programs. But the powers that be won't
talk to the Sioux about these options or about who
ought to participate in the first place. Meanwhile,
the fund grows. It will reach an astronomical figure
before any legislation is passed. I have quietly

discussed with some colleagues my genuine fear that the sum will be so large as to prompt Congress to withdraw from Sioux programing. There is such a thing as too much money.

The actor Marlon Brando says that he abhors the Hollywood Indian image, which is almost always "pro-Indian" in at least a juvenile sense. Brando had no qualms, however, in doing his best in "The Godfather," a magnificent portrayal, and so strengthen the criminal image of Italian Americans. This advocate gave AIM a useless plot of California hillside land saying something at the time that this kind of return was long overdue. The militants, who share so much of the responsibility for the sacred lands philosophy, quickly decided to sell the tract without consulting any Californians indigenous to the area, assuming any exist.

CHAPTER   THREE

"AN   INDIAN   DON'T   HAVE   TO   PAY   HIS   DEBTS."

A   tribal   councilman.

Nowhere   is   distortion   and   instant   tradition more   evident   than   in   the   realm   of   treaties,   and   in those   aspects   of   historic   and   contemporary   Indian life   that   are   perceived   to   be   treaty-related.   The uninitiated   members   of   the   dominant   society,   and   so many   of   those   within   Indian   society,   are   to   be forgiven   their   confusion   when   the   very   term   "treaty" is   bandied   about   with   such   impunity.   Misapprehension can   only   be   extended   and   the   mythology   enriched   by the   assertions   of   those   in   high   government   places, journalists   and   a   plethora   of   Indian   advocacy   groups to   the   effect   that   the   special   position   of   Indian tribes   derives   wholly   from   treaties.   The   authors   of these   constantly   repeated   statements   blithely   ignore the   reservation-based   tribes   who   have   never   entered into   a   treaty.   Among   these   are   the   Papagos   and Pimas   of   Arizona   and   the   Walker   River   and   Pyramid Lake   Paiutes   of   Nevada,   all   with   large reservations;   and   the   numerous   Rio   Grande   Pueblos are   included   among   the   non-treaty   tribes.   There   are no   treaties   with   any   Alaska   entities.   Those   who persist   in   the   error   also   usually   ignore   the   fact that   since   1924   all   Indians   have   been   full   citizens of   the   United   States,   many   having   previously achieved   such   status   through   special   statutes.

One   of   the   most   influential   "Indian" newspapers   in   the   country,   a   weekly   based   in   Martin, South   Dakota,   and   generally   of   value   to   observers   of the   Indian   scene,   is   the   Lakota   Times.   The editor-publisher,   Tim   Giago,   a   sociological   mixed blood   Oglala   Sioux,   seems   to   seesaw   between   the objective   and   the   informative   and   sentiments   that can   only   be   characterized   as   Indian   journalese.   As the   large   circulation   includes   not   only   Sioux   of many   tribes,   but   other   Indians,   and   many   non-Indians, it   is   noteworthy   that   the   editor   of   late   is approaching   new   levels   of   stridency.   It   should   be said,   charitably,   that   he   could   not   have   read   any

73

treaty. But he often speaks of treaties generically, and of the Sioux treaty of 1868 in particular. In an article, actually a second editorial, he opened as follows: "Treaties are legal contracts signed between governments. In the case of the treaties signed by the Indian tribes and the federal government, they were contracts between sovereign nations." (I am convinced that Mr. Giago inadvertently employed the past tense). Further in the article we find: "Maybe the terminology in some of these treaties is colorful, such as 'as long as the grass shall grow and the rivers flow,' but the meaning is quite clear. It means provisions of the contract are perpetual." The piece ends with the kind of fear-mongering that has become a mainstay of Indian journalese and increasingly a slogan for Indian political figures everywhere. "Our treaties are a matter of survival, and those who would destroy those treaties would also destroy the Indian people."[1] Mr. Giago has done this writer a favor by nicely encompassing so much of the treaty rhetoric in so few lines. He invites us to dispense with one basic piece of mythology immediately, this being the poetry, considered to be standard treaty language by the whole of the American public, about rivers (or water) and grass.

---

[1] Tim Giago, "A matter of Survival," in the Lakota Times, Martin, South Dakota (October 16, 1985).

Some aspects of the historical and legal background of the concept of modern tribal sovereignty are found in Felix Cohen, "Handbook of Federal Indian Law," U.S. Department of the Interior, Office of the Solicitor, Washington, Government Printing Office (1942), reprinted by The Michie Company, Law Publishers, Charlottesville, Virginia (1982); and U.S. Commission on Civil Rights, "Indian Tribes, A Continuing Quest for Survival," Washington, Government Printing Office (1981).

On August 12, 1861, at the Wichita Agency in the Indian Territory, the Confederate States entered into a treaty with the Comanches, Wichitas and other tribes. The Confederates, undoubtedly thinking that they were following the established practice of the Union, wrote in Article V that, "Each tribe or band shall have the right to possess, occupy and use the reserve allotted to it, as long as grass shall grow and water run ... "[2] Similar language appears in another Comanche treaty of the same day and two other Confederate treaties made that summer. These are the only instances in which this phraseology or anything resembling it is found in any American treaty or agreement with an Indian tribe. I am advised that it appears also in an English colonial treaty. No matter; neither the language of the Redcoats nor the Greycoats obtains in these United States. Journalists, including those who know better, simply refuse to abandon this fiction. Years ago I was invited to one of those Washington "lunches" by William Greider, then the Washington Post's "Indian" man. The subject between mouthsful was treaties. Among the elements emphasized were that, overwhelmingly, Indian treaty signatories were illiterate non-English speakers; that tribes, not being nation-states, could not bind their own factions or individual dissidents; and that the grass and rivers romanticism previously employed by him was a figment of everyone's imagination. Only days later, on a front page article by Greider, appeared the deathless poetry in reference to the provisions of the 1868 Sioux document, the most frequently cited and most garbled of all treaties.

A specialist in American frontier history has coined a very strong term embodying what have become the most unrealistic and damaging aspects of Indian and non-Indian perceptions of treaties. The scholar is Robert M. Pennington, introduced in the preceding chapter. The term is "treaty psychosis," which was

---

[2] "Jefferson Davis and the Confederacy," Ronald Gibson, ed., Oceana Publications, Dobbs Ferry, New York (1977), p. 138.

first used in an excellent paper titled "Broken
Treaties" delivered in 1975 at the Unitarian--
Universalist Church in Reston, Virginia. Professor
Pennington's only sin, but a mortal one, is losing
the original and failing to make a copy of this work.
I have not been able to persuade him to rewrite it.

Pennington, regarding the broken treaty
litany, offered a number of telling examples of
tribes, or large factions within them, blatantly
ignoring treaty provisions and proscriptions. Among
these he cited the treaty between the Cherokee Nation
and the Confederacy, the tribal leaders (who were not
illiterate) being quite conscious that in signing
that document they were breaking about 20 treaties
with the United States, the series having begun in
1785. Other tribes or significant portions of
tribes made treaties with the rebels and so broke
all of those with the United States. In addition to
the Cherokees, and the Comanches and Wichitas
mentioned above, there were the Caddoes Creeks,
Choctaws, Chickasaws, Seminoles (of Oklahoma),
Osages, Senecas and Shawnees (of Oklahoma, the
latter not to be confused with the "Loyal Shawnees"
then in Kansas), and the Quapaws. A fascinating
development is the treaty made by one group of
Kickapoos, that tribe being aboriginally from the
Great Lakes, with the Mexican government. Mexico
honors the treaty, made in violation of American
treaties, and recognizes a reservation in the State
of Coahuila for this group.

The Delawares, generally staunch allies of
the British, broke the first treaty and successive
treaties and were not pacified until the signing of
the famous Treaty of Greenville in Ohio in 1795.
That event followed General "Mad Anthony" Wayne's
defeat of the intertribal alliance led, among others,
by Little Turtle of the Miamis. The Ohio Valley
tribes, in particular the then powerful Delawares,
Shawnees and Wyandots, all broke the American
treaties of peace, and of some land cessions, made
by them prior to Greenville as they persisted in
their association with the British. That association
did not actually end until the British defeat in the
War of 1812. The treaties were broken by the warring
tribes for the laudable reason that they trusted

76

Britain to hold their persons and their property safe from the avaracious American upstarts, but they were broken nevertheless. Much later in American history, when some Navajos had in the public view become as much of a scourge as some Apaches to the Anglo, Mexican, and other Indian populations of the Southwest, a peace treaty, but not of cession, was made with them on September 9, 1849. Numbers of Navajos, particularly during the period of the Civil War, followed a raiding economy until the tribe's utter defeat in 1868. On June 1 of that year the second and final Navajo treaty was made, this providing for a large reservation. That reservation has had extensive lands added to it and all other provisions have been greatly augmented in terms of goods and services. Recently, while participating on a television panel, a White attorney for the Navajos was questioned by a viewer on the numbers of broken treaties. With neither qualification nor embellishment he replied: "Three hundred and seventy-one treaties made; three hundred and seventy-one broken."

Many treaties enjoin the participating tribes to observe the peace with everyone including ancient or new tribal enemies. Especially on the Great Plains these provisions were flagrantly broken but an interesting and widely repeated distortion has emerged from them. For example, a Selective Service officer called my office to inquire whether any treaty exempted Cheyennes from the draft, the potential draftee maintaining that his tribe's treaty forbade him to bear arms. Cheyennes, of all people, a warrior society par excellence. The last treaty made with any Cheyennes was in 1868. For years afterwards both Northern and Southern Cheyennes were fighting other tribes and the United States. Further concerning warfare or the bearing of arms, almost identical assertions, apropos nothing, were made before a large crowd by a Kiowa announcer at the July 1974 Smithsonian Folklife Festival in Washington, D.C. It was the quantity and quality of the response of Indian volunteers during the First World War that led to the Indian Citizenship Act of June 2, 1924.

In support of the utility of the term "treaty

psychosis" I can add, apart from purely historical considerations, that a casual visitor to many diverse Indian communities might very understandably come away with the impression that the people were treaty-crazy. At the very least, it is to be expected that such a stranger would be convinced that the Indian people were avid students of treaties. Nothing could be further from the truth. Always given exceptions, Indians who talk treaty, and plenty of Whites, have never read a treaty. If any such reading has been done, it is almost invariably very selective. Generally, any superseding treaties are neglected in favor of that which is most gratifying and, more important, superseding agreements or acts of Congress are equally neglected or dismissed from consideration. There is an almost universal unawareness of the existence of Kappler's compilation of all valid Indian treaties and agreements and many of the pertinent acts of Congress.[3] These editions, Volume II being the "treaty bible," were always within easy reach in our office. The availability usually impressed tribal visitors or delegates, but not everyone appreciated printed versions. A colleague reported that at one time the entire Oklahoma Seminole tribal council, more than forty all told, resolved to journey to the Nation's capital to view the original of their treaty (in singular, not specifying which one). Asked why this very expensive trip was necessary, the tribal officials responded that they would not otherwise believe that a treaty

---

[3] Unless otherwise noted, all treaties and agreements cited or quoted herein are found in Charles J. Kappler, "Indian Affairs, Laws and Treaties," Washington, Government Printing Office (1904).

The Institute for the Development of Indian Law issued an eight volume set, "The American Indian Treaties Series," plus a "Chronological List of Treaties and Agreements [etc.]," including both ratified and unratified documents, Washington (1973-1975).

existed. Whichever treaty they meant, it is of nothing but historical or documentary value such as in pursuing claims cases. The trip was never made.

The American penchant for treaty-making is a direct outgrowth of what had become a time-honored British colonial practice in dealing with the tribes. There are about 372 United States-Indian treaties, the imprecision due to the fact that in a few instances it is unclear whether some treaties were ratified by the Senate. The same treaties have nevertheless been recognized. No less than nine treaties were made, all in an attempt to pacify the allies of the Crown, prior to March 4, 1789, the effective date of this country's constitution. In the Constitution, Article I, Section 8, it is provided that "the Congress shall have power ... to regulate commerce with foreign nations, and among the several states, and with Indian tribes." Avoiding any argument about what "commerce" meant to the authors, it is indisputable that if Indians themselves were not expected to disappear there was little doubt at the time about the fate of tribes as such. However, since they were around, and armed, and with the capacity to produce not only war but furs for trade they had to be dealt with.

Contrary to what is often written in general historical publications, repeated by the news media, and firmly asserted by the Six Nations, the first treaty was not made with that confederacy but with the Delawares on September 17, 1778. This brief document set the tone and pattern for many succeeding treaties. Among other things, it provides for the cessation of hostilities, for the passage of U.S. troops through the Delaware country (then Pennsylvania and part of Ohio), for no punishment to be inflicted on either Delawares or Americans absent a fair trial by judges or juries comprised of both parties, and for the regulation of trade. It is established in Article VI that Delaware territorial rights guaranteed by "former treaties" be observed. This is obscure but included treaties with the English. No land boundaries whatever are cited, this being unusual. In the same article appears an extraordinary feature, one that would have frightened later United States representatives.

This is an invitation to the Delawares and "other tribes who have been friends to the interest of the United States" to form a state with the Delawares at the head--and with representation in Congress. A few other early treaties provide for a tribal delegate to Congress, but such was never implemented. Given the excesses of the treaty psychosis, some surprise is to be expressed in that this provision has not been unearthed by the militant Delawares of Oklahoma, an insignificant group. I say this only partially with tongue in cheek because even some conservative Delawares of the main body have disavowed their treaty with the Cherokee Nation, and have threatened to form a totally separate tribe. Twenty-four treaties were made with those Delawares who constituted the principal group that as of 1866 incorporated with the Cherokees. For most purposes, this same Delaware element no longer constitutes a tribe in itself and their language and traditions have practically disappeared.

The Piankeshaws, hardly among those tribes known in the past or present to the dominant society, have ten treaties, the first signed in 1795 and the last in 1867. Originally part of the Miamis, as a sadly reduced entity they in time merged with the Illinois and other remnants forming what became the Peoria Tribe. This northeastern Oklahoma organization is, along with some of its neighbors, and the Miamis of the same state, a "paper tribe" (my term). They are among the Whitest Indians in the country. Those who insist that the very existence of a single treaty creates full tribal sovereignty would have been seriously challenged to find a viable Piankeshaw society even well prior to their last treaty date. Why then was a treaty made with them at that time? The answer is because they were Indians, and with Indians you make treaties.

The treaty-making era did not end until 1871 when the House of Representatives decided it wanted in on a proposed Yankton Sioux treaty. Only the Senate had been involved in this peculiar practice in dealing with peoples (admittedly not citizens at the time) within the borders of the country of the true sovereign, the United States. The last treaties, most quite similar as reflective of the

"peace policy" of that era, were made in 1867 and
1868 mainly with hostile Plains tribes and the
Navajos. After withdrawing from the treaty approach,
"agreements" were entered into with the tribes,
these in format and otherwise hardly different from
treaties, but were incorporated in or confirmed by
acts of Congress. While it is true that warfare
with the United States, or hostilities between
Indians and White settlers or migrants, prompted the
drafting of many treaties, a very large number
involved tribes never or inconsequentially engaged
in any such hostilities. Such is the case with the
Potawatomies, originally all from the Great Lakes,
another Indian society never in the public eye but
whose several subdivisions have in aggregate more
than 60 treaties. The question asked by many Indian
leaders and spokesmen is also raised here. If
Indian tribes are sovereign why cannot the United
States continue to make treaties with them? A
related issue is how the United States can control
Indian tribes through legislation, if indeed they
have sovereignty, with or without a prior treaty or
agreement.

Very few treaties contain viable provisions.
The now token cloth payments to the Six Nations have
been mentioned. The formally constituted Oneida
Tribe of Wisconsin, originating in New York, long
ago arranged for its portion to be converted to cash.
Periodically, when the annuities approach a figure
deemed worthy of a per capita payment such is made
upon the request of the tribe. On a visit to that
community some years ago a former sailor told me that
he had received a cloth payment check in the amount
of $1.49. He ordered a beer in a San Diego tavern,
paid with this federal check, received change for
$149.00, and ran like hell. There are other
treaties, however, that have been interpreted to
contain continuing provisions resulting in very real
economic benefits for some Indians, and
sociopolitical problems for them and their White
neighbors. The most notable of these affect Indian
and the larger societies of the Northwest Coast, the
Plateau and the Great Lakes. The "gonzo" journalist,
Hunter S. Thompson, has done a better job than most
in painting the early scenes leading to some
startling judicial decisions. The action began in

81

1964 with a "fish-in" on the Nisqually River in
Washington. The then durable and dependable advocate
Marlon Brando showed up, but none of the other
expected screen luminaries. Thompson reports that
more than 50 tribes were represented and that "one
of the leaders said happily that it was the first
time Indians had demonstrated any unity since the
battle of the Little Big Horn." The Sioux and
Cheyennes of 1876 had never heard of these
fish-eating people, but such ethnohistorical and
geographical extravagance aside, there was
considerable Indian unity in supporting this
demonstration and others to follow. The
confrontation was prompted by a State Supreme Court
decision restricting Indians in the use of
net-fishing for salmon and steelhead, and so
challenging the Treaty of Medicine Creek of December
26, 1854. A Tulalip Indian embellished the usual
fictional treaty language in asserting that the
Indians "'could fish for eternity--as long as the
mountain stands, the grass grows green, and the sun
shines ... '" Thompson so rightly concluded that
the sentiments expressed at the fish-in "could have
wideranging repercussions."[4]

The Medicine Creek Treaty was made by Isaac
I. Stevens, as Governor and Superintendent of Indian
Affairs of Washington Territory, with the Nisqually,
Puyallup and other tribes. In the following year
Stevens made eight other treaties throughout the
territory. Many of these so-called Stevens treaties
included tribes now extinct as such. All of these
treaties contain language very similar to Article 3
of Medicine Creek which reads in pertinent part:
"The right of taking fish, at all usual and
accustomed grounds and stations, is further secured
to said Indians in common with all citizens of the
territory ... " Such fishing places included
Pre-Columbian sites off the reservations. Continued
demonstrations and some dangerous confrontations,

---

[4] Hunter S. Thompson, "Marlon Brando and the
Indian Fish-In," in "The Great Shark Hunt," Summit
Books, New York (1979), pp. 378-383.

and the jailing of some Indians for allegedly
fishing illegally, brought the matter to a head with
what is commonly called the Boldt decision. Judge
Boldt, in his 1974 injunction against the state, the
federal government bringing suit in its own behalf
and as trustee for the Quinault and other Stevens
treaty tribes, found the fishing rights viable. The
same decision holds that off-reservation fishing by
other citizens is "merely a privilege" governed by
the state "as the interests of the state or the
exercise of treaty rights may require." The treaty
Indians were granted up to 50 percent of the
harvestable fish passing through their recognized
grounds. Washington State and non-Indian commercial
and sports fishermen protested the Boldt and other
related decisions and the issue ended up in the U.S.
Supreme Court. That court affirmed the 1974 Boldt
decision.[5] Subsequently, it was judicially
clarified that the affected Indians are required to
be members of federally recognized tribes. Governor
Stevens could not possibly have conceived of
commonality in the same sense as the contemporary
courts. His sloppy draftsmanship is typical of that
found in many treaties.

Analogous to the Washington State cases are
the treaty-based hunting, fishing and trapping
situations found in the Great Lakes, Florida and
some other parts of the country. A most unhealthy
and ambiguous climate has resulted in the
interpretations made concerning hunting and fishing
rights absent any such specifics found in a treaty.
The prevailing judicial view, which causes many local
Whites, whether hunters, fishermen or simply
conservationists, to gnash their teeth is that such
Indian rights are either to be read into a treaty or
are intrinsically found in tribal sovereignty. Like
aspects of the Stevens treaties, these rights are

_____

[5] The Boldt Decision emerged from United
States v. State of Washington, 384 F. Supp. 312, 392
(D. Washington 1974); affirmed by Washington et al.
v. Washington Fishing Vessel Assn. et al., 443 U.S.
658 (1979).

not limited to the reservations, and most reservations contain non-trust ("non-Indian") land. Many either border on or contain important commercial and recreational waters and wildlife habitats. Indians, who may be essentially White (as in much of Michigan) and hardly dependent on the woods and waters, being permitted to ignore catch and seasonal limitations have given rise to racist bumper stickers in such places as Wisconsin and Michigan. These read: "Save a Deer, Shoot an Indian" and are similarly ugly concerning fishing. Spear-fishing, for example, so popular with northern Wisconsin and upper Michigan Chippewas, is considered to be a genuine threat to the pike and walleye. Local Whites, and national sports and conservation associations, openly scoff at the cherished myth of the Indian bond with nature and have been voicing real anger at federal and state agencies and courts. As these lines were being drafted I had the opportunity to discuss the fishing problem in Michigan with a student from Traverse City. Referring to his aunt and uncle fishing in Lake Superior he said, "They used to get lake trout and salmon every day, but like, the Indians used gill nets and cleaned it out." Genuinely concerned, thoughtful citizens feel that they have no recourse other than calling for the abrogation of all treaties and the imposition of full state jurisdiction. Such people are, expectedly, accused of "genocide" by Indian advocates. Meanwhile, as one friend observed, the courts seem intent on giving Indians guns (and gill nets and fish spears).

Particularly on the smaller reservations of the Northwest Coast and the Great Lakes where civil and criminal jurisdiction was assumed by the states, it was thought that conservation was also so controlled. With the recent emergence of often spiteful assertions of nativism these previously somnolent situations have become very problematic. Whites and Indians have been forcefully reminded that the Act of August 15, 1953, usually known by its Public Law number, 280, passed during the "termination" era, allowed states to assume certain jurisdiction on Indian lands but explicitly excepted hunting, fishing and trapping. A full legal discussion cannot be attempted here, but the courts have held that even with those tribes whose relationships with the federal government have been terminated, the treaty-derived hunting and fishing rights continue if not also specifically terminated. Exacerbating the entire situation is that treaty rights apply not only to the exterior boundaries of a reservation established by treaty but in many cases to aboriginal lands. These interpretations have led to violence in Great Lakes states and elsewhere. Returning to the terminated entities, most have been restored to the federal bosom by a contrite and embarrassed Congress, but even before the Klamath Tribe of Oregon had been restored in 1986, the hunting and fishing rights remained under the treaty of October 14, 1864.

Recently, a guest in our home said that he had just relocated to Florida and that the only thing he knew about the Seminoles was that they had never signed a treaty. The usual extension of this statement, delivered ad nauseum, is that they are, therefore, still at war with the United States. It is uttered by just about everyone, including casual tourists to the Sun Belt, and echoed by some Oklahoma Seminoles. Not long before I retired I thought I had a White official of the BIA cornered into a bet to the tune of ten dollars for each treaty the Seminoles had signed. Obviously, this would have cost me nothing. Because he became overly suspicious I lost a half interest in 70 dollars, the other half to be pocketed by the employee who had made the "wager" in the first place but who lacked the documentation. The first of the Seminole treaties was made on September 18, 1823, in Florida with the "Florida Tribes of Indians" but clearly meant only Seminoles, by that time entirely politically distinct from the Creeks. A framed copy of this treaty is displayed in the Hollywood office building of the Seminole Tribe of Florida. It is, as previously mentioned, the principal document serving as the source of the land claims award, yet the Seminoles and everyone else continue to bask in the romantic aura of still being at war. The treaty, incidently, was signed by "Miconope" (Micanopy), the principal chief as the name itself conveys.

The second of the Seminole treaties was also

signed in Florida but all the others were made with
the main body after removal to the Indian Territory.
Many documents concerning Florida Seminole business
in this century have been labeled "treaties,"
including the constitution and bylaws of the
"Miccosukee Tribe of Indians of Florida." In the
early 1960's a faction of Mikasuki-speaking Seminoles
on the Tamiami Trail persuaded Indian-interest
organizations, the State of Florida, Congress and
the BIA into accepting them as distinct culturally,
including in religious terms as non-Christians, and
linguistically from the newly organized Seminole
Tribe of Florida. The majority of all Florida
Seminoles is Mikasuki, a minority being Muskogee or
Creek linguistically. The small group recognized
separately is comprised of parents, siblings,
uncles, aunts and cousins of the members of the
Seminole Tribe. They have had a Baptist church on
the reservation for almost 30 years. They are also
among those who maintain that they have a "buckskin
treaty" securing for them all of extreme south
Florida including the Everglades National Park. The
Seminole treaty mythology is so widely and strongly
accepted that Florida Seminoles were thought to be
immune from the draft during and for some time
following the Second World War. Until the 1950's
only one Seminole had been in uniform, Howard Tiger,
a volunteer.

The Florida Seminole reservations are wholly
tribal in ownership. Long prior to their
establishment by virtue of a series of purchases
made by the Secretary of the Interior, and gifts
from the state, the Seminoles were to a large extent
supporting themselves by the sale or trade of plumes
and skins. They surely played a role in reducing
some wildlife populations to the extent that
supposedly iron-clad legislation had to be passed
and promulgated to avert extinction. In February of
1986 a Seminole friend resident on Big Cypress
Reservation in the Everglades emphasized to another
friend, a visiting White grade school teacher, "I
can hunt _anything_ on my reservation." The tribal
chairman, James Billie, fully agrees.

Mr. Billie was arrested for killing a panther
on Big Cypress Reservation. The tribal chairman

admitted shooting the "protected" animal, one of a very few of the Florida species, but claimed that prosecution constituted infringement of religious freedom and treaty-derived tribal sovereignty. Thus far Mr. Billie has gotten away with it, the judge finding that neither the federal government nor the state has jurisdiction. Concerning assertions that Seminoles use panther parts for religious purposes, the court understandably avoided such matters on the basis of the overriding issue being one of sovereignty.[6] Among other treaties and statutes, the judge cited Article IV of the 1823 Seminole treaty, this pertaining to the reservation granted at that time. The lands are well north of any twentieth century Florida reservation and all historic Florida Seminole reservation lands were lost through an 1832 treaty that resulted in the forced removal of practically all of the Seminoles. The U.S. Fish and Wildlife Service is not happy with the _Billie_ decision, particularly as the judge also cited a federal Fifth Circuit decision that treaty rights obtain. This conflicts with a Ninth Circuit decision to the effect that no one is permitted to hunt a species to extinction. This _imbroglio_ came before the U.S. Supreme Court in _United States v. Dion_, a decision rendered on June 11, 1986. Dwight Dion, a Yankton Sioux, shot four bald eagles on that tribe's reservation in eastern South Dakota. Claiming unrestricted hunting rights under the Yankton treaty of April 19, 1858, Dion was advised in the decision that the Eagle Protection Act abrogated said treaty. Eagles are further discussed in Chapter Seven along with a variety of popular misconceptions, but I do not know the full implications of _Dion_ on the Florida case or other similar controversies. Florida having Public Law 280 civil and criminal jurisdiction over the Seminoles is immaterial to those egrets, panthers, alligators or elephants found on any of the Florida reservations, not one of which, I repeat, is treaty-

---

[6] _State of Florida v. James Billie_, Case No. 83-202 (_Circuit Court for 20th Judicial Circuit_, Hendry County, dated and decided June 28, 1985).

derived. *The creatures have reason to tremble. The
Seminoles are also notorious for hunting by
jack-lights mounted on swamp buggies. They do not
basically differ from all too many Whites and Blacks
in this respect, or from the Fort Berthold people in
North Dakota who take a ceremonial sweat bath, mount
their pick-up trucks, and proceed off the
reservation to drive deer onto the reservation so
others in the party can shoot without regard to
state licenses or limits.*[7]

    *Among the many of my personal experiences
that can be characterized as being within the realm
of the treaty psychosis are the unforgettable
assertions of an Eel Clan mother of the Onondagas.
This tribe served as the historic "keeper of the
fire" or center of the council of the Six Nations
Confederacy. In no Indian communities, including in
South Dakota where many Sioux are given to shrill
treaty rhetoric, is the treaty psychosis more
evident than in upstate New York. The Onondagas,
numbering no more than a few hundred, are among
those Iroquois who assert full and complete
sovereignty and consistently deny that they are
citizens of this country. The clan matron, who found
me alone in my office after everyone else had left
for the day, was accompanied by the Eel Clan chief,
her son whom she had appointed, and her husband, a
Mohawk. This extremely articulate lady explained
that she was interested in researching treaties. I
reached for the treaty bible and quickly turned to
those treaties that confirmed the title to the
Onondaga Reservation and provided for the cloth
payments. The clan mother, with a disdainful wave
of the hand, said that she was not interested in
"trifles" but in the treaty she had with her. A
three by four inch piece of slick paper was produced
containing what she insisted was part of a treaty
providing for the total sovereignty of all tribes on*

---

    [7] *Interesting observations in these contexts
are found in "Indians, Animals and the Fur Trade: A
Critique of* Keepers of the Game*," Shepard Krech III,
ed., University of Georgia Press, Athens (1981).*

a par with the United States and Canada. There was on this scrap of print no heading, citation or other identification but it did so provide. I maintained that it could only be a portion of something that had been proposed. From time to time various individuals write "updated" or revised versions of treaties. Some Indian spokesmen insist that the United States should continue to conduct all business with the tribes on a treaty basis, making new treaties as the occasion arises. The talk with the three visitors turned to citizenship at which point my remarks were met with increased disdain. The "delegation" left, bearing with them the sacrosanct, neatly clipped portion of a fantasy.

The attitude of the Onondaga matron is to be classified somewhere near that of the individuals who are members of tribes or aggregates having no treaty whatsoever but who think and behave as if they do. I discovered that a large, young Northern Paiute element believes that a Paiute treaty exists and will not be disabused of this notion. Although several general meetings were held in Nevada at the Carson Indian School to discuss the combined Northern Paiute land claims awards no mention was made of a treaty at any of these gatherings, not even by those who shouted that acceptance of the funds would result in the loss of land title and the termination of their tribal existence. With the development of a proposal by the claims committee for the utilization of the more than $20 million (a full per capita payment), a Hearing of Record was held at Carson in the spring of 1974. Young people had been conspicuously absent at the meetings but turned out in force at the hearing. Little testimony was offered on the proposal but fierce oratory was directed to the awards themselves. It became clear that most of those in attendance, particularly young, longhaired males, were convinced that a treaty guaranteed them the continued title to the extensive acreage in northwestern Nevada and nearby areas that was the subject of the three awards. The only treaty made with any Northern Paiute or Paviotso people is that of December 10, 1868, with the so-called Malheur Paiutes. The aboriginal Malheur lands and their short-lived reservation were entirely situated in Oregon. In fact, their land claims award was processed separately and well prior to Northern Paiute. This treaty does not appear in _Kappler_ since it was never submitted for ratification. It was not cited by the Northern Paiute militants but doubtless would have been if they had been aware of its existence. Any treaty will do, whether non-existent or totally inapplicable.

Lest I be taken to task for being too hard on Indians who indulge themselves in treaty fantasies, an observation concerning the Southern Cheyennes is in order. Two anthropologists, who shall remain unnamed, aided and abetted a faction of Southern Cheyennes, self-styled as arch conservatives and religious traditionalists, in forming a state-chartered corporation apart from the official government of the Cheyenne and Arapaho Tribes of Oklahoma. At a symposium in New Orleans several years ago these worthies discussed this development making no pretense about its political nature. When I inquired as to why the traditional, including religious, principles and activities could not be protected and sponsored by the constituted tribal organization, one of these "action anthropologists" responded that tribal councils were "set up by the government to make treaties."

The document epitomizing treaty fantasy is the previously referenced Sioux treaty of April 29, 1868, the date representing the first signing at Fort Laramie in Wyoming. It was signed at Laramie later that year as various Sioux (and Northern Arapaho) leaders were invited to do so, including Red Cloud, and still later at Fort Rice on the upper Missouri. It is very often confused with the Northern Plains Laramie treaty of 1851 mentioned in the preceding chapter. This 1868 treaty, actually similar in format to others made that and the previous year, is nevertheless characterized as a unique instrument. It is represented as a staggering defeat for the Sioux; as a total victory for Red Cloud as "the only Indian who won a war with the United States"; as a shameful action that effected the loss of most western Sioux lands (which it did); as a treaty that secured their lands forever; and, finally, as granting the involved Sioux tribes full sovereignty. These contradictions,

and many more, are sometimes uttered by Sioux and
non-Sioux in practically the same breath.

During the summer of 1955 I had to explain to
a then middle-aged Brule Sioux woman that the Wounded
Knee tragedy of 1890 occurred <u>after</u> the defeat of
Custer (in 1876), and that both events post-dated
the subject treaty. This same woman, styled as a
"tribal elder" and an "oral historian" assisted the
young Sioux militants by testifying in court in their
behalf. The unfortunate woman had lost her son
during the Wounded Knee occupation of 1973. He was
the only Indian killed; the second "Indian" was a
White posing as a Cherokee. She asserted in 1955
that Red Cloud was drunk when he signed the treaty
(the clerk making an 'X" while the chief touched the
pen held for him, the usual treaty practice). She
insisted in court, however, that the treaty granted
tribal sovereignty at least as concerned all of
western South Dakota and so made the militants
immune from prosecution. They had not only staged a
heavily armed occupation of Wounded Knee but had
been responsible for violence elsewhere in South
Dakota.

The numbers of Sioux who honestly believe
that their leaders were under the influence when
"touching the pen" are legion. For some years at
Pine Ridge Agency a canvas of the signing was
displayed in Lone Dog Cafe. It depicts Indians
cavorting while brandishing bottles before a group
of White officers. The Whites are anachronistically
sporting tri-cornered hats and eighteenth century
swords and other accouterments while seated at a
table bearing the treaty. The painting has, happily,
disappeared along with the cafe. Red Cloud, an
avowed enemy of alcohol, was totally sober when
signing on the sixth of November after requiring
three days of explanation and interpretation. The
other band chiefs and warrior fraternity officers
were not drunk either, but all did lose a vast
territory, keeping a large but greatly diminished
reservation comprising western South Dakota with a
small area east of the Missouri.

The 1868 treaty is the historic basis for the
Black Hills claim and, together with the 1851

Laramie Treaty, for the claims case designated as Docket 74 as originally filed with the Claims Commission. The United States Claims Court found that the Sioux ceded by the 1868 treaty a huge aboriginal area east of the Missouri in the Dakotas, and most of the west Missouri lands that actually constituted their first reservation as described in 1851. This judicial decision was not easily made because of a number of complexities, one being that the cession language of the treaty is so ambiguous as to border on the contradictory. The ceded west Missouri portions were located contiguously in North Dakota, Montana, Wyoming, and Nebraska. It is noteworthy that in dealing with certain of these areas in South Dakota and Nebraska the government on two occasions gave Ponca lands to the Sioux. The court in 1985 awarded more than $39 million for the Sioux cession. The plaintiff tribes will not accept the award, maintaining that the 1868 treaty is inviolable. They demand, therefore, that this vast acreage in no less than five states be returned to them. In this totally unrealistic atmosphere the award is being appealed by both the tribes and the defendant United States, the latter in an attempt to reduce the sum.

It has been stated that an 1877 act implemented a very faulty 1876 agreement and took the Black Hills in violation of the 1868 treaty. Article 12 of the treaty requires the consent of three-fourths of the adult male population for further land cessions, similar provisions appearing in other treaties of that period. Nothing resembling the required number of signatures was obtained, neither the federal commissioners nor the chiefs and head men bothering with the commonality. The other men did not raise the issue either. The contemporary tribal leaders, including those who have formed now old "treaty councils" and who greatly resent the elected bodies, and friends as far away as Austria, delight in publicizing a patronizing and legally worthless utterance of the Supreme Court in reference to the violation. The demand for the hills, which had been overrun by gold prospectors, was accompanied by a threat to deny rations to the dependent Sioux if they did not relinquish title, this aptly called the "sign or starve policy." The Supreme Court on page 15 of the previously cited June 30, 1980, decision, repeating the language of the Court of Claims, said: "A more ripe and rank case of dishonorable dealings will never, in all probability, be found in our history, which is not, taken as a whole, the disgrace it now pleases some persons to believe." The statement is cited up to and including the term "history," but no further. What is not cited, ever, by Indians or their "friends" or in Indian publications, is this devastating sentence found on the first page of the decision: "In 1877, Congress passed an Act ... implementing this 'agreement' and thus, in effect abrogated the Fort Laramie Treaty." The emphasis is mine.

The 1868 treaty does not contain a single currently effective provision. If not abrogated by the Act of February 28, 1877, it was clearly superseded, the Great Sioux Reservation being greatly diminished by the loss of the hills but actually increased to some extent by adding a North Dakota tract. The Act of March 2, 1889, broke the reservation into six separate reservations and opened large portions of the original to settlement. Still later acts of Congress resulted in the settlement by Whites of parts of the separate reservations. Even the 1868 annuity provisions have run out of the period specified. Some friends and colleagues, including attorneys specializing in Indian law, agree that the treaty is essentially dead but insist that the education provisions obtain--and apply through graduate school. One such attorney will not accept that the states are responsible for Indian education and regards such states as Montana, where almost all Indian children attend public schools, to have adopted a gratuitous stance. I find this utterly wrong. If the U.S. Supreme Court declared that Texas is responsible for the education of illegal immigrant children surely the states are responsible for Indian children.[8] Most Indians, including those resident on reservations, have for a long period been attending public schools.

---

[8] Plyler v. Doe, 451 U.S. 958 (1982).

The 1868 treaty is very much alive in the minds and hearts of Indian people, White students and others far removed culturally and geographically from any Sioux societies. Article 6 provides for adult males to be entitled to homesteads of 160 acres on land outside the described reservation "which is not mineral land, nor reserved by the United States for special purposes other than Indian occupation ... " This language was actually unearthed by the militants, most of them decidedly not Sioux, and their non-Indian student comrades, to support the illegal and dangerous "takeover" of Alcatraz Island in the 1960's. Among the more vociferous leaders was a Canadian Mohawk who waved this American Sioux treaty around like a banner--and whose young daughter who had been kept out of school fell to her death from one of the abandoned federal prison's concrete tiers. The father, who became a fugitive, was later shot and killed by a California policeman.

The takeover mentality is best exemplified by those Mohawks from Caughnawaga in Quebec and St. Regis in Quebec, Ontario and New York who cited American Iroquois treaties to support their claims to lands in New York and Vermont. They first "repossessed" a site in upstate New York involving a series of violent incidents, including the shooting death, possibly by accident, of a young White girl. Continued litigation, characterized among other things by the incredible ignorance of New York officials, led to the "relocation" of the Mohawks to an Adirondack state park tract in 1977. They practice what they perceive to be traditional life in this the second home that they have named Ganienkeh. These people derive from Mohawks and other Iroquois (and Abnakis and other Algonquians) who divorced themselves from their tribes and the Six Nations Confederacy to become French Catholics. Their reserves on the St. Lawrence River, as stated earlier, date from missionary centers, these centers then being within French Canada. They had no part at all in the treaties made between this country and the Iroquois, whether the latter were friendly to King George or to George Washington, an indisputable fact forgotten by them and by the Six Nations nativists of New York who support them. It is

94

apparently also unknown to New York State authorities and a small army of social scientists. Perhaps it should be said that all or most of these people are deprived in that they had no nuns in New York City to introduce them to Kateri Tekakwitha, the now beatified "Lily of the Mohawks," who left her tribe and her confederacy for a St. Regis convent. I was taught that she prayed barefoot in the snow offering this penance for her pagan relatives who had burned French Jesuits at the stake. These were the same pagans who remained in the Mohawk Valley in New York until the end of the American Revolution.

Tom Beaver, an Oklahoma Creek journalist whose tribe does not have reservation status but does have some tribal trust land and certainly claims full sovereignty, writes in his column so inappropriately titled "Building Bridges": "Indian nations should begin to seek foreign aid for their underfunded programs, develop trade agreements with other nations and even begin sending ambassadors to Europe, South America and Asia. All it takes is the will to do something Indian nations haven't done before."[9] I am aware of only one entity, the small Lummi Tribe of Washington, that has followed this outrageous exhortation in the form of applying for a portion of their reservation to be designated a foreign trade zone. However, some other tribes are not far behind in like manifestations of sovereignty. The Red Lake Band of Chippewas, whose reservation in northern Minnesota is entirely comprised of tribal land, has declared that a "passport/license" is required for all visitors doing business on the reservation (see following plate). The Oglala Sioux Tribe recently attempted the issuing of tribal auto licenses in lieu of those issued by the state, while South Dakota plans to assume jurisdiction of all highways and even local roads on all reservations in the state. The list grows with each passing day to the edification of those Whites avidly seeking a

---

[9] Tom Beaver, "Building Bridges," in the Lakota Times (November 13, 1985).

NOTICE

NO TRESPASSING

The Red Lake Reservation is a closed reservation. A passport/license is required to anyone who wishes to conduct business of any sort having to do with any person, agency, department, company or corporation must first contact the Red Lake Tribal Council to make an application for a passport/license approval. Passports/Licenses will be granted upon Tribal Council approval. Violation of this order constitutes a punishable offense against the Red Lake Band of Chippewa Indians.

Prepared and paid for by the Red Lake Tribal Council
Roger Jourdain, Chairman

As appeared in the *Lakota Times* (December 11, 1985).

confrontational issue that will end all vestiges of tribal authority and the trust status of Indian land.

This chapter can hardly purport to be a treatise on the labyrinth of Indian law, but some historic issues are unavoidable. They are presented here with the continuing caveat that all Indians are now citizens, and the observation that few individuals of any stature in the last century could or would project that viable Indian societies would be in existence today. In my view the disappearing Indian myth colors everything. The first Indian to serve as Commissioner of Indian Affairs, a Tonawanda Seneca, had been General Ulysses S. Grant's aide during the Civil War. His presence at Appomatox Court House was initially questioned on a racial basis by Robert E. Lee. This New York Iroquois, Eli S. Parker, had some telling things to say about Indian sovereignty. He stated in 1869:

> A treaty involves the idea of a compact between two or more sovereign powers, each possessing sufficient authority and force to compel a compliance with the obligations incurred. The Indian tribes of the United States are not sovereign nations, capable of making treaties, as none of them have [sic] an organized government of such inherent strength as would secure a faithful obedience of its people in the observance of compacts of this character. They are held to be the wards of the government, and the only title the law concedes to them to the lands they occupy or claim is a mere possessory one. But, because treaties have been made with them, generally for the extinguishment of their supposed title to land inhabited by them, or over which they roam, they have become falsely impressed with the notion of national independence. It is time that this idea should be dispelled, and the government cease

the cruel farce of thus dealing with
its helpless and ignorant wards.[10]

Parker spoke just after the making of the last
treaties. Although his statement is loaded with the
cliches of yesterday, and today, such as the
references to wardship and Indians as roamers (the
Iroquois, for example, were sedentary), his attitude
is quite clear. These days Parker, who both held
the traditional title of a councilor in his tribe
and was a graduate engineer, would head the list of
the "Uncle Tommyhawks" or "apples" (being White on
the inside).

By the time the Cherokees were faced with
removal to the Indian Territory confusion concerning
sovereignty became truly confounded. I am referring
specifically to the famous, and to me now very
anomalous decision of Chief Justice John Marshall,
often quoted and variously analyzed. Justice
Marshall, in 1831, characterized tribes as "domestic
dependent nations" and acknowledged the peculiar
relationship of the tribes to the United States. He
spoke of such relationship as "that of a ward to his
guardian" and made other similar statements that
hardly support tribal sovereignty.[11] Nevertheless,
the advocates of full sovereignty can be counted on
to cite this particular decision, sometimes
qualifying in terms of the relationship being closer
to that of trusteeship. A much less popular Supreme
Court decision, virtually unknown to Indian people
and long preceding the Black Hills case, was
prompted by the complaint of the Kiowa chief Lone
Wolf and others of the combined Kiowa, Comanche and
Apache tribes of Oklahoma.

---

[10] Annual Report of the Commissioner of
Indian Affairs for the Year 1869, Washington,
Government Printing Office (1870), p.6.

[11] Cherokee Nation v. Georgia, 5 Pet. 1
(1831).

The Medicine Lodge Treaty of October 21, 1867, with the Kiowas and Comanches, fully involving the so-called Kiowa Apaches in a separate treaty made just afterwards, is one of those providing for the consent of three-fourths of the male population for any further land transactions. The reservation established by the treaty was allotted to the tribesmen, that is, individualized, and the surplus lands opened to White settlement by virtue of an 1892 agreement that, apparently, failed to secure the required consent. Controversy over the value of the surplus lands and other issues delayed implementing legislation until 1900. Following this move by Congress, Lone Wolf filed suit. The resulting Supreme Court decision made clear that Congress has the power over the tribes to abrogate a treaty. The court said that "Congress has always exercised plenary authority over the tribal relations of the Indians and the power has always been deemed a political one not subject to be controlled by the Courts."[12]

In contradistinction to the treaty rhetoric, Indian treaties are not inviolable and do not constitute the "supreme law of the land" since Congress has plenary power over the affairs of the tribes. And, despite any upholding of tribal sovereignty by the courts, whether or not treaty-based, such sovereignty exists only at the whim of Congress. It is, therefore, not "sovereignty" as perceived by so many Indian people and the general public. However, within the climate generated by or generating the treaty psychosis are found numerous individual Indians and often practically entire tribes, and individuals from all sociological classes within the dominant society, who maintain that the tribes are true nation-states. The same people vehemently deny that Indians are citizens--or affirm that they occupy a special or dual citizenship status. We who bother to read the constitution of the United States find only two

---

[12] Lone Wolf v. Hitchcock, 187 U.S. 553 (1903).

individuals in the country who have special
citizenship status. They are the President and the
Vice President; both must be natives.

With far too few exceptions, the quality of
reservation life is visibly deteriorating while
these lines are being written. Alcoholism, endemic
diabetes, drug abuse, broken families or the absence
of a family structure, homicide and suicide are
forming what is becoming the norm in reservation
Indian society, and much of non-reservation society.
Despite all this, tribal governments, who spend
money like it's going out of style, exhaust their
energy and resources not in meeting these frightening
sociopsychological problems but in the pursuit of
the trappings of sovereignty. The listed social
diseases, and many more wholly or closely related
such as the staggering auto accident rate, are simply
not perceived to be as much of a threat to Indian
society as the omnipresence, in the Indian mind, of
the end of special Indian rights and privileges.
Beyond the scope of this book is any detailed
analysis of the field of tribal civil and criminal
jurisdiction, but with all too many tribes this is
among the manifestations of sovereignty that occupy
them to the loss of a suffering resident membership.

Samuel J. Brakel has studied the tribal court
system in depth, many tribes maintaining either
these or, to a much lesser extent, the federal Courts
of Indian Offenses that still operate on some
reservations. Brakel states in his publication,
subtitled "The Costs of Separate Justice," that the
tribally operated courts "are white American
creations, and quite recent ones at that" (the
so-called Five Civilized Tribes no longer have
courts but their European-influenced systems began
in the Southeast and were transported to the Indian
Territory). Brakel contrasts the attitudes of
tribal leaders with those of the average reservation
residents concerning tribal police and tribal courts.
The latter have little interest in maintaining this
expression of sovereignty. I add in a personal vein
that it is also an expression of Indianness. Among
the strongly asserted conclusions in this politically
very unpopular report are that a distinction between
"Indian justice" and "White justice" is little more

than a cliche, and that Indian police and judges often behave more like Whites than the Whites. He concludes also that, "Integration is the only approach with real promise, and it is inevitable in the long run."[13]

I agree wholeheartedly with Mr. Brakel's findings and conclusions. Tribal civil and criminal jurisdiction, fortunately absent in .Oklahoma and other states with large Indian populations, is a sham. The courts are not empowered to handle the major crimes such as homicide, rape and arson but only the "kid stuff," and do not have criminal jurisdiction over non-Indians including those who reside on trust land. They do, however, have jurisdiction over Indians who are not members of the tribe. Any BIA police operating on a reservation also have such extended, and limited, jurisdiction. A visiting Winnebago from Wisconsin can be arrested for drunk driving on the Navajo Reservation (where is found a most elaborate court system whose only important Indian trait is, apparently, the use of the tribal language), convicted, fined and incarcerated in tribal jail. A White, Black or Hispanic equally irresponsible can at best be only held for state authorities. For a long time I have wondered what the same or other tribal courts would do with a triracial party recognized by North Carolina as an Indian, or a "terminated" Northern Ponca. But this is idle conjecture because such an individual undoubtedly would be declared a non-Indian after any initial confusion. This aspect, more than any other found in the system, renders it not so much an extension or trapping of tribal sovereignty as a racist farce. Only recently have two Indians,

---

[13] Samuel J. Brakel, "American Indian Tribal Courts: The Costs of Separate Justice," American Bar Foundation, Chicago (1978).

Alternative views are found in Vine Deloria, Jr. and Clifford M. Lytle, "American Indians, American Justice," University of Texas Press, Austin (1983).

one in Arizona and another in North Dakota, questioned the authority of tribal courts over non-members. As these very new cases are in early 1989 before the federal appeals courts further comment would be premature. The issue will undoubtedly be before the Supreme Court. Tribal member or not, and I interject that a number of tribes still have nothing resembling official, current rolls, no Indian arrested by tribal police has yet formally raised the issue of American citizenship.

Although the term "sovereign" nowhere appears in the text, the Indian Reorganization Act (IRA) of June 18, 1934, conveyed to many tribes a heightened sense of sovereignty. However, to many other tribes and many of the members of those who organized under it, this legislation inspired a real fear of the loss of sovereignty and the protection of the federal government and so to be left to the mercies of their own people. In my view too much has already been written and spoken about the IRA. There are not any significant distinctions sociopolitically or culturally between IRA and non-IRA tribes, and the dominant society understands even less about the act than Indians. It is, though, blamed by some Indians and Whites for every conceivable social and economic problem. Often called, misleadingly, the "Wheeler-Howard bill" after an introduction that was substantially reduced by Congress, the resulting act was touted by Commissioner of Indian Affairs John Collier and other New Dealers as the social, political and economic salvation of the tribes.

The Indian Reorganization Act became the accepted title, but in itself it is an act "to conserve and develop Indian lands and resources; to extend to Indians the right to form business and other organizations; to establish a credit system for Indians; to grant certain rights of home rule to Indians; to provide for vocational education for Indians; and for other purposes." It was amended on June 15, 1935, to include the Oklahoma tribes who were in political limbo after statehood. Section 16 of the IRA provides for the adoption of a constitution and bylaws by the tribes. Most of the *tribes electing not to come under the act have, nevertheless, written, formal governing instruments. The two largest tribes, the Navajos with a reservation and the Cherokees without reservation status, and other large tribes, are not organized under the IRA. Some professional observers, among them BIA officials, are still, like Collier and his friends of years ago, clucking their tongues over the non-IRA tribes. In the last analysis the non-IRA tribes, and those with no formal governing documents at all, have as much administrative potential such as forming housing authorities, and as much or as little sovereignty as those under the IRA. John Collier apparently thought that most Indians either basically resembled the Pueblos or had the capacity to develop similar sociopolitical institutions or practices. He particularly regarded Taos Pueblo as a model for the IRA. Ironically, while the Taos people voted for the application of the IRA they have retained their ancient religious and Spanish colonial political system. The Cherokees and the other Five Civilized Tribes, who now generally eschew the adjective, had in the Indian Territory and some of them in their aboriginal homes what would have been considered almost model IRA organizations.*

Immediately upon organizing under the act many of the affected tribes embarked upon a course of political embroilment that is unceasing. The quality of campaigns, election and post-election battles, bickering and open warfare within the councils and with those out of office, and with the Old Dealers who have never accepted constituted government inspire contempt from White neighbors and the tribal members themselves. The latter, regardless of how ill-informed they may be, find comfort in their belief that whatever the excesses of their tribal government their treaties will keep them safe. I have, throughout my career, heard and read innumerable poignant statements from those now usually aged individuals, both Indian and White, who strove mightily to make the IRA function as intended. These critics tend to wring their hands over the abuses of power evidenced by so many tribes, and the general absence of social and economic growth. In reference to the tribal councils in the Northern

Plains, not exempting that of his own tribe, an extremely professional Sioux who delights in speaking polished Lakota said, "We created a monster." An Omaha woman echoed the simplistic sentiments of many in saying that "Collier set the Indians back a hundred years." More thoughtful observers wonder whether this trip was necessary, and ask if it is too late for the tribes to form truly civic-minded local organizations geared also to the proper utilization of their lands and other physical resources.

In the midst of the disappointment voiced about the IRA, or the continued championing of the statute and its actual or potential good, Congress instituted in the 1950's the termination policy. In brief, termination sought to not only end the special relationship of the tribes with the federal government, and in actuality their political status as tribes, but the disposal of tribal land, timber and other assets. It meant also the termination of special Indian programing and services. It was a mindless and uncalled for move with tragic results for most of the relatively few tribes so stricken. For the Menominees of Wisconsin it was a genuine disaster; for the Northern Poncas of Nebraska, who no longer formed a viable community, it meant little. As said, the policy has been reversed, with most of the formerly terminated tribes, including Menominee, having been "restored." For how long? ask Indian people.

The termination policy was replaced in the early 1970's by the hollow slogans of "self determination" and "government to government relationship." I was present when an anthropologist in the employ of the BIA, who had genuine contempt for anyone who expressed concern about tribal cultural distinctions, wrote the first slogan for President Nixon. The view persists that tribes ought to do as they please with their own property, and who has the temerity to raise any question? But tribal land remains inalienable (unless Congress decrees otherwise) for which every tribal member should give thanks. Most tribal funds are still held in trust by the Secretary of the Interior and the tribes are generally dependent on the federal government for funding, often including the support of their governments. Try as they might, neither Indian leaders nor anyone else can truly equate the tribes and their governments with any of the sovereign states of the Union. A White friend with impressive scholastic credentials has read the first treaty, that with the Delawares, and has an unpublished paper urging the establishment of an Indian United Nations with the objective of forming something resembling a state and so ending any threat of termination. He and I know that some member of Congress is capable of airing a notion like this, but if anything gives the lie to tribal sovereignty it is the history of caprice as expressed by the solons and the executive branch, to say nothing of a maddening and hopelessly tangled judicial skein.

The Oglala Sioux, whose attitudes so reflect the treaty psychosis, form an IRA tribe, although many of the members adamantly proclaim that the tribal council is at best playing games, the "treaty" being the sole governing authority. In the 1960's certain storekeepers or "traders" on the Pine Ridge Reservation began to do more than chafe under the burden of credit accounts with Indians, these entrepreneurs being invariably White. This omnipresent problem was brought again to a crisis by threatening to deny further credit to some of those in arrears. Most of the involved customers were very poor, but had nonetheless accumulated some impressive bills for groceries and gasoline. During a meeting at one of the largest reservation centers the problem was discussed amidst quite damning accusations directed to the storekeepers. Finally, a councilman representing that district arose and said in English, "An Indian don't have to pay his debts; that's in the treaty." The response was delivered in the form of a resounding chorus of Hau from the men and traditional expressions of assent from the women. I was not in a position to question this astounding declaration. My father-in-law was not among those being vilified but he was a reservation storekeeper. The Superintendent was present but said nothing. While driving back to the agency he said "Such statments should be responded to." Well, why didn't he? In those days the Agency Superintendent was still a demigod.

CHAPTER FOUR

"IT'S ONLY FORTY ACRES."

An Indian bureaucrat.

There is a valid statement made by the fear-mongers who plague Indian people. They rightly point to maps locating reservations and remind all their listeners that the boundaries as delineated are often deceptive. The official BIA map is one of the worst examples since no attempt is made to convey that within the exterior boundaries of a given reservation more than half of the land may have passed out of tribal and individual Indian ownership. This situation, particularly prevalent in the Great Lakes region, throughout the Plains and in Oklahoma, is the result of well-intentioned policy as much as it is of White agrarian need and greed. During most of the last century and continuing to the present there have been few Americans who have not supported the philosophy and all of the attendant techniques of turning Indians into nice, quiet, harmless dirt-grubbers. To this end, with the support of the White House and all involved federal agencies, and the general public as represented by the clergy and the do-gooders of eastern High Society, Congress passed a number of pieces of legislation that carved-up the tribal patrimony. The most far-reaching and damaging of these was the General Allotment Act, also known as the Dawes Act, of February 8, 1887. The emphases of that statute, and others such as the 1889 Sioux Act, were to create detribalized, ruggedly individualistic Indian families who were expected to quickly achieve self-sufficiency. A disaster everywhere it has been imposed, especially in those many instances in which the allotment was eventually "fee patented" (removed from trust status), the system has not even worked with horticulturalist tribes like the Creeks and Choctaws. Most allotments have been sold to Whites and highly acculturated mixed bloods; with the latter they often remain in trust and therefore not taxable.

The tracts that were fee patented were usually the first to be acquired by Whites. "Supervised" sales of allotments held in trust, together with fee patenting, account for the "checker-boarding" of both large and small reservations that were often already reduced by legislation providing for White settlement. Patents were sometimes forced on Indian owners, particularly mixed bloods, and the tracts then sold without their knowledge or consent. This was the cause of the loss of much of the White Earth Chippewa Reservation in Minnesota. The IRA forbids any further allotting of reservation land. The proponents of the IRA anticipated that Indians throughout the country would enthusiastically salute that particular proscription, but I and many others have heard numerous Indians bemoan the fact that they were born too late to have received allotments.

Some Indian people made and continue to make strenuous efforts to preserve their allotments or portions that they have legally inherited, reside on them and actually utilize them economically. Others have never seen the land that was sold. Some have significant interests in land that exists for them only in the form of a periodic grazing or farming lease or minerals royalty check. A very conscientious Agency Superintendent who was concerned about the loss of Indian land had, at the same time, few illusions about the utilization of such land by the owners. He frequently referred to any large lease checks received by either resident or absentee owners, including those who resided on the reservation but nowhere near their land, as "unearned income." Deploring the flow of requests made by usually elderly full bloods to sell their land at below appraised value to a mixed blood or a White "friend," or to sell it out of an economic grazing unit composed of contiguous allotments, he said more than once that he felt saddled with "the strangest landlord situation ever." This man, who was White, would personally counsel full bloods who had no income other than their lease money, and he very rarely approved land sale applications made by owners in that category.

In Oklahoma the pressure, including outright threats, placed on full bloods and Freedmen to sell their lands is too well-known to bear repetition here. A celebrated case involved a Seminole who spoke little English and who was known to me during the last years of his life. He killed and literally "fed to the hogs" a local White who tried to steal his land. Convicted and imprisoned, he was later pardoned by the Governor. His stance is to be contrasted with those who are eager to sell the very tract upon which they reside, and who bitterly denounce any tribal or federal authorities preventing them from so doing. For generations the pattern of land utilization on the larger reservations, whether subjected to the allotment system or not, has been that of mixed blood or White stockmen and farmers leasing tribal land and combinations of tribal land and allotments, their cows grazing around the homes of full bloods who often enough raise only dogs. Exceptions are found among Navajos, Pueblos and some Apaches where full blood sheepherders, farmers and stockmen are in evidence. On the Plains where, as always, there are the starkest contrasts, the successful mixed blood ranchers and farmers are often publicly reviled by the full bloods, and by landless mixed bloods. Indian people living on, for example, 80 acres rutted by the constant movement of cars and pick-up trucks, with the ancestors of the same vehicles rusting all around the acreage and a few yards from the house, and with trash of every description underfoot, have real difficulty understanding why someone else's cows are grazing on the same site (if it has any grazing value). Their resentment and incredulity are heightened by the proximity of a White farm on land identical in every basic respect to theirs and which, in fact, may be leased from an older family member. I once spent an evening in Fort Totten, North Dakota, with two Canadian brothers-in-law who were there pricing farming equipment. Their complaints about the totally idle lands on a Manitoba Indian reserve adjoining their operation are among the angriest I have ever heard. What was worse, exclaimed one of the pair, "that's Crown land and you can't touch it," meaning buy it.

Every conceivable technique has been brought to bear in the interests of making agriculturalists of Indians. Some of these would resemble games if they had not been so serious and cost so much money and time. The usual result was an increase in the bitterness or at least the sense of failure exhibited alike by the Indian participants and those charged with the execution of such programs. I refer to such approaches as giving an individual, or even a community or a tribe (the Rousseaunian nonsense again), a bull and a number of cows or a genuine herd. Many people, including Indians, resident or employed on reservations chuckled delightedly as each animal was slaughtered, left to starve or thirst or to succumb to disease. The not so funny, but very typical, remarks of a Creek mixed blood who had supervised one such program among traditional full bloods ended with the rhetorical question, "How can Indians think they can start a herd after they eat the bull?". A hilarious and yet very instructive novel by Dan Cushman revolves around the eating of a bull on a Montana reservation.[1] This invaluable publication is largely unknown to the present generation, but it is frequently found in the more acculturated Indian households where there may not be anything in the way of the history or the traditions of their own tribe or any other. I pause to say unequivocally that Indian people from the most varied cultural backgrounds have a marvelous sense of humor and delight in recounting the foibles of Indian society. If there are any weaknesses in this they are more than compensated for by the strengths. It does not mean, as so many members of the dominant society who live and work in Indian country think it means, that Indians are happy with their lot.

The emphasis on farming, ordinarily meaning gardening, was more intense than any other land utilization program. It was hardly successful, the produce from fields and gardens rarely lasting for even part of a winter. Exceptions are found among Pueblos and others where no federal stimulus was needed to encourage such activities. A good Indian

---

[1] Dan Cushman, "Stay Away, Joe," The Viking Press, New York (1953).

was someone who planted and tended a garden; and a real good Indian was able to display prize squash or other produce at a reservation or community fair. One of the most touching scenes I have ever witnessed involved a highly respected old traditionalist who was trying in vain to get the attention of some impatient agency employees. Yelling, which was quite uncharacteristic of him, that he would not be treated "like an Indian," in his desperation he nevertheless added that he "put in a garden every spring." When a BIA functionary finally indicated that he was listening, this man in lower tones began to speak about his problem, apparently some money he thought was due him. This was more than a decade ago when gardens had become a rarity on his reservation. Today they are almost nonexistent.

"Well, all Indians were roamers," apologized the Secretary of the Interior's special Indian representative. She was referring, tangenitally, to the high mobility of Indians contributing to their unwillingness to use their land. The woman is an Oklahoma Choctaw. In their aboriginal home in Mississippi her ancestors were renowned as the preeminent agriculturalists of the Southeast, the immensity of their fields of corn, beans and other crops never failing to impress European and American visitors. The perception of Indians as nomads, despite the existence of gardens or even fields, was nevertheless adopted by Europeans primarily because the indigenes who planted also hunted and gathered to an extent that to them spelled savagery. Since Indians were also heathens, the perception was strengthened. Heathen equates with savage, and savage equates with instability. The rationale naturally proceeds to nomadism--and shiftlessness, all of these epithets irrationally coexisting with the Noble Savage myth. Indian people have adopted similar views of their past though even Californians and Great Basin people who planted nothing aboriginally were hardly nomadic. The tipi-dwelling buffalo hunter has influenced practically everyone, and the practically everyones don't know that on the Plains some tribes secured as much of their food from their hoes as from their bows. It was the same people, convinced that all Indians were nomads, who were intent on instilling in them the European peasant and early American agrarian values of their forebears. If it is of any consolation to both the Indians and the Whites who hold fast to the stereotype of nomadism, it can be said of numerous Indians that with the advent of the automobile they quickly put to shame any of their ancestors who might have been truly nomadic. The resources of a family, often a very extended family, expended in getting a car to move through and out of the larger and more isolated reservations can scarcely be conveyed to a stranger to such phenomena. I have accompanied Indian families on hundred-mile round trips for a case of beer, and to distant dance and rodeo encampments returning several days later to find dead cattle and gardens trampled by living cattle and horses.

During the winter of 1959-60, in the midst of a well-orchestrated program conceived by the Association on American Indian Affairs of New York City to frighten the Oglala Sioux into a realization of just how much land they had lost, I was invited to a meeting in a small, little-known community. In the capacity of adult educator and community development worker I was requested to review the kinds of activities in which I was engaged. Most of these were briefly covered, but little interest was sparked until I reached what was deliberately called the "tribal village development program." Taking some pains to distance this approach from the rhetoric of the New York association (an old Indian-interest group), it was explained that where people had clustered (in reality squatted) on tribal and in one instance BIA school land we were attempting to formalize and improve such situations. We were encouraging the residents to organize for the purposes of securing valid tribal assignments, potable water sources, establishing recreational areas and in general bettering what had largely developed into "dog patches." The program was the direct outgrowth of an unacceptable situation in another part of the reservation where a number of families had settled at random on the day school grounds and were, among other naughty things, tapping the school's very limited water supply. My first specific assignment with the BIA, other than *being employed as a laborer during two previous summers, was to assist these people in establishing a village on a nearby tribal tract that, although the only one available, was not the most appropriate site. The assignment proved a nightmare, that community hardly boasting the human resources found among the group I was addressing. It was, however, accomplished and later attracted many other families who found it convenient to live there.*

The people of the Sand Lake community (a not too imaginative pseudonym) had some limited knowledge of what had been initiated with the people who were required to vacate the school grounds. I was asked specifically what had already been done, which was little as the program was embryonic, and what was projected in the long run. After a presentation that included some crude blackboard diagrams relating to the other group, the community chairman and several others politely asked why they had not received similar attention. I expressed my surprise that such needs existed among them as I had been told that they were residing on their allotments. The community officers and others present countered that they were crowded on the allotments of ancestors, that is, "heirship" land, or on the lands of living, older relatives. They added that their roads were often difficult or impassable and, further, that only one well served the whole community, the water unsafe and the pump in disrepair. When asked what they had in mind the response was swift. They wanted to establish a village on the site where we were meeting, federal school land in the immediate vicinity of their homes. These people elaborated that although some families would be expected to remain where they were, the village facilities would serve all. Much was accomplished in that first meeting, surely one of the most gratifying in my memory.

Heirship land, federal reserve land, and tribal land in this context are all terms that demand some attention before proceeding. The Sand Lakers, many of them, were at least utilizing heirship lands. These are allotments in multiple ownership. The original tracts were granted late in the last century to most Indians from allotted

113

reservations and early in this century to the Western Sioux. The causes of multiple ownership are easily understood; the results are accountable for the ill health of some of the bureaucrats who have tackled the problem. Numerous allottees simply failed to make the wills that were something unheard of in Indian society. Their descendants followed suit. As a consequence such items as annual grazing lease checks for a dollar and a few cents are familiar to many affected heirs, with the whereabouts of many others remaining unknown. This problem worsens with each passing hour and the government doesn't know what to do about it. I know; by legislative fiat the land should be returned to the tribe from whence it came if it is of any value in a designated tribal development area. A lifetime estate can be provided for any heirs actually in residence on the tract and who desire to remain. This approach would be consistent with existing law as it has been decided that tribes have jurisdiction over allotments. The matter came to a head with a suit brought on by the Oglala Sioux Tribe's tax on individual grazing lease incomes.[2] The tribe won, to the continuing resentment of the older, full blood allottees. As said earlier, it is so often the Sioux who set the stage for Indian policy and law. Further concerning heirship tracts, if too remote for inclusion in any development area I believe that they should be declared taxable, which was the intent in the first place, if such lands have been abandoned. If an heir has established residence, however, again a lifetime trust status estate can be created. Lest any of this sounds simplistic, I hasten to add that I remain aware of the formidable legal and sociopsychological problems inherent in any moves of this sort. Meanwhile, the handwringing and moaning about heirship continues; but I have never heard anyone say that it is the heirship problem itself that is responsible for the retention of much Indian trust land. In some cases these tracts are in

---

[2] *Iron Crow v. Oglala Sioux Tribe*, 231 Fed. 2d 89, Eighth Circuit (1956).

blocks, well situated or potentially so for
community development programing.

The proposed Sand Lake village tract
consisted of 40 federal acres, school reserve land
that had, of course, been carved out of the original
tribal patrimony (as recognized by the 1851
treaty). There were, in addition to the allotments,
some contemporary tribal tracts in the vicinity and
a lot more acreage that had been sold out of Indian
ownership. In short, the area surrounding the
community was, and still is, checkerboarded as is so
common on many reservations. The federal reserve
land in question contained at the time a frame
building that originally housed a BIA day school but
had subsequently been made available to the county
for a public school. This was the building in which
we met. Other, smaller school buildings and a
softball field were situated on the tract, but
nothing else. I was requested, as a preliminary, to
approach the responsible agency and tribal officials
about the possibility of restoring this tract to the
tribe for the purposes of satisfying the needs of
the local community. I did so with alacrity. An
agency realty officer, a tribal member who knew and
admired the Sand Lake people, promised full support
saying, "Give it back to the tribe; it's only forty
acres." By this he did not mean merely that the
land was worth nothing to the government, but that
it did not resemble a large, taxable agricultural
tract. At that time any attempt to remove land from
the tax rolls was anathema to White residents of the
Northern Plains and their congressional
delegations. The picture is not much changed
today. Legislation, passed about four years after
the start of the project, was actually needed to
restore the land to tribal ownership.

With the blessings of the BIA and tribal
officials it was decided to move ahead while the
machinery was in operation to secure the site. It
should be remarked that if a community development
figure is expected to act as a catalyst in such
situations, my role as far as that was concerned was
nothing but a continuous joy. It surely was not
with many other equally needy but truly apathetic
and virtually leaderless groups. Local communities

within reservations can offer the most boundless contrasts. Sand Lake's only important deficiencies were that it was too small and too isolated socially and geographically to serve as a model. However, as things progressed the people themselves did much, sometimes consciously, to influence others. They attained an enviable position despite any isolation factors. The agency employment assistance man, who much later became the chairman of the Yankton Sioux Tribe, sanitation workers and engineers and others with the Indian Health Service all offered unwavering support on both the professional and purely personal levels. They shared my view that the small Sand Lake group had if anything too many excellent leaders, both male and female. It also boasted husbands and fathers who actually worked at whatever was available.

A few more words are in order about the community setting at the beginning of the program. This was a sociological full blood group; the children conversed among themselves in the tribal tongue. The one really aged lady in the community, mother and grandmother of many of the residents, was never seen without shawl, moccasins and a sheathed knife at her belt (a war trophy; a swastika-embossed German dagger). She and an old gentleman, also a community ancestor, were among the most respected people on the reservation. Their children were the movers and leaders. At Sand Lake, formerly uninviting in any physical sense, fathers and uncles played softball with the kids. Later, as the group began to give public evidence of their vitality, they not only sent forth fierce challenges for softball and baseball games but formed what became one of the better known traditional dancing societies. They constructed a "shade" (a pine-covered, open circular arbor) near the school house and quickly became famous for hosting Sioux dances.

Together with all of the evident or potentially good features, the Sand Lakers were burdened with a one-room grade school with one teacher, a well-meaning, energetic Sioux college graduate whose English was execrable. Within a year they began thinking the unthinkable--to close the school and bus the children to a public school in

116

the nearest town. That school had classrooms for all grades and, at that time, an overwhelmingly White enrollment. The move was made; the school house was turned over to the tribe and, renovated by the local people, became the community building. Today most of the children of this presently much larger community attend, where many excel, the public grade school and high school. It is with pride that I note in news of the schools the same surnames as those with whom I worked. They are the children of the Sand Lake children of the 1960's, the same who did not run and hide at the approach of strangers, the usual behavior of those who lived on remote homesteads. They were not only free from dangerous drunks in their own community; they had plenty of responsible people around to protect them. Shortly after the closing of the school the teacher entered tribal politics, abandoned his young family, and then contributed to the positively frightening reservation highway death toll. It is difficult to blame that unfortunate, so ill-prepared man for anything; but surely Dante, writing today, would reserve a very special place in the Inferno for those who handed him a degree and teaching certificate.

A milestone was reached with the Health Service's drilling of a well and installing an electric pump, a utility afforded all the village projects within the new program. The Sand Lakers, like the other village groups, elected a "Water Commissioner" to collect the small but psychologically important usage fees. People had selected small lots on the site, obtained formal assignments, and began moving in. There was no housing program at the time, the residents buying and moving usually old houses to their lots or building houses as best they could. The greatly expanded community features new housing on the land added but not contiguous to the original village. The only thing that I discouraged was a "community garden," meaning a cooperative, proposed by some women. I simply reminded them that such projects had been dismal failures, with which they promptly agreed. Other activities such as renovating the houses and providing furniture needed scant encouragement from anyone. To this day I fondly recall the women, assisted by an Indian extension service lady, making curtains and restoring furniture in what had been the canning kitchen, another relic of the agency farm program days. The community chairman's family was among the first to occupy a lot. I apologize to nobody for the intense pleasure I experienced when happening upon him mowing his lawn for the first time, and I hate caring for lawns.

The Sand Lake and other village projects were at varying developmental stages when the Association on Indian Affairs' efforts gave birth to a noisy grass roots move to end land sales. Accordingly, a confused and fearful tribal council prevailed upon the BIA to halt a scheduled land sale. As I predicted, and got myself into a lot of trouble for so doing, the movement was not grass rootsy enough. Some of the tribal members calling for the moratorium on land sales were among those who raised hell when actually confronted with the loss of the anticipated funds. The supervised sale was, therefore, eventually held. What is relevant to the present discussion is that the Sand Lakers and many others began to recognize that only tribal land was truly secure, something that had not greatly occupied them previously. One very active woman at Sand Lake remarked at a community meeting that "this is the safest land around," and went so far, I think to her husband's consternation, to say that even if the lots were eventually taxed they would be able to easily absorb the expense. This is, after all, not Manhattan Island "front inch" real estate. All concerned, however, had to exercise much care in view not only of the confusion engendered by the moratorium rhetoric but the exacerbation of the fear of land taxation. Such fear, as applied to the tribal village development program, often manifested itself in the caveats issued by people convinced that the sites would quickly become incorporated towns. Given such factors the greatest pains were taken to employ the English term "village" but never "town," and to assure the people that they were not being enticed to a place where they could lose their homes and their identity. Just prior to a Sioux style celebration serving as the official opening of the settlement, I had a sign painted that read SAND

LAKE INDIAN VILLAGE and was decorated with tipi outlines. The very pleasant, young Episcopalian minister who was derisive of the Indianness conveyed by the tipis simply did not appreciate the intensity of the fear-mongering with which we had to contend. The Sand Lakers enthusiastically accepted the sign, none of the many Indian visitors of the following day registering any objection either. The man who dug the holes for the sign posts, a descendant of Chief Conquering Bear, served as the community vice-chairman and one of the drivers of the local school buses.

Of course there were some disappointments, and some failures, but hostile dependency, apathy and factionalism were never in evidence at Sand Lake to the extent found elsewhere. I was not too concerned, but some other BIA people and some tribal officials were, when the community and the tribe derived only a pittance from a tribal hay meadow. This was a nearby tract that had been regularly leased to a White rancher. The Sand Lake people made an arrangement with the tribe to bale the hay. I remain convinced that if the community had sole rights to the production they would have done well, if not that year then the next. Everyone knows what happens to such funds when emptied into the coffers of "the tribe," that entity often being more distant from a local, natural community than the federal government, the county or the state.

Several years later, while employed with the Seminole Agency in Florida and on vacation with my family, I visited Sand Lake in mid-summer. I met a vivacious White VISTA worker who had been there for some time and was about to return to graduate school. This young man was knowledgeable about the sequence of events at the village to an astounding degree. He explained his own role in the most candid manner, concluding with the observation that the atmosphere had become moribund and that "a new crisis," like the lack of water, was needed. This student left early the next day. Much earlier that morning the old frame community building burned to the ground, the fire injuring no one and damaging nothing else. It did not reach the nearby shade within which was to be held a feast and a dance for

a man and wife who had died years before. (The
dance aspect was "funny" as one old lady opined. It
is a new observance in honor of the old, powwowism
now reigning practically supreme in Indian
country). I have long since forgotten the VISTA
worker's name, and statute of limitations aside I
would never utter it anyway; but no one is going to
tell me that he was not responsible for the
conflagration attributed to "old wiring." No, I did
not put the idea in his head, but this arsonist
deserves a medal.

I had been invited to the memorial feast and
dance, held despite the community tragedy and
well-attended. A local lady who had been unstinting
in her support of the program, and who had provided
a fine model for the whole community, was weeping
copiously over the loss of the building. I referred
to her by name during a lull in the ensuing dance,
but after securing the permission and encouragement
of the principal mourners. What I said basically,
the community chairman interpreting for the sake of
formality, was that there was no need to cry and
that the Sand Lake people were capable of erecting a
much larger and fireproof community hall. The fund
was begun with an embarrassing four dollars from my
wallet, ceremonially turned over to the chairman.
The immediate response was of the kind only Indian
people can make and the Sioux in particular. That
very afternoon and evening contributions poured in
from locals and members of many other communities.
One of the means of obtaining donations, of a
strictly Northern Plains Indian nature but invented
on the spot, was to sing in honor of the license
plates of the many cars ringing the dance shade. A
year later the community officers proudly escorted
me into a new but not quite completed concrete block
building. There were some good days in that
business even though I was no longer employed there.

Admitting fully that the Sand Lakers
comprised an extraordinary group of poor, rural
people, be they Indian, White, Black or otherwise,
what is the point of all the above? It is that the
original 40 acres, including the ball field across a
gravel road that was, finally, maintained, are of
more value to more Indian people than huge portions

of reservation land. The participating bureaucrats from a variety of agencies deserve commendation for the inspired realism they brought to this project in social engineering. Their attitude can be sharply contrasted with that of a longtime BIA functionary whose staff in Washington, D.C. was examining the programing potential of an Eastern Sioux land claims award. This man said of his own tribe, which was one of the recommended beneficiaries, "Forget programing at Sisseton; there's not enough land to bother with." Sisseton (Lake Traverse) Reservation in extreme northeastern South Dakota was one of the first to be allotted; fee patents were then issued with a vengeance. A totally non-traditional but very "Indian" ceremony, concocted to encourage the acceptance of fee patents, made its appearance at Sisseton and later was employed in the western Dakotas. Male heads of families and other adult males were invited to stand on a wagon bed and shoot an arrow, thus symbolizing the release of any restrictions on their allotments. Trust status, therefore, flew with the arrow, or perhaps arrow should be pluralized. I have never been able to learn whether the bow and the arrow or arrows used were authentic, how many of the enfranchised knew how to nock and release the arrows, or how many arrows were broken or lost. These kinds of questions occur to an ethnographer, especially one who knows how long it takes to make a Sioux style arrow. However unauthentic that peculiar ceremony might have been, it is quite verifiable that most Sisseton land quickly disappeared, and with the opening of the reservation for settlement by Whites land was not retained for tribal purposes. The tribe has since purchased or otherwise acquired land, but in the 1960's the only tribal land was a small tract that had been the site of the agency. The not enough land to bother with was the home of a local community and is still called Old Agency village. Some other not entirely unrelated points should be made. Ultimately, Sisseton programing was made possible through that particular claims award; and most Indian employees of the BIA are just as insensitive as most non-Indians to distinctions, not to mention interrelationships, between people and natural resources.

In his testimony some years ago before the House Subcommittee on Indian Affairs, the chairman of the Cheyenne River Sioux Tribe made an impassioned plea for assistance in securing more land. Unlike Sisseton, White Earth, the former Oklahoma reservations and many others, Cheyenne River has in addition to allotments large quantities of tribal land. In reality representing the stockmens interests, the tribal official was unaware that one of the subcommittee members, with only one small tribe in his own state, had taken the trouble to quietly visit Cheyenne River and other reservations. His views were very similar to my own. He did not much like the contrasts he found between the residents of full blood communities and other tribal members who were engaged in ranching and other operations supported by tribal land. The Congressman was close to hostile in saying to the tribal chairman that he for one was tired of hearing about the need for more land "as if that is going to solve all your problems," to slightly paraphrase him.

The Congressman did not specifically refer to any communities on Cheyenne River but I know that he had in mind, among others, a very remote entity in the western part of the reservation. I visited there after the tribe had received extensive funds and programing for the loss of lands flooded by the damming of the Missouri River, their eastern border. Largely Mnikonju (Minneconjou), one of the four historic Teton divisions that formed the modern tribal political entity, these people are among the few on the reservation who have retained their identity in the historic band sense. The members of this community were mainly residing on tribal land, but that is essentially all they got out of the tribe. The village contained a two-teacher BIA grade school that fortunately was operated by a very dedicated, professional Sioux couple. The people were occupying clusters of ancient log cabins, old shacks, and new shacks constructed through some program made available as a result of the condemnation of the land along the Missouri. The place reeked of poverty with the usually squalid house sites scattered aimlessly. The village contained a small general store run by a White family. The village also contained nothing but

122

alkaline wells, absolutely putrid water including
that produced by the school house pump. This
sizeable populace was generally hauling drinking and
cooking water from the Cheyenne River.

An unforgettable village facility was the
"community hall," a small, old BIA warehouse. It
was so narrow that during the Flag Day celebration
the dancers were obliged to move in confined lanes
until they reached the end of the building at which
point they made a sharp turn. These conditions did
not seem to diminish the festive air and the
vitality of the crowd, but a visitor whose ancestors
had often fought those of his hosts was moved to
promise aid in establishing a decent community
center. The Sand Lake project had gotten off the
ground by that time but we were all still anxious
about the status of the tract. The community
described above already had tribal land; they and
their representation in the tribal government would
have done well in spending some time at Sand Lake.

Ideally, and theoretically in the legal view,
whole reservations are comprised of tribal land
since they have never been allotted. Manifestly,
individual holdings are frequently treated like
allotments except that they are never sold or
otherwise conveyed to non-members of the tribe. The
members of the larger society who think that tribal
reservations are perceived of and utilized by Indian
people as if they resembled a Chinese commune or an
Israeli _kibbutz_ have a lot to learn. Called
"possessory holders," individual Eastern Cherokees
have leases with the operators of tourist
attractions, one tribal member laughingly relating
that she was assailed by Christmas carols all summer
long. The New York Iroquois reservations also are
tribally owned, but many eyebrows were raised during
the Kinzua Dam controversy that resulted in the
condemnation of extensive acreage within the
Allegany Reservation of the Seneca Nation. The
Seneca families who had occupied tracts, often for
generations, descended on all the involved offices
and agencies, especially Congress, demanding huge
sums for their lands and improvements. The
extensive claims of impossible numbers of farmers
were ludicrous, the Senate determining that about a

123

*double handful could be realistically classed as
such. The Seneca Nation, although protective of all
of the valuable lands that were being lost, made no
move to question the private land owners, and for
all practical purposes that is what they were. The
tribe and the individual land owners were
compensated through legislation, but not to the
extent of their original demands. Aboriginally, the
Iroquois and everyone else with gardens or fields
worked their own plots within tribal or clan areas.
They also harvested the plots themselves, the
produce in some tribes belonging to the women.
Northwest Coast and Plateau people treated their
fishing platforms in similar fashion; and Plains
Indians identified their buffalo kills by individual
arrow markings.*

*The Governor of Zuni Pueblo in New Mexico did
an excellent job with a slide presentation of the
impressive new projects sponsored by the tribe. He
was addressing a large audience in the auditorium of
the Department of the Interior headquarters.
Arriving at the efforts underway in the area of
housing, he made an observation that to me was
startling and bothersome. The Governor, a very
articulate leader, said concerning the housing site,
"We never had to pay so much for a piece of land."
Why, since all the land is tribal? I learned
shortly after the presentation that the housing
project was on clan land in a general sense and more
specifically the property of an individual within
that particular clan. The acreage had been, in
fact, in the nature of an individual holding within
a clan since time immemorial. So much for all the
official maps and charts of reservation lands that
never go beyond the designations "tribal,"
"individually owned (referring only to allotted),"
"federally owned" or "non-Indian owned."*

*The basic definition of contemporary Indian
tribalism is founded upon the existence of a
recognized tribal political structure and the
possession of tribal trust land. For purposes of
this discussion Alaska Native villages would be
considered as tribal trust lands. In the legal and
administrative connotations I find no difficulty
with this definition. Ethnologically, however, it*

can be unacceptable, a group like the Narragansetts of Rhode Island being admitted to the federal fold partly on the basis of an insignificant church tract that was accepted as tribal land. A more complex situation is found among the Winnebagoes of Wisconsin. Unlike the Narragansetts who are essentially Black and whose "tribalism" is a sham, the Wisconsin Winnebagoes are among the most traditional Indian people in the country. Residing generally in scattered communities, sometimes on public domain homestead allotments in trust status, they had no reservation. In the 1960's one such homestead, an isolated, unoccupied, wooded tract, was discovered to have been willed to the tribe although that entity had no formal organization. With some legal gymnastics it was concluded by those on high that this tract constituted enough of a "reservation" to enable the tribe to organize under the IRA. In retrospect it seems to have been a lot of nonsense as any other piece of land could have been taken in trust to satisfy IRA requirements. Other, much more useful land for housing and other projects was, in fact, acquired after the Winnebagoes adopted an IRA constitution on the strength of the original gift. The lands later made available are within the Black River Falls area, a principal Winnebago center that became the tribal headquarters.

The Winnebago project can be compared with the Miccosukee situation in Florida. There the people organized under the IRA with much fanfare, federal, private and state agencies being convinced that they were a tribe separate from the Seminoles. That they had no reservation at the time they organized was ignored or not fully understood. The group had a permit to occupy a portion of the Everglades National Park and an arrangement to utilize some state acreage. Not until about a decade ago was land taken in trust for them by the Secretary of the Interior. Sociologically, culturally and racially both the Winnebagoes and the Tamiami Trail Seminoles are distinctly Indian and maintained tribal societies absent reservation status. One of the arguments in support of formal Winnebago organization and land acquisition was that such developments would pave the way for the extensive programing of their anticipated claims award. The Wisconsin funds, the award shared with their Nebraska reservation-based cousins, were paid out on a hundred percent per capita basis. They adamantly maintained that although organized with reservation status they were too scattered to derive any good from programing. When the move was on to organize the Miccosukee element it was naively expected that all the "non-Seminoles," the Seminole Tribe of Florida having already been formed, would join. As has been said, the rest of the Trail Seminoles refused to join either organization. Much more numerous than the Miccosukee tribal members, some have obtained title to the small pieces of land they have occupied for generations. On some of these are found tourist shops and other attractions with some authentic features and others like totem poles that belong nowhere but among the Northwest Coast societies.

Returning to Oklahoma where there are more than 30 tribes, and where most of the individual tribes each had a reservation, we find some extremely traditional communities but no reservations. (I am aware of the ambiguous official position, but I cannot accept that the Osage Tribe of oil-rich fame has a reservation). Anthropologists and other professional students of traditional Indian life notoriously fail to inquire into the nature of the land supporting the ceremonials that are of interest to them. I always do, and long ago was introduced to a remarkable phenomenon. The Oklahoma tribes, who along with all Indians have been officially encouraged since the 1930's to use their resources to enhance their traditional identity, have made little or no effort to preserve ceremonial sites. The "stomp dance" grounds, which are the places where the sacred fires are lit and ancient ceremonies are performed, are among the Oklahoma Cherokees, Creeks and Seminoles all situated on allotments or what is left of the originals. Some of the principal traditionalists of those tribes are not at all anxious for the tribal governments, in however passive a capacity, to be involved. The Christian leaders, who are often themselves very traditional in behavior, are either not interested in or are hostile to the concept of preserving anything resembling so public an affirmation of the old religion. There is, however, probably no obstacle to dealing with the state to ensure that these places remain inalienable. The Cherokees, Creeks and Seminoles, and other Oklahoma societies such as the Absentee Shawnees and the Loyal or "Cherokee" Shawnees, have not made arrangements along these lines with either tribe or state, yet they all have viable and ultra-authentic ceremonial grounds. These ceremonies, like the Creek and Seminole annual Green Corn observances lasting several days, and the Shawnee Bread Dance, are not to be confused with powwowism. However, in this context it should be noted that numerous, large intertribal powwows are not held on Indian land but on municipal fairgrounds or in parks. The Green Corn ceremonies of the Florida Seminoles are held in very remote, off-reservation places. The Creek-speaking Brighton Seminoles conduct their Green Corn Dance on the property of a White friend, outside of Fort Pierce, where they have done so since long prior to forming the Brighton reservation settlement.

As discussed further in these pages, I am a member of the minority that views with distaste the current tribal high stakes bingo enterprises. Whatever the sociopsychological, economic and political considerations, and whatever the nature of the involvement of White business interests, the question arises: how much land is needed for this type of money-maker?

CHAPTER FIVE

"THIS IS WHAT THEY DO WITH THE FISH
FACTORY MONEY."

An Indian bartender.

The simplistic view that all that Indian
people need, like more land, is more jobs--or just
jobs--is voiced alike by impoverished Indians who
have never worked and workaholics in the dominant
society. If things with non-White Americans were
that easy there would scarcely be found, in
consideration of the unemployed Black element, a
single recently arrived Hispanic, with or without
green card, cooking, washing dishes, waiting on
tables, landscaping, sewing hems or maintaining
high-rise residential or office buildings. There
is, obviously, something very wrong with that
situation. Anyone who thinks that the participating
White employers have intrinsically a greater
affinity for non-English speaking, Indian-appearing
Central Americans than for native Blacks is enjoying
a very peculiar form of self-delusion. The
politicians, bureaucrats and businessmen who either
shrug or throw up their hands at the spectre of
Black unemployment, especially among young males,
nevertheless seem convinced that they have the
answers to similar or identical problems found in
Indian societies. The casual visitors to
reservations, no matter how professional in
background, are surely among the worst offenders.
The usual absence of realism and the breakdown of
professional analysis characterizing much of what is
offered by White "experts" is very frequently
mirrored by tribal leaders genuinely concerned with
getting their people to work.

Among the most predictable observations made
by people confronting Indian poverty is that the
subject Indian populace ought to be producing
handicrafts or that they ought to be hosting
tourists. The extension of this philosophy is that
Indian manual and finger dexterity, regarded as

129

supreme among all American ethnic entities, ought to be employed in factories if not in the production of crafts destined for sale to tourists. Many of these declarations find their way into lengthy, expensive reports and recommendations produced by federal agencies, and by consulting firms that deliver this kind of paper to the tribes or the same federal agencies. Defying quantification, a good portion of these paper products are, in my view, at least unconsciously based on the "Indian shyster" myth as exemplified in innumerable cartoons and screen depictions. No Indian stereotype is more enthusiastically accepted by the public, and none is more baseless, than that of "Hawkeye," the longhaired con man, replete with Cadillac, of television fame. Some Indian friends delight in this caricature. Some, who know better, would like to think of Hawkeye as being typical. I have known only two individuals who resembled, including physically, this and similar screen figures. One was a Yaqui in New York City who posed as a Navajo under the incredible name of Hill Canoe. A very glib, colorful silversmith and huckster, he died a pathetic alcoholic. He was also a kind and generous man.

Many reservations, remote socially and geographically as they may be, constitute overcrowded islands of poverty and squalor in the midst of agricultural areas. Often, other reservations or in fact the same ones are found within tourism centers or at least nearby and on route to such attractions. Some such Indian islands are within or near urban areas and very negatively affect the Indian image, most of their urban kinsmen being employed. With most Indians now residing in the metropolis, increasing numbers are creating more handicrafts in urban and suburban centers than are produced on their home reservations. For some people these and related activities, in addition to their psychological worth, form an important income supplement. The now well established situation, to which I was introduced in my youth in New York City, is that other than Pueblo potters, and some other specialists like Navajo weavers, most of the best and most authentic craftsworkers are found in cities.

However, at the risk of offending Indian people everywhere, there are some observations to be made concerning certain categories of material culture. I have reference to the weaponry, ceremonial regalia, the highly decorated clothing and such items as equestrian paraphenalia of the last century. Particularly as applied to the Plains and Plateau culture areas, and to a lesser extent the Iroquois and Chippewas of the Woodlands, for truly well made, authentic replications of these artifacts one does not seek an Indian artisan. If pieces inspired by museum specimens are desired, featuring for example not the more modern Czech but the old style Italian beads, and such items as old trade cloth, only White hobbyists can be prevailed upon. The present chapter concerns the dynamics of the problems of Indian unemployment, and I am not suggesting that significant numbers of Indians can make a living at producing these items. However, a Crow beadworker cannot be expected to provide, let us say, an 1870 vintage Crow rifle scabbard; but a White friend of mine from Baltimore, Leslie Gay, is one of the better known enthusiasts who can. White hobbyists like the Laubins, husband and wife, have devoted their lives to the study and production of items of Indian material culture. Their publication on tipi design and construction, this ingenious nomadic shelter being so much a part of the international Indian scene, is an ethnographic delight.[1] Much of the hobbyists' crafts finds its way into Indian hands, very often as outright gifts.

None of the above should convey that Indian people have nothing to offer collectors, ordinary shoppers and tourists. And surely no viewer of any of the more extensive museum collections can come away with anything but a sense of awe of the industry, skill and adaptability so much in evidence. However, contrary to popular expectations, individual Indians ordinarily have

---

[1] Reginald and Gladys Laubin, "The Indian Tipi; Its History, Construction, and Use," University of Oklahoma Press, Norman (1977).

nothing available in the way of hand made souvenirs and, all too often, a startling unawareness about how to deal with an eager visitor to the community. Indian people, in fact, often make guests of tourists rather than patrons. Indian entrepreneurs on many reservations, including those on tourist routes, are often nonexistent, the Wisconsin Winnebagoes being among the exceptions. This absence rather than presence of peddlers or operators of such things as stands catering to vacationers or other travelers is much in evidence. Related to this problem is that, lamentably, many makers of decent crafts charge entirely too little. Very recently a friend of mine purchased from an aged Florida Seminole woman a fairly large, colorful, authentically dressed doll for only four dollars. The price should have been at least twice that much.

Pine Ridge Reservation boasts of being on the way to the Black Hills, one of the two main highways going west to that area running through this home of thousands of Indians. Despite the Oglalas forming the best known and largest subdivision of the most famous North American Indians of all time, the Sioux, for years the only person actually "on the street" with anything to sell was a lady offering "tommyhawks." These were miniature stone headed war clubs with beaded handles. She rarely stated a set price for these replicas and in fact her usual technique was to beg, invariably saying that she needed to sell in order to buy bread. Most of her customers were visiting bureaucrats with business at the agency. This very poor woman, whose whole family lived in a commercial, walled tent, was to be admired, as well as her disabled husband who fashioned the soft stone heads and fitted the thin wooden handles. A sign, shade, table, and for effect a sweat lodge, were provided for them alongside the highway very near their tent. They expressed their gratitude, this being during the summer season, and occupied the "complex" for no more than part of one unrewarding day. They were, among the thousands of sociological full bloods on that reservation, the only people I have ever known who consistently made such souvenirs with the intent to sell directly to the public. Few had anything to sell to the four or five stores that handled authentic crafts. The well known glazed "Sioux" pottery is anything but authentic. What is more pertinent is that for a long period it was produced by only two women, sisters, one of whom had a combination kiln and sales shop at the agency. She was quite uninterested in involving anyone else.

Speaking as someone who has sat through and tried to contribute to numerous meetings and conferences on tourism, I have long since concluded that in general Indian people and their advisors either have some fantastic notions about tourist potential or cannot take advantage of a situation ready-made. Never, to my knowledge, has anyone talking or writing about the subject recognized or admitted that the main obstacle throughout the Dakotas and in Montana and Wyoming is simply that the reservations are on the way to, or ironically too close to, such attractions as The Devils Tower, Mount Rushmore and Glacier National Park. The secondary factor, which in some cases is surely the primary negative factor, is that few Indian communities are anything but slums. Browning, Montana, the center of the famed Blackfeet Tribe, does not deserve to be singled out in this respect. It is no more unlovely than other Indian towns but it is distinguished in being located on the flats right up against the eastern edge of Glacier. It certainly took me long enough to bow to the reality of tourists not having much desire to stay longer than momentarily on an Indian reservation, even if facilities and entertainment existed, when all the comforts may be found an hour or less away. The Havasupais are residing right on the floor of the Grand Canyon. A very poor, small tribe with severe social problems, the only thing they have to offer visitors to this internationally favored area are horseback rides down the canyon into their village.

The same hardbitten businessmen turned consultants, who fully accept that corner grocery stores in Washington, D.C. will not be owned by Blacks but by Koreans and other Asians, have not given up on Indians. The Whites and White Indians who authored a thick report containing thin recommendations for the administration of Ronald

Reagan are not that much different from the proponents of the IRA.[2] Reduced to its basics, the document preaches that the business of Indian tribes should be business, and the same should hold for as many tribal members as possible. The authors, and so many others of quite different political persuasion, remain unaware of such mundane factors as what Indian people can do to a relative who has a seemingly unlimited supply of cash, gasoline, groceries and soft drinks, and who might actually have a tourist trade in the bargain. Those who rightly bemoan the dependence of Indian people on federal officials and federal programs usually don't know how quickly such dependence can be transferred to tribal officials and tribal programs. With the latter the kinship factor is, of course, even better institutionalized. For many, Indian or not, altruistic or not, and with varying degrees of expertise, their perceptions of Indianness are bound to affect every initiative and every means of implementing anything designed to provide employment. Unemployment on reservations is all too frequently attacked in a manner that ignores the surrounding and often closely neighboring world of the dominant society. The bureaucrats and the tribal governments that I have in mind are, therefore, unceasingly preoccupied with creating jobs for Indians with a peculiar Indian flavor, when everyone else in the area who wants to be employed may be busy. The creation of activities and enterprises removed from the local socioeconomic atmosphere, that is, conceived to draw Indian people away from the established local economy and to the bosom of reservation and tribe was and still is most visible among the Florida Seminoles.

Prior to being enticed to reservations, beginning as late as the 1930's, most Florida Seminoles were occupying scattered camps, families often distant from other Seminoles and everyone

---

[2] Report and Recommendations to the President of the United States, Presidential Commission on Indian Reservation Economies (November 1984).

134

*else. The late 19th and early 20th century history
of this remnant, bereft as it was of Seminole town
sanctions and residing in isolated places, is
unquestionably in large part the source of much of
the interpersonal hostility so evident in their
crowded contemporary reservation settlements. They
were relatively ignored administratively until the
highly publicized formal organization of the
1950's. The Dania (later Hollywood) Reservation
served as the headquarters of the tribe and agency
and was billed as "the showplace" of the Bureau of
Indian Affairs. An elaborate IRA constitution was
drafted and adopted, and an IRA corporate business
charter, very few tribal members being able to read
or at any rate digest either of the documents for
which they had so enthusiastically voted. What is
relevant here is that all business enterprises were
to be controlled by the tribal corporation or
"board" comprised of the president (who is vice
chairman of the tribal council), a vice president
(who is chairman of the council) and one
representative from each of the Hollywood, Big
Cypress and Brighton reservation elements. What is
also relevant is that for years the corporation head
was not only totally illiterate but a lousy
businessman. In addition to the interlocking
directorate and the appalling lack of sophistication
among the members of the council and board, there
were other peculiarities that did not lend
themselves to any realistic approaches to
socioeconomic problems. The political figures, and
the board members were indeed political, were
derived almost exclusively from the newly converted
and therefore newly emerged Baptist leadership. The
council chairman was pastor of one congregation on
Hollywood and the board president the pastor of
another across the road. Poor conditions prevailed
throughout most of the sixties while BIA people,
state representatives and local old ladies
organizations all proclaimed to each other, to the
Seminoles and to the world that things were simply
wonderful. The social situation, especially on
Hollywood, was a disaster and every tribal
enterprise was in the red. With the advent of new
leadership certain aspects changed, and overnight,
but all basic elements continue to deteriorate. The
recent bingo windfall is discussed later.*

While Brighton and Big Cypress remain well off the beaten track, the latter still remote despite now easy access to "Alligator Alley" running across South Florida, Hollywood Reservation is practically surrounded by the city of that name. Any tribal member may live there, but I would not recommend such a move to anyone. Hollywood is, of course, almost on top of Fort Lauderdale and the rest of the burgeoning no-end metropolis of that portion of the Atlantic Coast. The reservation name was changed from Dania to Hollywood at the insistence of the Agency Superintendent, this for the edification of Hollywood City notables and to secure their support for a reservation golf course. Against this, fortunately, the board prevailed. The area is crawling with golf courses. No Seminole has ever sought employment with them in any capacity, and that fact is reflective of the heart of the matter.

Although so close to what would be regarded as a made-to-order situation, duly considering any literacy or other disadvantages, and emphasizing that Seminoles were present at the birth of the modern south Florida economy, they have been at best barely on the fringes. Those relatively few Seminoles, mostly young married men, who had however superficially entered the Hollywood--Fort Lauderdale economy, were lured to the then usually mediocre jobs with the Bureau and the tribe created as a result of the showplace atmosphere. The people were not encouraged to literally walk across the highway to seek employment with any of the service businesses. They have never, insofar as I know, been counseled or assisted to any serious extent to go a little farther than across the street to the hotels, restaurants, tourist shops, water attractions or anything else for which the peninsula has long been world famous.

One of the features included in all the hoopla was a living Seminole village and a large crafts sales shop housed in an attractive building. This development, replete with a hamburger stand, was situated on one of the most inappropriate sites in the entire area, Hollywood Reservation being in a primarily industrial and cheap service zone and too far from the beach resorts. The complex was, in fact, across the highway from a large truck stop (this small reservation's tribal residential area is contiguous with an urban pig farm, such things being possible in the City of Hollywood). No Seminoles worked at the truck stop. The crafts exhibitors and others working in the "Okalee Village" (as redundant as "pizza pie"), virtually all women, were paid a pittance and they and others were not paid much more for finished sewn "patchwork" (cloth bits forming geometric designs) skirts, aprons, dolls, crude carvings and the like. I am at this point reminded of the oft repeated comments praising the high level of industry of many Seminole women in view of the long hours spent at their sewing machines in the production of patchwork embellished items. Often, this to me more than suggested a form of escape, many of the same intent ladies being surrounded by sickly children and squalid conditions in chikee camps (the clusters of traditional thatched-roof dwellings) or in and around more conventional houses. The patchwork designs, a 20th century Mikasuki Seminole invention, are by the way often inspired and very attractive; and chikee construction demands real skill and labor. It should also be noted that the traditional camps of some older people are as neat as they can be.

The village's main attraction was alligator wrestling. Neither Florida residents nor visitors are willing to believe that this is decidedly not an aboriginal Seminole sport. There was also a large pit containing huge specimens of these reptiles where tourists could view them devouring chicken necks. One of them inhabiting the narrow, artificial canal running through the village devoured a little old touring White lady's poodle. A wrestler who was in the habit of running for a few beers between bouts was slightly bitten while taunting an alligator that was, fortunately, about one-fifth the size of the creature depicted on the tribal billboard. All of the alligators wrestled were small, a detail that would have had no relevance for Roy Nash, a BIA special investigator of 1930 who has provided us with invaluable and truly candid observations of what was essentially pre-reservation Seminole society. The Okalee

Village, pertinently, also included a small zoo with a cougar and bears and other delights in cages. One morning the pappa bear ate the just born baby bears before either the mamma or the Seminoles could rescue them. About this kind of thing, so totally ignored by his BIA successors who encouraged and subsidized it, Nash wrote:

> *To the commerical [tourist] villages in Miami, St. Petersburg, and others which may spring up, I would grant no quarter. I am well aware that there are things to be said in their favor--where could a Seminole desiring to spend some time in Miami stay if Musa Isle and Coppinger's Tropical Gardens were abolished? He would be welcome in no hotel, he has not the money to go to a hotel if he were welcome. But these places point the road to stagnation and death. I am not so concerned with the venereal problem as with the fact that earning one's living in competition with rattlesnakes and alligators leads nowhere ...*

> *During the past summer Coppinger's village was deserted, except on the weekly occasion of the docking of a certain boat which brought sightseers. Regularly a truck was sent to the reservation at Dania to take a load of Indians down for the day. I consider that the end justifies cutting off the rations of all Indians who accept this demoralizing employment.[3]*

---

[3] *Roy Nash, "Survey of the Seminole Indians of Florida," U.S. Senate, 71st Congress, Third Session, Document No. 314, Washington, Government Printing Office (1931), p. 81.*

The village struggled along for more than a generation, together with the crafts shop, and finally all was shut down about ten years ago.

Some of the most instructive failures in the history of these made-for-Indians projects involved the Brighton and Big Cypress people. The Creek-speaking Brighton people had never fully accepted the Mikasuki-originated patchwork, but at the instigation of the agency where was the dress and blouse factory established? Not at Big Cypress but at Brighton; and even if it had been in the hands of the Mikasuki Seminoles of Big Cypress or of anywhere else the making of a conventional dress or blouse is quite distinct from a Seminole style blouse, cape or skirt. Patchworked as they were, the garments were often misshapen. Simultaneously, a woodworking shop was put in place for the Big Cypress people where generally young men were employed. Most of the production consisted of junk souvenir cypress knives and tomahawks of the same wood, these items and those from Brighton destined for the Hollywood sales shop and non-Indian establishments. On Big Cypress the toll on the cypress knees cut to produce the tomahawks was serious indeed. During the course of about two years the inventory from both factories reached alarming proportions until a new tribal administration ended the operations and somehow got rid of the items.

During this period tribal grocery stores with gasoline pumps were constructed at both of the remote reservations. In a relatively short time individual tribal members leased the stores and in 1986 the shelves of the Big Cypress store were bare, the owner-operator and his family obviously offering little more than gas and hamburgers. The fate of the Brighton store is similar; it is something less than a convenience operation with sales mainly consisting of soft drinks and gas. Among other forms of blindness exhibited by both Whites and Indians who engineer such operations for isolated Indian communities, and who deplore Indian money being spent off the reservation, is their inability to see that Indian people, like most other rural people, will furnish themselves with any excuse to go to town. It is immaterial that the town may itself possess only the most primitive services. It may at least have a bar or two and afford in other ways a welcome change from the reservation environment.

"If I wanted to give away the land I'm sure I could easily do so," declared the thoroughly agitated agency realty officer. An electronics company had been attracted to Hollywood Reservation and was given an amazingly generous lease, for 99 years, on a choice tract. The justification for this move was simply that the plant would be filled with Seminoles, including large numbers from the outlying reservations and the few tribal members living in Immokalee, then a hideous farm labor town. They were all considered to be in a sweat to relocate to Hollywood to sit on benches and assemble parts. A large plant was very quickly erected by the company while extravagant announcements were being made by the company officials, BIA chiefs and city and county bigwigs. One of the company's cute magazine ads included a color portrait of the board president wearing a patchwork jacket. It said that he had never signed a treaty with the United States but was happy to have one with the company. Even I was surprised at how quickly every one of the comparatively few Seminoles who signed up for the on-the-job training at the plant, financed by the BIA, vacated the premises. The building was quickly filled by local lower middle class White women, some of whom had only to walk across the street or a few blocks onto tribal land. The apartment complex constructed to accommodate part of the expected horde of Seminole plant workers became so notorious for drugs, drinking, prostitution, fighting, vandalism and the nonpayment of rent that the units had to be converted to tribal and federal offices. A local White who dealt in old Seminole and other Indian artifacts was stupefied upon discovering these buildings. He actually stopped his car to gaze, saying, "My God, instant slums for the Seminoles," and this was before the notoriety. They never ask the right people.

The picture does not always have to be so bleak, but there is little in the way of useful analysis as to why a given employment project or industrial program works with one tribal society and not another. By all accounts the Mississippi Choctaws are performing astoundingly well, they like the Florida Seminoles being from a group that stayed behind when the main body of the tribe was removed to the Indian Territory. The Choctaws, however, were spared the experience of the devastating warfare that accompanied the removal of the Seminoles. Like the Seminoles they are scattered on tribal tracts, but have little resembling the romantic image of the Seminoles. The Choctaws are not part of the popular consciousness and do not attract many tourists. Philadelphia, which is the capital of Neshoba County, the Choctaw homeland, justly achieved a bad image during the civil rights movement of the sixties.

Possessing dynamic and informed leadership, and evidently the ability to confront the effects of illiteracy, grinding poverty and a classic racist climate, the tribe has lately emerged as the largest employer in the county. Involved in greeting cards, automobile parts and a tribal construction industry, the complement in these plants, factories and other enterprises is more than 60 percent Choctaw. The remainder is comprised of Whites and Blacks, this in itself thus far spelling a monumental social success. As part and parcel of this spectacular picture of rejuvenation the Choctaws maintain a variety of cultural and educational programs, their tribal fair and other activities known for authentic color and now drawing large crowds. What is right in all this? I for one don't know anyone who knows and the answer will probably require intensive examination over a period of years.

Very early on a bone-chilling morning, 13 Oglala Sioux men, mostly young and married and full blood, sat anxiously in an unused dining room of an old BIA building lodging agency employees. They were waiting to learn whether they would be employed at something to do with sporting goods that, they were told, demanded a high degree of manual and finger dexterity, and a lot of patience. We who were meeting in the Agency Superintendent's office with him and two of the officials of a Denver-based firm had known, prior to this gathering, no more than the men sitting less than 50 yards away. About three weeks before this eventful morning the agency employment assistance officer, the state agricultural extension worker and I had been summoned by the Superintendent. We were told that representatives of a sporting goods firm specializing in fishing tackle and employing only women would be arriving to test a dozen persons of that sex. We were also advised that if the company were impressed sufficiently the employment figure might escalate to as many as several hundred. Specifically, we were directed to carefully select 12 women who were known for their ability in handicrafts and in other respects, in our judgment, capable.

The three of us, all close friends and personally familiar with most of the artisans on the reservation, immediately met in the employment assistance office and in a matter of minutes developed a monstrous fabrication. What had greatly unnerved us was the prospect of several hundred women employed, who knew at what, with a large population of male baby sitters being produced as a result. Only too cognizant of the destructive history of male roles in most Indian societies, especially all of those of the Plains, we were intent on saving the situation for the men. We conspired, in direct violation of that aspect of our assignment, to quickly seek out men, preferably young men with families, and only men. Nobody was going to even suggest to us that men could not perform whatever was in the offing (and, for that matter, men from any ethnic background). Further, we sincerely believed that the Oglala sociological full blood men, given certain props, would exhibit more stability than the women, full or mixed blood, in a plant or factory setting. We ourselves didn't know how right we were.

The scene was structured accordingly as in no time at all we contacted the men we had in mind. All were unemployed. Most had never worked at much more than seasonal or odd jobs. All except one, the thirteenth, an older mixed blood who showed up very early that morning, were craftsmen (we had agreed

142

not to take any chances on this initial crew). We
admitted the older man not only because he was so
early but because he had a background as a ranch
foreman and, we figured, what the hell--if they go
for 12 men they'll go for one more. The gentlemen
from the company explained that the principal
activity was the snelling (hand-tying) of fishhooks,
plastic leader being used, with other products like
reels a possibility. The preliminaries over in
minutes, they were eager to meet with the
prospective trainees. We told them that in the next
building were 13 men equally eager to begin. No
objection at all was made concerning the number, but
both men were quick to express their dismay at the
absence of women. One said in a tone of finality,
"Men can't do this work." It was I who told the
filthy lie that we simply could not find interested
women. All three of us offered assurances that the
men, beginning with the craftsmen we selected, could
produce. With some misgivings the Denver gentlemen,
and a glowering Agency Superintendent, were escorted
to the old dining hall. I silently conveyed thanks
to the several men waiting outside for not saying a
word as we passed by them. They had heard about
some kind of job and had also presented themselves
early that morning. We duly noted their names and
swore that if things went well they would be the
first among the next crew members. We were as good
as our word and so were they. They could not have
been more understanding. In fact, two of the
originals selected did not appear. These extra men
quickly agreed about the order of arrival. We were
able in the most amicable manner to pick up two
candidates but still emerged with a baker's dozen.
These males who would not or could not do "womens
work," with hands suspected of being too big or too
rough, were immediately snelling fishhooks with a
speed that amazed the trainer. Some of them were
snelling along with the trainer as he began
instruction, and they were not fishermen. If memory
serves, this was a Wednesday. By Friday afternoon
the immensely pleased company men had selected a
temporary foreman, the assertive older man who was a
bit clumsy, and advised concerning production quotas
for the next week. Every worker had at least met
the increased quota prescribed for each day of the
three-day period.

Meanwhile, the whole reservation was in a terrible state. The Denver people had, in the strongest terms, warned about any visitors to the building. It was made only too clear that this operation, insofar as possible, was to be kept secret. That included members of the tribal council who were dying to get in (I threw one of them out, to the applause of the workers). To this day I marvel at my own naivete. Certainly I was among the last to realize the extent of the fear of the company about unionization. The Three Musketeers who actually had to do the hiring and firing until a company manager was installed (a Sioux from the adjoining reservation) were willing, along with a lot of other people, to put up with practically anything in the interest of introducing a male-oriented wage economy. An astonishing percentage of the employees was receiving significant bonus pay, and very proud of the production that merited same. The company, in very short order, arranged for an extended BIA on-the-job training contract, requested a factory building at the agency and, in time, selected two more sites, one at Wounded Knee and another at Kyle. The Sand Lakers, caught up in the excitement, registered keen disappointment when informed that their numbers and the dimensions of their community building were too small to sustain a factory.

The response of the tribal and Bureau officials and personnel was deserving of the highest praise. BIA buildings at Pine Ridge Agency and at Kyle, a community quite distant from the tribal and agency headquarters, were made available and quickly renovated. At Wounded Knee, a community notoriously recalcitrant and with by then an old history of practically every sociopsychological complaint, a crippled, aged traditionalist, Charlie Shot To Pieces, arose at a crowded, spontaneous meeting and in his own language, in stentorian tones worthy of the Senate of Rome, demanded that the old log community building be made immediately available. Many of the Wounded Knee men, including some of the elderly, mostly unpaid but provided lunch and coffee by the local storekeeper and served by the women, were feverishly engaged in readying the grounds and the building itself. Assured that brand new Indian

144

Health Service outhouses would replace the existing relics, two newly married young men meekly asked if they could take them home. I replied that I couldn't see any outhouses and asked a local representative to the tribal council if his vision was any better than mine. He said that there was no such thing in sight and wondered aloud how anything nonexistent could be moved. We both gazed into space as the outhouses were loaded onto a pick-up truck. The men who transported these priceless examples of very functional carpentry returned in minutes to resume their labors on the hall's exterior. They were among the first to occupy the new "fish factory." The company resisting every entreaty to display signs or logos on or in the buildings, that is what they were ordinarily called. The Sioux people were thus deprived of the sense of working for a designated firm within the private sector, meaning an entity identified as such and distinct from tribe and federal government. The presence of myself and the other two conspirators did not help either. This was indeed a damned shame, but one of the many unpleasantries with which we were willing to contend.

Prior to the opening of the two "country" factories, we who had by then become inured to repeating the canard that the company did not employ women were delivered a stunning blow. The widow of one of the firm's founders had learned of the absence of women and reacted as a true sister, especially in view of the fact that all of their other plants constituted a totally female operation. The Denver representatives, delighted with the performance of the men, sheepishly announced during one of their infrequent visits that they were constrained to include the fairer sex. We warned them, and the trouble began with the first female crew. Unlike the usually patient men, as soon as the word was out the agency and tribal offices were besieged by women who with indulgence might be called insistent. Within two or three weeks the company people returned to admit that they were good and sorry that they had not taken our advice and stood up to the widow. The women fought among themselves and badgered the men. They accused male co-workers and especially the supervisors of

145

almost every conceivable thing including sexual harrassment in the physical sense. Totally unlike the men, some women accosted the company's officers whenever they made an appearance. Men were fired for absenteeism, drinking on the job, or lack of production; women were fired for insubordination or rabble-rousing. Of course, not all or most of the women exhibited such behavior, but the situation became so bad that the sexes had to be separated physically and different roles had to be established. Most of the women became the carders of the fishhooks.

Most assuredly, some of the men drank up much of their wages. Most did not, duly spending the check for family needs. Some were able to do both. A woman whose husband was a well known drinker deplored the increase in drinking as a result of the new employment but remained philosophical, or perhaps it should be said that she was merely resigned. She concluded her lament in saying, "They could lay out all weekend as long as they go to work." Her husband did lay out all weekend but he was working steadily, something to which his children, like so many others, were not accustomed. Given that in Indian societies, to varying degrees, property is very personal in nature (and thus is not to be confused with generosity, Sioux or any other style), the younger, unmarried workers were under no obligation to contribute to the support of the household. In this respect youth employment programs among Indians are generally disastrous. Those who make loud noises in support of such activities for Indian and Black communities seem to think, however, that they are dealing with immigrant youth of two generations ago--and the fathers who controlled them.

Many of the newly employed women could and did drink freely and publicly. The off-reservation bars were loaded with women on the company's weekly pay day. Married or not, with kids in tow or on the streets or waiting in cars, these women appeared to be intent on making up for lost time. The din in the bars is impossible to convey and so is the desperation of the drinking, all in full view of very many kids. A bartender, a tribal member, had

146

never seen anything like it and neither had I. While trying to serve several drunken women shrilling simultaneously at each other and at him he leaned over to me and said: "This is what they do with the fish factory money. Are you the guy who started this?" It hurt; it will always hurt. Some people cannot handle money however hard they have worked to earn it.

There were men who were burdened with problems unknown to White, middle class society, and unknown to those who think that all that Indian people need are jobs. Among them was the poor soul, a full blood with several children, whose sickly wife refused to believe that his daily absence, unprecedented, was due to employment and only a quarter of a mile away. Reminded that as an ardent member of the Native American Church and a non-drinker he responsibly brought home his pay check she remained adamant. She was not alone in having a husband whose usual work history was in activities in sight of the whole family, such as picking potatoes on Nebraska farms. Workers of both sexes, but particularly men, suffered from hypochondria characterized by a great variety of ill-defined complaints like a "bad stomach" that probably defied distinction between the real and the imagined. This sort of thing has the strength of a cultural pattern in Indian society and is apparently aboriginal in origin. It is, most certainly, aggravated by all of the exigencies of contemporary Indian life. The woman who sat with a small child in a pick-up truck the entire day, except for lunch hour, while her husband was working in a plant across the road was not contributing to her own health, her child's or her husband's. The family would find a local relative's house for lunch. The numbers of people who indulged themselves in this gross disfunction of traditional kinship obligations were so excessive that I and others were besieged with complaints from residents in and around the agency. I told my father about those employees who never seemed to bring a lunch bag. He countered with descriptions of Blacks on construction jobs who, in contrast with Italian immigrant laborers suitably shod and bearing tantalizing sandwiches, arrived wearing "dancing shoes" (like patent leather), *without a thing to eat, and no money to buy same.*

None of this was easy. A lot of it was as gratifying as it was difficult and short-lived. No one, to my knowledge, ever mentioned unionization. The company, though, began irresponsibly laying off whenever it so pleased, a whole plant at a time being affected. The officers would then courageously resume the on-the-job contract provisions in rehiring with the workers not having previously exhausted the training period limitations. Some five years later the operation ended after repeated stops and starts that totally confused and frustrated the Indian people. The firm very graciously left the light fixtures, benches and tables to the tribe. I am reliably informed that the inventory, consisting of boxed articles, was easily removed in a single truck. I still buy this company's hooks. They are now snelled in Mexico, the Philippines and Korea. On the same reservation in 1986 a modest electronics industry was anticipated for one of the districts. Guilelessly, the initiators, mainly tribal members, announced that the local people "don't want to leave to find work" and that "the industry can contract for work and get it done cheaper if its [sic] done in small communities ... where there are no unions and people are willing to work for the minimum wage."[4]

We return to the beaches, palm trees, retirees, tourists and neon lights of Florida. The Seminole Tribe, with White partners, was a pioneer in the wave of high stakes bingo games now sweeping Indian country, with some tribes like the Otoes and Sacs and Foxes of Oklahoma going well beyond bingo to actively pursue track racing on their lands. Thus far, the Seminoles and the more than one hundred other bingo tribes have, in exercising their sovereignty, resisted all efforts by the states to prevent, control or tax these gambling enterprises. Not long after the bingo game got into full swing on the Hollywood Reservation the tribal council

---

[4] *The* <u>Lakota Times</u> *(March 19, 1986).*

chairman was questioned by journalists about the
absence of tribal members in the operation. He
responded that every effort had been made to employ
Seminoles but they did not stay with it. He
indicated further that he could care less whether
his people were involved in any employment sense;
he was intent on constructing a tribal pool with the
bingo proceeds. This facility was, in his view,
evidently of much more value to his kin than a
ready-made opportunity to enter the wage economy and
simultaneously learn to deal with Florida tourists
and residents in a manner and on a scale
unprecedented in Seminole experience. I am aware
that bingo supports such Seminole programs as
education assistance and law enforcement.
Nevertheless, an attitude like that expressed by the
chairman is very disturbing. Whatever the tenuous
legalities of tribal bingo casinos, and despite the
sudden and artificial character of these
enterprises, there are some places where they have
resulted in meaningful employment. The operation I
visited on the very small Shakopee Reservation in
Minnesota, near the Twin Cities, was almost entirely
run by young, very neat appearing Mdewakanton Santee
Sioux of both sexes. That tiny tribe is also
utilizing the proceeds for some impressive
programing. I traveled on the newly paved roads
leading to every household. What should be
emphasized, however, is that regardless of the fate
of tribal bingo the work-training experiences for
individual Indians will have been invaluable.

The Miamis of Oklahoma, historically from
Wisconsin, Michigan, Ohio and Indiana, are among the
peoples of the Prairie and Great Lakes areas who
lost most of their traditions even prior to arriving
in the Indian Territory. The Miamis are not only
essentially White in every respect but the legal,
they have no tribal land. Undaunted, the tribal
government moved to cash in on the bingo adventure.
The tribe announced that a contractor had been found
and that acreage for their bingo casino, to be taken
in trust, would be purchased in a suitable locale--
in Ohio. This artless display of what we New
Yorkers call "unmitigated gall" is among the
phenomena that have forced an Interior Department
ruling that no more land would be taken in trust

outside of reservation boundaries. For the Miamis this evidently means beyond their former Oklahoma reservation. As usual, the necessary specifics concerning historic boundary alterations can be addressed on a crisis basis. The bingo labyrinth, including repeated accusations of the involvement of organized crime, has resulted in the issuance of Congressional guidelines, as late as April of 1986, to the effect that all tribal bingo management contracts would be reviewed by the Secretary of the Interior. Self determination, this means, has gone too far. Some observers think that it has just about gone far enough to prompt the Congress to impose total state civil and criminal jurisdiction on the tribes. Ross Swimmer, the former Assistant Secretary for Indian Affairs who announced the issuance of the guidelines, is no friend of tribal bingo. Also the former Principal Chief of the Cherokee Nation of Oklahoma, having served for ten years, he vetoed his own council's bingo proposal. He has unequivocally stated: "'It sends the wrong signal--that there is a quick way, a fast buck to be made, that economic development simply means dollars in your pocket instead of people development' ... "[5] Bravo! But Mr. Swimmer is well known for his devotion to creating and enhancing stable tribal enterprises to provide both tribal and individual self-sufficiency. There remains a nagging question. If so many Indians won't work for a local store, hotel, ranch, farm or factory, why are the same Indian people expected to perform for the tribe or a federal program or activity benefiting the tribe? Concerning charges of racism in this regard, they exist; they are valid; and they all too often form a very convenient defense. In this connection it should be observed that young, <u>uneducated</u> Whites leave areas like the Northern Plains in droves partly because they will not work for what the locals are willing to pay. This factor in itself is responsible for the existence of large Indian islands in states that do not even have a natural

---

[5] *Cass Peterson, "The Federal Report," in the* <u>Washington Post</u> *(January 9, 1986).*

growth rate. Indians do leave these areas as has been said and will be discussed further.

Returning from a very brief trip to the Northern Cheyenne Reservation in Montana, a place populated in large part by the descendants of those who survived in 1878-79 one of the most terrifying military pursuits in the history of Indian-White relations, I discussed some of my impressions with an old Indian Service hand, Gordon Macgregor, who had served as the Agency Superintendent. Among the experiences I found interesting was meeting a relatively young man who owned and operated a filling station and who was extremely well versed in Cheyenne cultural history. A full blood, he displayed in the auto parts area some authentic replicas of old warrior fraternity staffs and other related artifacts. He was quite familiar to Macgregor who was gratified to learn that he appeared to be well adjusted. Macgregor said, however, "If he wants to stay there he has to be a good Cheyenne." By this he meant that anyone in such circumstances would be expected to support a small army of his and his wife's relatives, and Macgregor knew this to be the man's burden. On the border of the adjoining Crow Reservation, in the town of Hardin, a most personable, intelligent young full blood from an extremely traditional family was employed with the local newspaper. His boss told me that a parade of relatives passed through the establishment. There are few Indian societies in which this condition does not prevail. It does not, however, among the Florida Seminoles to any great degree. It can be so severe, though, that in a community of any size, a few hundred being very large, any enterprise that results in the hiring of only a few places on those few enormous pressures. Windfalls like claims awards and lease money, poor health, welfare checks, and peculiar forms of envy and fear also militate against employment. So do such sporadic activities like fire-fighting in which Indian crews excel.

Concerning the factors of envy and fear in the areas of industrialization and employment, a situation not bizarre for that culture has been reported for the Navajos. Similar phenomena can be *expected to be evident in others of the more traditional Indian societies. I am speaking of witchcraft, something quite foreign to the larger society but very much a part of the life of such unrelated peoples as Navajos and Seminoles of both Florida and Oklahoma. In 1979 the National Indian Youth Council, a militant group then still active, sued the Secretary of the Interior in an effort to prevent the strip mining of coal on the Navajo Reservation. An anthropologist submitted a lengthy affidavit, one of two, concerning the probable harm that the proposed strip mining might have on a local Navajo community.[6] He observed that "there is no doubt that the prospect of a coal mine opening in (the community) has caused anxiety and depression among individual Navajos in (the community) and divisive social conflict within the community itself ... " In brief, the very ancient Navajo technique of social control, witchcraft, made its appearance in spades as a result, in part, of the threat of relocation and the loss of the traditional sheep herding life-style. Community members believed that they were the victims of witches, including those who welcomed the prospect of jobs at the mine. Some who resented opposition to the mining were intent on securing whatever might be had from the mining company's buying out of relatives' grazing leases. Concerning one woman in particular, the affidavit states: "She became very distressed when I asked if she would mind the graves of her relatives being relocated. She said that since the coal mine had been proposed she was constantly worried, because if the dead were disturbed then the living would suffer. She said she would never permit her sons or grandsons to work at the mine, because if they accidentally disturbed a gravesite they would become ill and die." The same participant-observer makes clear that drinking in the community during that stressful period reached an explosive level.*

---

[6] Affidavit of Jerome Hasenpflug, National Indian Youth Council, et al. v. Cecil D. Andrus, et al., U.S. District Court for the District of New Mexico, Civil No. 78-586-C (1979).

The consumer advocate Ralph Nader, for whom I have respect, has no notion what he's talking about when it comes to things Indian. He is one of those critics who mindlessly contends that the BIA relocation program (from reservations to certain cities) of the 1950's and 60's is responsible for the numbers of Indians established in urban areas, and for all of the problems found within urban Indian society. Simple arithmetic is enough to give the lie to the first accusation; and Indians are usually no better adjusted to isolated, rural agricultural life than to urban life. In consideration of the fact that often ill-prepared Indian people usually avoid small towns in favor of making the great leap to the metropolis, they have adjusted surprisingly well. They are surely much better employed as a result. Cognizant that Nader's non-involvement in Indian affairs reached a peak in the late sixties, and making allowances for the outdated statistics, the intensity of his knee-jerk reactions leads me to conclude that they would not be substantially different today. He is assuredly a professional figure, but I have heard on innumerable occasions similar comments from individuals who make no pretense to that classification. Interviewed in Playboy *magazine, a publication as good and as bad as many others in perpetuating the great American Indian myth, Nader stated in response to what the federal government might do to alleviate the reservation situation: "The awful thing (is that) it could be* easily *improved (emphasis his). There are only 400,000 Indians on the reservations and 200,000 in the cities ... The opening up of only 45,000 new reservation jobs could put Indians on the road to economic self-sufficiency and social health. The Government could provide some of these jobs, and others could be created by an imaginative program spearheaded by the Government and the private sector."[7] He has all the answers; he was speaking not long after the demise of the fish factory. Nader also delivered himself in the same interview of an assertion that, while hardly*

---

[7] Playboy, *Chicago (October 1968).*

original, never fails to inspire trepidation in this
observer. "The Indian's lot would improve vastly if
the Bureau's annual appropriation ... were paid
directly to Indian heads-of-family, instead of
undergoing its customary bureaucratic attrition."

    Moapa is a Southern Paiute tribe of less than
400 members with a reservation of that name situated
right on the highway about 25 miles from Las Vegas.
Land recently added to their reservation did them no
good; the tribe's enterprises like greenhouses
failed; and by 1982 federal cutbacks in programing
resulted in the loss of most employment. Claiming
their action to be one of desperation, the Paiutes
announced that they were going into the world's
oldest business by entering into a lease with the
operator of a brothel. Obviously writing with
tongue in cheek, Mary Thornton of the _Washington
Post_ reported: "Tribal officials say that they
expected both the prostitutes and the customers to
come predominantly from off the reservation;" and
that, "The Indians say that the operation would have
been heavily regulated--from the cleanliness of the
sheets to the limit of three red lights (no more
than 200 watts each) to be allowed in front of the
establishment."[8] In his capacity of trustee of
tribal land and resources (and morals?), the
Secretary put the lid on this one, tribal
sovereignty or self determination notwithstanding.
I do not think, though, that any of his
representatives suggested to these inspired people
that they could easily commute to Las Vegas for
employment and with, I cannot resist, nary a red
light to contend with on that desolate stretch.

---

    [8] Mary Thornton, "Tribe Seeks Green Light for
Red-Light Venture," in the _Washington Post_
(September 28, 1983).

CHAPTER SIX

"WE'RE GETTING RID OF ALL THESE
                    HONKIES."*

                    An Indian to an Oriental.

        "-- And that means you, too!" He who fired
this barb was a young mixed blood with a law degree,
then newly employed with the BIA at its headquarters
in Washington. His target was a full blood, an
American totally of Japanese ancestry, a Nisei born
in California. This "Honkey," unlike the bearer of
the law degree, had many years of professional
experience in the administration of Indian affairs.
She had also, along with her entire family,
experienced the supreme injustice and ignominy of
internment during the Second World War.

        Again in contrast with the belligerent Indian
American who cannot speak the language of his tribal
ancestors and is divorced from their traditions, the
Japanese American is fluent in her ancestral tongue
and fully literate in its complex writing system.
Many tribal visitors, because of her physical
features and the obvious non-European character of
both her given name and surname, regarded her as
Indian, and probably do still. They were confirmed
in their belief to a large degree by the genuinely
personal attention she gave to all the many tribal
delegations with whom she came in contact.

        This confrontation between the two employees,
if it can be so-called, occurred at the beginning
stages of the new emphasis on Indian preference in
the BIA and the Indian Health Service (IHS). Many
people, Indian and non-Indian alike, found that

---

        * This chapter, slightly altered, is being
published in "The Invented Indian: Iconoclastic
Essays," James A. Clifton, ed., Transaction
Publishers, Rutgers University (1990).

particular threat to be highly amusing. I did not, but an Afro-American co-worker became almost hysterical at the prospect of attaining honkeyhood. Half-jokingly, she resolved to find Indian ancestry in her genealogy but was warned that this would not suffice. Indian preference had been limited to one-quarter blood for initial appointments in the BIA, and later in the IHS when health services became separated from the Bureau. We all thought that with preference extended to promotions and training the same quarter-blood criterion would apply. The situation, however, became even more unpalatable and unworkable than it would have been if limited to the mythology of blood quantum.

These developments came during the mid-1960's, with the opening of the abuses of affirmative action (i.e., officially sanctioned discrimination) in academia, in government, and in much less formal institutions of American society. The BIA, close to the seat of federal power and particularly vulnerable to the wants of its own special interest lobby, reflected the attitudes and policies of the dominant society sooner and quicker than other institutions. Affirmative action, meaning Indian preference, was bound to rear its ugly head but, as always in the field of Indian affairs, with a peculiar visage. In an official sense it began with a memorandum of May 3, 1966, from the Commissioner of Indian Affairs to all BIA chiefs. Most employees shrugged; a surprising number had forgotten it; I and others saw the handwriting on the wall.

As will be recalled, a confused, blatantly racist, extraordinarily offensive atmosphere had surrounded the seating of Bennett in the Commissioner of Indian Affair's chair. Bennett's first Bureau-wide memo, mentioned above, was titled "Indian Employment." One cannot ignore the impression that this member of the society of professional Indians, a person reared in the Bureau's Haskell Indian Institute, had been waiting a long time. The document stated in its most pertinent part:

We have always considered that Indian preference has applied only in the initial appointment process. We have taken the position that, as in the case of veteran's preference, it has no force in connection with promotion and training opportunity ... I am sending this memorandum to you because I believe we have not been concerned enough with the Indian after he is employed. We have let his employment drift along after having given him his preference in appointment. I do not believe we can continue this. Too often I have seen an Indian and a non-Indian compete for promotion and the opportunity goes to the non-Indian because he is better qualified. While we must always endeavor to select the best qualified person for the job, we also must help the Indian to be among the best qualified.

During the next two years quarter-blood preference was applied in the filling of vacancies and in general recruitment in a growing climate of inconsistency and fear. Among other unsavory features was the spectacle of people who had never seen a tribal roll, and who did not know whether they were enrolled, feverishly trying to establish their blood quantum. To achieve a quarter-blood status they were enlisting the services of Whites who were familiar with useful records, including some with a flair for genealogy. Some of the exercises performed in that discipline, and in pedigree mathematics, were ludicrous. Tales of the individuals who added a 7/32nds father to a 3/64ths mother to achieve a better than one-fourth "blood" status are legion.

Then a blockbuster hit--a Memorandum of Agreement dated April 26, 1968, between the BIA and IHS. Titled "Maximum Utilization of Indians," it was co-signed by Commissioner Bennett and the Director of the Division of Indian Health. Reaching all the way back to an Act of June 30, 1834, a

century earlier that the Indian Reorganization Act
(which statute would have in itself sufficed), this
poorly drafted paper confirmed our suspicions about
the future of professionalism in the specified
agencies, and in other positions in Interior and
Health, Education and Welfare within Indian program
fields. Using a quarter-blood cut-off earlier in
the text, the second "Policy" point read:

> Maximum use will be made of trainee
> type positions and restructuring
> positions when feasible to permit
> Indians to qualify for appointments.
> For non-professional positions, in
> particular, when positive efforts have
> failed to produce a fully qualified
> candidate and there is an Indian
> preference eligible [i.e., applicant]
> available who is believed to possess
> the ability to perform the duties of
> the position satisfactorily but who
> does not fully meet the established
> qualification standards both agencies
> will utilize every means available to
> restructure such positions in an
> attempt to permit the Indian
> preference eligible to meet the
> requirements of it (emphasis mine).

I submit that no other federal agencies would
have countenanced such a monstrous declaration.
Forgetting for the moment the non-Indians directly
affected, exceedingly few individuals regarded this
policy statement to be offensive to Indians.

Although indisputably many of his fellow
Haskell alumni and other Indian staff actively
supported the Commissioner, others were derisive.
They were professionals with varying backgrounds in
tribal traditions, or none at all. They appreciated
the first preference that had been extended to them,
but although most began their careers as clerks they
had risen to responsible positions. In my view,
some remained clerks regardless of grade, and far
too many remained "country boys (or girls)," but

this has nothing to do with Indianness. It is, indeed, a major problem encountered throughout the federal bureaucracy.

Those from Haskell Institute were loyal to the old school tie but some thought it had outlived its usefulness. Some were thoroughly critical of the speech and work habits of the younger graduates. This institution, located in Lawrence, Kansas, began as an off-reservation boarding school with a curriculum aimed at preparing reservation Indians for participation in the national work-force. In practice, it trained young Indians for careers in the BIA. My own mother-in-law, her brother, and two of her sisters graduated from Haskell; and all but one sister entered the Indian Service in low-level jobs, for example as typists. Lacking the legally required one-quarter blood minimum, they were, however, permitted to attend, as were many other marginal "Indians." They were all at the time strangers to any Indian community other than that formed by the Indian Service bureaucracy itself. Indeed, there is such an animal.

Haskell has for some time been a glorified high school with nominal community college status. One reason that young Indians--from reservation communities or elsewhere--are drawn to it is simply that tuition, board, and room come free. There are still many students enrolled who do not derive from reservation communities. The "old guard" Haskell graduates, many of whom were essentially Euroamerican in both ancestry and culture, have practically disappeared from the Indian scene, and some of them from this world. Among them were, as contrasted with many of today's professional Indians, competent, conscientious, and hardworking administrators. One, for example, was an Oklahoma Choctaw who was noted for being "unalterably opposed to spending a dime for off-reservation Indians" (his words in my presence). He was high-ranking and influential, and personally went out of his way to help in establishing a much-needed child welfare program for Florida Seminoles (it was a failure, however, through no fault of the Bureau). Not atypically in this respect (but we can't all be perfect), he also said of a BIA--multi-tribal conference, "It was a real nice affair--no Indian dancing or stuff like that." Oklahoma Cherokees and Choctaws were the most visible and powerful of this old guard. One such "Choctaw," whom I first met at a Sun Dance in South Dakota, admitted that he had no Indian ancestry whatsoever but he did exhibit a healthy appreciation for tribal traditions among those who did. Unfortunately many were they who had no such sentiments and cared less. A few were, as privately labeled by Gordon Macgregor, "culture destroyers," and he certainly was including non-Indians in this condemnation.

I am suggesting that Indians, genuine or spurious, are no better qualified than others to understand the dynamics of Indian societies and to gauge and cope with their needs. For instance, a Nisei with an anthropological background, Hiroto "Zak" Zakoji, achieved much success and well deserved respect for his grassroots person-to-person involvement with and sensitive analysis of some truly staggering sociopsychological conditions among Plateau and Northwest Coast tribes. (No, the Bureau is not and never has been loaded with Japanese Americans).

I am not suggesting that Indians are intrinsically less qualified, but if non-Indians need highly special training, experience and sensitivity in confronting these often exceptionally difficult problems so do they. Such knowledge and skills are not acquired through biological inheritance. The older Indian element, graduates of Indian Service schools or not, would generally agree. It need hardly be said, however, that it is a great rarity for younger Indian people of any level of sophistication to admit today that any qualification beyond that of an Indian identity is needed. Much of all this is lost on the poorer, less educated but mature reservation residents. Typical of their attitudes are the comments of several Florida Seminole women who approached me in a group before the beginning of what was to be a greatly enhanced summer recreation and learning program. These ladies, all mothers of teen-agers, were working or visiting at the tribal commercial village. When I mentioned a few names, including a

160

college graduate and some graduating high school seniors, one woman said unqualifiedly, "Don't get any Indians." All the other women present echoed this sentiment but I was constrained by my own and BIA policy to ignore them. I did add, as volunteer workers, a young White couple pursuing graduate degrees, and another young White woman borrowed from a county program. That the Seminole mothers knew what they were talking about was shown by later events, itself a sad commentary. The Seminole counselors would not try and could not control the kids enrolled in this program. On the other hand, the non-Indian volunteers tried and were unsuccessful, with painful results: both of the dedicated young women were assaulted.

Louis R. Bruce succeeded Bennett as Commissioner. Immediately upon Bruce's confirmation, during Richard M. Nixon's first term, the Indian preference policy reached new levels of stridency. About a year after he took office, Bruce said in Binghamton, New York, that of the 23 top positions he found in the Bureau none was occupied by an Indian, but under his aegis soon there were 20 such positions, 17 of them filled by Indians.[1] His claims were preposterous. Although their ranks had been thinning, the old guard Indians were veritably much in evidence when Bruce took office, and the Deputy Commissioner on deck, John O. Crow, epitomized the Haskell influence. But Crow was no friend of Bruce and his ilk, who loudly proclaimed that at last Indians had taken over the BIA. During the same Binghamton address Bruce said also that Indians are "fighting only to be heard. We don't want to hurt anybody--just to be recognized. That's what our red militants are doing." Bruce's appointees were not only by and large militants and total strangers to administration, novices intent on reinventing the wheel, they actually sanctioned the use of federal office space, support facilities, and travel expenses for representatives of the American

---

[1] *Steve Morello, "Getting 'More Than Words'," Binghamton New York Press (October 27, 1970).*

Indian Movement. To show their gratitude, in 1972 these young militants occupied and wrecked the BIA building, provoking the demise of Bruce and company, and ending as well Deputy Commissioner Crow's distinguished career of service to Indian people. The situation was so bad under Bruce that we lesser, long-service fools in the Bureau thought that the discriminatory Indian preference policy would go out the door with him. No such luck! The pressure that Bennett, Bruce and Interior Secretary Rogers B. Morton responded to with this racial preference policy continued, as did the policy itself.

On June 26, 1972, Secretary Morton together with Bruce issued an edict containing the boldest statement yet: "Where two or more candidates who meet the established requirements are available for filling a vacancy, if one of them is an Indian, he shall be given preference in filling the vacancy." As noted by a then newly organized group of BIA employees, Dedicated Americans Revealing the Truth (DART), the statement "who meet the established requirements" did not mean equally qualified. Just before the application of this new garnish to the preference policy, the National Federation of Federal Employees had protested vigorously to the Secretary in opposition to any discrimination based on race. Later, however, this employees union proved unwilling to do real battle for the BIA's non-Indian segment of its membership. Non-Indians then began to pay increased attention to the activities of DART.

During this turbulent period federal government agencies, state institutions, and larger private employers everywhere were experiencing the thrust of affirmative discrimination in the form of quotas, or the threat of them, or of arbitrary employment decisions that produced the same results. Even before the Morton-Bruce declaration some highly irrational things were being said and done, absent any official sanction, to promote the interests of selected Indians. When a professional White branch chief expressed his frustration about filling some positions, his supervisor--a White Haskell Cherokee--advised that she "always thought there was a lot of talent in the Mail Room." The

Mail Room and some other operations in the BIA
headquarters were almost entirely filled with
individuals, usually young and uneducated, recruited
directly from reservations. These and many
secretarial positions were and are truly low-paying
jobs.

Yet even with Black unemployment the problem
it is in the Washington metropolitan area the Bureau
has no compunction about filling these slots with
people who have to be transported from places as
distant as the Navajo Reservation. The protesting
branch chief was engaged in extremely complex work
pertaining to tribal government. Needing skilled
and experienced help, he was not friendly to
suggestions that he canvass the Mail Room. Further
concerning Blacks in this context, I have discussed
the nature of Indian preference with only a few
Blacks, including a federal personnel officer. All
except one woman, a BIA employee, fully accepted
Indian preference in the capital city and everywhere
else. For a long period my own small branch
contained no Indians, but did include two Blacks and
two Nisei, one of the latter a clerk-typist whose
output was nothing less than prodigious. When
acting as branch chief for an extended period I was
chided for maintaining an "integrated shop." One of
our people was a young, dark complexioned, historian
with somewhat craggy features. Our regular chief of
many years once said half-seriously, "I sure wish
Mike looked more like an Indian." This kind of
thing is really not funny. This young man, a Ph.D.
candidate and a specialist in Indian political
history, got out when it became only too evident
that professional advancement in the Bureau was
impossible for anyone who could not or would not
claim an Indian identity.

Those were the times that saw the beginnings
of the placing of "natives" in Indian cultural
studies programs. It was also the era of such
witless concepts as the development of courses in
Swahili for Black students. American Blacks largely
derive from West Africa. Swahili began as an East
African Bantu language laced with Arabic. The
Swahili classes emptied as quickly as college
classes in Indian languages. On a much lower

academic level, a woman from a British Columbia reserve expressed her shock at discovering that the Teton Sioux language was being taught to children in a grade school in the western part of the state of Washington. The proponents of this form of fake nativism were unable to find an instructor in the local tribal language, but the kids were learning "Indian." This is not funny, either. On a South Dakota campus a dear friend and colleague, a White native of that state who had spent his life in the study of Northern Plains ethnohistory, was summarily replaced by two thoroughly Americanized mixed bloods who proceeded to achieve fame in the development not of meaningful Indian studies classes but some astronomical travel and telephone bills.

The Honkey world, having witnessed such excesses only briefly mentioned above, riveted its attention on the <u>De Funis</u> and <u>Mancari</u> cases. Marco De Funis is a Sephardic Jew and Carla Mancari is an Italian. These American citizens challenged the emerging policy of affirmative discrimination, or reverse racism. Mancari battled furiously as gladiator in this legal arena, where the better class Christians, instead of joining the victims of discrimination, played the part of hungry lions. Although an organizer and later a shop steward of the union representing the BIA, I resigned because when things became truly intolerable that organization did not perform as expected. I was also one of the most vociferous opponents of Indian preference, but I did not formally join Mancari in her suit; and that I will always regret.

Mr. De Funis was the student who, graduating <u>magna cum laude</u> in 1971 from the University of Washington, applied for entrance to law school there. After being rejected he learned that 36 applicants with lower test scores than his were admitted. They were Blacks, Hispanics, Filipinos, and Indians. De Funis sued, a lower court finding in his favor. The Washington law school then appealed and was upheld by the State Supreme Court. Meanwhile, court orders enabled De Funis to attend law school. The case reached the U.S. Supreme Court in 1974 but was declared moot because of De Funis' admission to law school. He was by that time in the final quarter of his last year, the school assuring the court that he would graduate. We who were selfish enough to wish that he had not been admitted found ultimately, as described later, that insofar as Indian questions were concerned it would not have mattered anyway. William O. Douglas was one Justice who dissented, saying, "If discrimination based on race is constitutionally permissible when those who hold the reins can come up with 'compelling' reasons to justify it, then constitutional guarantees acquire an accordion-like quality."[2] The _Mancari_ suit had already reached the Supreme Court. Our hero was Justice Douglas who was going to save the Indian people from further patronization, and the rest of society while he was at it.

Carla Mancari was, at the time, one of many non-Indian education specialists at the BIA's Albuquerque, New Mexico, Southwestern Indian Polytechnic Institute. She was a founder of DART and a principal behind the effort to place a hold on all personnel actions until the courts were able to settle the Indian preference issue. Her courage is unquestioned, but she knew little of the workings of Indian society, especially of tribal governments and the history and nature of the definitions of tribal membership. I like to think that I and others knowledgeable in the fields of tribal organization and enrollment would have been able to contribute data and analyses beyond the racial issue. But the suit brought by Mancari against Secretary Morton was, I must admit, essentially of a racial nature in the minds and hearts of all concerned. Indian views did not much differ from ours. Whatever proclamations disguise or legitimize this form of government sanctioned discrimination it remains fundamentally a question of racism. The U.S. Supreme Court thought otherwise.

A decision in _Mancari_ was reached soon after

---

[2] _De Funis et al. v. Odegaard et al._, 416 U.S. 312 (1974).

the disappointing and frustrating *De Funis* case.
Mancari had won in the District Court on the grounds
of Indian preference being implicitly repealed by
the 1972 Equal Employment Opportunity Act. The case
was, as anticipated by all, appealed to the Supreme
Court. That body held on June 17, 1974, among other
startling things, that the Equal Employment Act, as
an extension of the Civil Rights Act of 1972, was
"largely just a codification of prior
anti-discrimination Executive Orders, regarding
which Indian preferences had long been treated as
exceptions ... "[3] Indians are bound to be, in just
about everyone's view, different. Indians are not,
as many Americans especially Mormons persist in
believing, descended from the ancient Israelites. I
am, however, in examining the extraordinary image of
Indian people in this country and Canada, frequently
reminded of the old story of the Jewish boy who asks
his scholarly grandfather if Jews are like other
people. The old gentleman lifts his eyes from his
talmudic studies to reply, "Yes, but more so."

The *Mancari* decision was unanimous. Justice
Douglas, therefore, let us down, but along with the
other eight magistrates did so in a manner that
beautifully skirted those constitutional issues
about which so many watchers expected a thorough and
conclusive review. Stripping the decision of
historical elements and jargon, what emerges from
the bare bones of *Mancari* is that indian tribes do
not constitute ethnic, sociological or racial
entities but self-governing sovereignties; and the
United States is responsible for the positioning of
members of such sovereignties in those federal
agencies charged with the enhancement of such
sovereignty. What a far cry from the honest
paternalism expressed to me on a June afternoon in
1954 upon arriving for the first time on Pine Ridge
Reservation. Although hired as a summer laborer, I
was admonished by the second in command at the
agency that particularly because of my interest in

---

3 *Morton et al. v. Mancari et al.*, 417 U.S.
535 (1974).

Indian tradition I was expected to "make life better for our Sioux people." I was not in much of a position to do that but, urged on by my new friends, I did take advantage of my non-Indian status, in nearby Nebraska, to illegally buy an awful lot of beer for their consumption. In fact, I did so the first night there, in the company of my great friend the late Clarence Janis, bearer of one of the oldest French names known to the Sioux and one of the finest traditional Sioux singers.

In the *Syllabus* of *Mancari* two basic findings are cited: firstly, that Congress did not intend to repeal Indian preference by the Civil Rights Act (as if it had been given any thought); and secondly, that Indian preference "does not constitute invidious racial discrimination in violation of the Due Process Clause of the Fifth Amendment but is reasonable and rationally designed to further Indian self-government."

If it is reasonable to apply Indian preference wholesale on a purely political basis, then it is eminently unconscionable to have Navajos involved in the affairs of Blackfeet or Crows, and so forth. It would be reasonable, however, for the entirety of Crow Agency to be staffed by Crows, the Minneapolis Area Office to be populated by all the Chippewas necessary to handle strictly Chippewa business, and precisely the same divided arrangements prevailing in the Washington headquarters. The Pine Ridge IHS Hospital would, we should expect, be staffed with Oglala Sioux (except that medical officers are exempt from the preference policy, fortunately for the patients). God forbid that a Crow orderly be employed at that hospital. Such would not only tend to violate principles of Oglala self-government, the Crows have a healthy penchant for recalling intertribal warfare. Ridiculous? Of course it is; but since the court said nothing to Congress or the Secretaries of Interior and HEW about the implementation of the policy many ridiculous actions were taken. Some of these really approached the nonsense sketched above. I do not know of any that strengthened the capacity for self-government of the several tribes but they certainly--hardly in keeping with the impossible idealism and romantic abstraction

167

of the court--strengthened Indian racism. _Mancari_
in truth elated most Indians but neither they nor
non-Indians immediately realized how loose and newly
extended a definition of Indianness was made
possible, indeed, virtually mandated by the
decision. When legal and other minds were agonizing
over the drafting of implementing regulations it
remained clear that the affected agencies were still
thinking in racial terms. "Certificates of Indian
Blood" were for years after the 1974 decision still
being required of Indian applicants with little
attention being given to the factor of tribal
membership _per se_. Only slowly did managers,
applicants and others begin to grasp that the
political nature of the matter allowed for Indian
preference to be extended to all members of
tribes--White members, Black members, four-fourths
blood members, thirteen-sixty fourths blood members
and the many thousands who would have to dig deeply
for an ancestor with an Indian name. Not until the
end of 1977 did the BIA at last publish rules for
the definition of the term "Indian" for employment
purposes. Long before then the racist climate had
become completely unbearable.

Characteristic of the blatancy of some of the
abuses was the notice of a combined Bureau of Indian
Affairs and Indian Health Service party, to which
only Indian employees were invited. I must remark
that the only "Indian" item on the reception's
limited menu was "fry bread." I have never seen the
proper adverbial form "fried" employed in any of the
innumerable meeting and Pow Wow notices that mention
this item. Most Indian people and members of the
larger society seem oblivious to the Pre-Columbian
absence of the makings of this distinctively modern
Indian delicacy. There was no wheat cultivated in
the Americas, this form of bread being adopted by
Indian people from the French and Spanish.

It was not necessary to travel any distance
beyond our own modest division in the BIA's
Washington offices to find examples typical of the
repressive racist atmosphere. Abuses in personnel
actions were not unknown before the coming of
Bennett and his policies, nor was it unknown for the
Indian Service to harbor both Whites and Indians who

had contempt for reservation people. There were, however, Indian and non-Indian bureaucrats who in those days said "no" to Indian leaders when any other response would have been patronizing. There were Indian and White Agency Superintendents and other officers who took their jobs damned seriously. They seemed to have had some silly notion that they were employed not by the tribes but by the federal government, in service to all Americans.

Truthfully, well before Bennett's arrival on the scene and absent any fanfare there was a move on to recruit qualified Indian graduates, not always with complete success. Representatives of a large Midwestern university, while arranging contractual services for our division, advised us that a recent law graduate there employed, a Chippewa called a "real whiz," might be attracted to the field of tribal government operations. Both Indians and non-Indians involved were anxious to recruit this man who arrived without delay, lugging his omnipresent, massive, bulging briefcase. He was given a specific and complex assignment, made an appearance late on a few afternoons, and then disappeared--to the great relief of those personally responsible for him. It was learned soon afterwards that he had a severe problem with alcohol and had produced nothing for the university. The Bureau had, in a word, been conned.

Not long after the formal announcement of the expanded racial preference policy there arrived, again in the same office, a young man who supposedly was a member of one of the many tiny southern California "tribes." To me and others his claimed identity was extremely suspicious, not only because he appeared and behaved as non-Indian as was conceivable. I checked. The group from which he derives is totally unorganized and has no membership criteria. The official enrollment ended with a 1940 reservation census. He was born in 1941; his name was added to the census by a White field staff member only when he showed up seeking Indian preference. This invididual who is not, and under the circumstances cannot be, a member of any tribe, and who has little Indian ancestry, has had--in addition to his initial appointment--at least two promotions based on Indian preference. He was, moreover, incompetent and his ignorance of Indian society reached a level just above that of bed-rock. Two or three doors away from his shop was another new employee who was in his own speech "a Indian" working on his "doctorial dessertation" [sic], his academic program being federally funded. Although assigned to tribal enrollment activities he flatly refused to continue an important enrollment research project, admittedly tedious in certain respects. This work was to have been performed under my supervision; I completed the portion that was expected of him and most of the rest of this lengthy project. No one would touch him, least of all his White branch chief, a professional of many years experience who had acquired a real fear of those Indians on her staff. She and I and others who declined to make an issue of the matter were all wrong. The employee eventually went on to better things in Indian programing, always by virtue of Indian preference, and in time was indeed invested with a doctorate (or is it "doctoriate"?).

By no means exhausting the horror stories within our own corridor (as this is about aspects of the Indian world I have not mentioned cases like that of the psychotic White secretary), I vividly recall the "summer student," a longhaired boy from Oklahoma with distinctly Indian features. He positively refused to return so much as an ordinary greeting delivered by any White staff member and sulked throughout the employment period. After his return to school were found in his desk copies of letters and memoranda he had written. They had been directed to the Equal Employment Opportunity Office and bitterly complained about the absence of Indians among the women who ordinarily supervised him. This unfortunate young person was tragically depriving himself, all the more so because he wrote excellent prose.

Anyone who thinks that such painful experiences as those few described above further Indian programing, tribal self-government, or the aspirations of young Indian people eager to work and to learn has several more guesses coming. On one

170

occasion, when lunching in the Interior cafeteria, I was treated to an unsolicited condemnation of Indian preference voiced by a tribal leader seated at the adjoining table. Indian both culturally and phenotypically, he was justly proud of his success in steering programs toward his previously neglected tribe. He fully admitted that he had strongly supported Indian preference, anticipating that the policy would attract specialists with a genuine knowledge of social and economic needs. Observing that, "We expected the best and got the worst," the strongest such charge I have ever heard, he ticked off the names of several undesirables also known to me. The rest of his remarks echoed the points made in a paper a few of us Honkies signed and delivered to Interior Secretary Andrus. We wrote that it was nearly impossible in our branch to fill vacancies left by two non-Indians. We said that this was becoming endemic to the Bureau, and "as a result of the ambiguous manner in which the Indian preference policy is administered the situation can only rapidly worsen due to attrition." There was no response.

I am among the ranks of those who have often begged for the opportunity to select and train Indian students and newly graduated individuals in all the fields in which I have been employed, beginning in adult education and community development on Pine Ridge Reservation. The closest I ever came to any such opportunity was to help in "sensitizing" sanitation engineers in the Health Service (but they were my age and White), and training a young, totally acculturated Indian woman in the processing of Indian claims awards. She was not selected by me and although she proved to be an excellent worker, I would have sought someone with a background more characteristic of reservation Indian society. On Pine Ridge there was at that time no chance to train an Indian assistant or even to establish such a slot. My successor was the whitest of Whites, a run of the mill shop teacher looking for the promotion he received with no affinity whatsoever for adult education or community work. I understand that he functioned largely as a truant officer, something I had avoided like the plague. Added to the irony was that he got to use the brand new agency car that was delivered one week before I transferred. My position had not been assigned a vehicle. For more than three years I had to borrow the Superintendent's car, catch rides from other BIA staff or from IHS people with similar destinations, or use my own.

At the Seminole Agency in Florida the tribal member on my staff whom I considered to be most promising became the president of the tribal board less than a year after I arrived. He spoke both native languages used by the Seminoles, and was much more aware than I could ever have become about the overwhelming sociopsychological problems of many individuals and whole families. On a Florida reservation one of the more public drunks, an alligator wrestler when he worked, produced children by both of his wife's daughters from a former marriage, and twins by one of his daughters from that wife, all living in the same household. Immediately after my arrival in Florida, I began arrangements for transportation and other business involving Seminole children scheduled to attend BIA boarding schools in Oklahoma. When I registered concern about the disproportionately high numbers being shipped away from their homes, my assistant explained that many of those being processed were the victims of severe family situations. She took pains to point out that the agency regularly sent the youngest teen-age girl from the incestuous family away to school to save her from the fate of her sister and half-sisters. (What is done for other Floridians to combat this kind of horror, not having a Bureau of Indian Affairs?).

The lady lamented, however, that neither she nor anyone else had ever been able to persuade the girl to remain in Oklahoma through the summer months, although a job for her could be arranged through the boarding school. The following year I mentioned to this girl's half-brother, well educated in the formal sense, that I intended to do everything possible to place her in an Oklahoma job, appropriately supervised by Bureau field staff (I failed; she came home as usual). He conveyed to me that he could not understand why I was so intent on keeping her away from home. This man succeeded to *my position. The tribes and the local communities have little hope, except accidentally, of being competently served and educated, in the broad sense of this word, absent the careful recruitment of individuals who are qualified well beyond any position description sheets. Today all such advertisements emphasize detailed Indian preference statements. The local, often isolated Indian communities starving for information, attention and encouragement ordinarily do not care where any employees come from or about their racial characteristics. Of course, most tribal politicians can be counted on to say that they do.*

Kelsey T. Kennedy, personnel officer at a Bureau field installation, wrote a letter of August 11, 1975, to all members of Congress enclosing a copy of a "petition," really a paper titled "Indian Preference--An American Apartheid." The covering letter states that the enclosure "seeks an end to the discriminatory, inequitable, and un-American policy of total Indian preference as practiced in the BIA today." Kennedy says also, "Although I do not presume to speak for Indians, I believe this petition is in the interest of Indians and of all Americans." Noting that at the time it was being circulated the federal government was fighting for the desegregation of Boston's public schools, the paper reads in an opening paragraph:

> *Although the government's apartheid policy for Indians is being pushed with equal vigor, most Americans are not aware of this policy because it has little impact on their lives. When this policy does attract public attention, efforts are made to conceal its malignant and pernicious nature and to make it appear benign and beneficial.*

> *Such slogans as "Indian self-determination," "Indian involvement," and "tribal assumption of programs affecting Indians" have become the catchwords to disguise Indian apartheid. Out of a*

*vague sense of guilt and without any
first hand knowledge of the situation,
most non-Indian Americans react
positively to such expressions as
clear evidence of their government's
determination to improve the lot of
Indians.*

Kennedy brought the house down with the following
observation, the most protracted applause coming
from those of us who were sickened by the political
games being played with the lives of Indians:

*Although Indians have been the victims
of many past injustices, the solutions
to today's Indian problems will not be
found by turning back the clock or
trying to undo the past. Solutions
must be found within the context of
the total American society of today.
The popular stereotype of the Indian
brave riding his trusty steed and
shooting buffalo with his bow and
arrow has no resemblance to the
current realities of American Indian
life. The future belongs to the
Indian who can understand, adjust to,
live with, socialize with, cooperate
with, and compete with his fellow
Americans of all races. The
assumption that the Indian can be made
whole by apartheid, by insulating him
from his non-Indian neighbors and
creating special Indian-made and
Indian-operated social and political
mechanisms to serve him is an unproved
and unsound assumption. It smacks of
social experimentation (emphasis mine).*

Referring to the Morton-Bruce announcement of
June 1972, Kennedy, who was surely knowledgeable of
the BIA employment situation, held that with Indian
preference limited to first appointments the 18,000
BIA force of the time was, nonetheless, two-thirds
Indian. He emphasized that Indians, therefore, had
achieved the 66 or so percentage employment in the
Bureau's work-force through merit. When Kennedy was

writing, the quarter-blood criterion was generally still being employed. With the dissemination of the 1977 regulations, Indianness in this context was expanded to all enrolled tribal members, consistent with *Mancari* and irrespective of the degree of their European or African ancestry.

As previously stated the Oklahoma Cherokee and Seminole tribes still contain enrolled Freedmen. I do not know of any such enrolled "Indians" who have applied for Indian preference--but I am waiting. The regulations, however, *inconsistent* with *Mancari* and fundamentally racist, are based on the language of the IRA, which includes persons who are descendants of members of tribes who were residents of *any* reservation on June 1, 1934. My wife has never lived on any Chippewa reservation, having been raised among her tribe's ancestral enemies, the Sioux. If she had been born just a little earlier our children would be afforded Indian preference; and that would be ludicrous. The preferential list, again following the IRA, includes people of Alaskan Eskimo and Indian descent, making clear that any quantum of blood suffices without regard to tribal membership. It further embraces anyone of one-half blood derived from tribes indigenous to the United States. This means that, for example, persons with New York Seneca fathers but White mothers are still given preference if the father is classed as a full blood.

What have been the employment results of the bitterness, the confusion, and the damage to Indian programing of all these years beginning with Bennett's first memorandum? During the fiscal year 1985 the total Indian complement of the BIA was just over 77 percent. This includes a great many fully acculturated, phenotypically White individuals, legally Indians or Indians "by definition," who are, more significantly, not the products of any Indian community. Naturally, no statistics are readily available for such variables. As the employment grades descend, the Indian percentage rises (so, too, does the level of cultural traditionalism). The higher reaches of BIA positions are reserved for those least Indian culturally, while the percentage of Indians at less than Civil Service Grade 6 is

175

almost 97. In the BIA education office we find the lowest Indian figure, roughly 43 percent, this despite the incessant din created by those who insist that only Indians can possibly understand Indian children. These days practically all BIA Agency Superintendents and Area Directors, and many of the IHS field office heads, are Indians. In early 1989 the IHS Director was a White Kiowa and the BIA head a White Cherokee.

More than 25 years ago the Associate Commissioner of Indian Affairs, a White anthropologist, told a gathering of his colleagues that the Superintendents had become "handmaidens to the tribal chairmen." He should have included the Area Directors, and if he thought that the picture was bad at that time he would have been truly repelled if he had stayed around for a few more years. There was a time when serving one's own tribe as Agency Superintendent was anathema, a notable exception in the 1940's being Crow Agency.

A specially debilitating feature of Indian preference, a practice preceding Bennett's tenure, is that of tribal councils reviewing and passing on all candidates for the higher level field positions, and many of the lower ones. Often, the tribes demand and get their own members for Superintendents and other positions, with the question of conflict of interest being raised--and ignored--every time. But this practice is, after all, entirely consistent with Mancari. The tribes are usually getting, including Area Directors, individuals who are more Americanized than the old Haskell elite. Together with all other exacerbated problems, nepotism, an old story in the BIA, has reached an alarming rate with whole families being employed, often at the same installation. But they are all "Indians," more-or-less. Yes, but the involvement and influence of individual Indians is thereby lessened. Leave it to the Teton Sioux to set a standard that, fortunately, has not so far been followed by others. Some years ago on Pine Ridge the posts of tribal chief and agency chief were shared by full brothers, tribal members, but their mother was a Creek.

176

Congress by the late 1970's at last began to examine the Indian preference mess insofar as some problems were concerned, one of which was the plight of non-Indian BIA and IHS personnel. Members of Congress noted that morale was shattered; many highly qualified staffers had left; others had nowhere to go and, denied promotions themselves, had to endure the spectacle of the advancement of the new and the less competent. It became acutely embarrassing for managers, Indian and non-Indian, to turn away well qualified non-Indian applicants (or to quietly advise them, as I did, not to bother responding to a position advertisement). The powers that be, still entrenched, had developed a technique disbelieved by non-Indian applicants. For a given position opening, assuming several non-Indian candidates and one Indian candidate, only the Indian, despite minimal qualifications, would appear on the certification list presented to the selecting office. However, in a few offices non-Indian professionals were actively, if surreptitiously recruited. In one of these shops, almost wholly and compromisingly White, an applicant was quickly assisted in establishing his remote Cherokee ancestry and, in this instance, his tribal membership. He is a highly professional person, but an Indian in no more than the legal sense. Federal court decisions and administrative practice are causing otherwise proud, well qualified people to graft new roots on their family trees, solely to achieve positions they deserve on the basis of their merits.

Congresswoman Gladys Spellman from Maryland and Senators Stevens from Alaska and Percy from Illinois, among others, became aware of the injustices and the gross failures of the whole system and began to allude to the dissatisfaction also expressed by Indian leaders. Simultaneously they were of a mind, reluctantly so because of the potential of setting a bad precedent, to ease the burden of the affected non-Indians. I do not know of any politician who seriously considered amending the Indian Reorganization Act and other statutes containing Indian preference provisions.

The so-called remedy, for which we all are

177

*expected to remain grateful, was to legislate the
"Honkey Out Act" of December 5, 1979. The
legislation made retirement for non-Indians within
certain categories almost attractive. In my own
case it permitted an early retirement--without full
benefits--after 25 years of service regardless of my
age. It also provided for those employees who
reached 55 years of age within five years of the
date of the act to make a decision about taking
advantage of the provisions, unless a waiver was
secured for one year. The act was recently (and
very, very quietly) amended to permit those who had
reached the mandatory class to continue for another
five years. Today there is only a handful of these
die hards left, since the legislation encouraged an
exodus of the "Old Honkies" in December 1984.*

*I followed the crowd two months later. With
their passing, and mine, the BIA soon fell apart, a
fact only entering the consciousness of journalists
and the Congress. I have much respect and sympathy
for those few professionals, Indian and non-Indian,
still with that agency. There remains an unjust and
as usual unforeseen ramification. I refer to the
Indian employees who never received Indian
preference in any form, including initial
employment when the quarter-blood criterion was in
vogue. They are being told they cannot retire under
the act. Included are the employees who became
officially enrolled tribal members long after they
entered the Indian Service. Often enough the tribes
only lately established formal enrollment criteria.
These people are among the innocent victims of these
discriminatory policies. So, too, are most of the
others who have been granted preference in hiring
and promotion on the basis of race, although they
and patronizing Americans may not yet be aware of it.*

*Nowhere else within the minority preference
syndrome, legal or otherwise, has the principle of
affirmative discrimination been so applied. In its
first BIA applications it was unique; and it is now
found in every federal agency containing an "Indian
desk" or even an "Indian interest" of any kind, such
as Housing and Urban Development and the Smithsonian
Institution. It is also found in state agencies
handling special Indian programing of all types, and*

includes our universities, private and public. And it is found in the Vatican. When Kateri or Catherine Tekakwitha was approaching beatification, the step before canonization, the Church admitted that there were no _bona fide_ miracles to be ascribed to her intercession. In all other cases miracles had been necessary to achieve beatification--but not for an Indian, and there were no other Indian candidates. She was beatified in 1980 amidst much pomp and ceremony including a Catholic Indian pilgrimage to Rome to see the Pope who had waived the standard qualifications, expressing the Church's own version of affirmative discrimination. I was unaware of any ethnic or racial preferences to be found among the company of saints. Non-Indians who have made their way up through the ranks, like San Francesco of Calabria of whom it is still said that a day he did not work a miracle was a miracle, are fortunately not concerned about promotions.

CHAPTER SEVEN

"SO   I   BURNED   HALF   MY   RESERVATION   DOWN."

> *A young woman from a southern*
> *California tribe.*

 *I made smoke signals a long time ago, and I
was not the only kid in the Bronx to have done so.
Damp oak leaves piled on a decently hot fire made
the densest, yellowish smoke, and burlap bags made
do for blankets or buffalo robes. (Some of us
"Indians" made blood brothers too, but of that more
later). I have discussed the romance and the
fiction of smoke signals in as distant a place as a
city in southern Italy when questioned about the
practice by a relative, an engineer who avidly
viewed on television everything available within the
genre of the American western.*

 *The most memorable of such discussions,
however, took place in the BIA headquarters when I
was asked to address some visiting high school
students. In this I joined several other employees,
mostly Indians. Always quick to take advantage of a
virginal group, I launched into a polemic on the
great American Indian myth and included among the
examples the business of sending smoke signals. I
explained that with the possible exception of a
pre-arranged column of smoke (which has never been
proved to my satisfaction), I had never found any
hard evidence that any American indigenes
communicated in this fashion. (North Americans
never used drums for this purpose either, but such
peoples as Jivaros of tropical Ecuador do so with
large, hollowed, notched logs). The students
apparently accepted what I had to say, but as soon
as I had finished a very striking young lady from
one of the smaller southern California rancherias
related, without any reference to my spiel, an
alleged anecdote from her childhood. She said her
grandfather took her to the top of a hill to
instruct her in the art of smoke signalling, and
that the fire had gotten out of hand and threatened*

to consume the reservation. A White colleague who was present found this incident amusing, observing that I had "no chance against a cute little Indian girl like that."

At the risk of belaboring the issue, I hasten to remark that professional colleagues have taken me to task on smoke signals; most anthropologists who are at all interested seem to believe that such a trait existed. I will concede, with no conviction whatsoever, that the practice, again limited to a simple column of smoke, was conceivable on the Great Plains and among Apaches of the Southwest--if the so unpredictable winds of those regions would cooperate. I will not swallow anything resembling deliberately constructed puffs of smoke.

The ethnographer James R. Walker, to whom students of Teton Sioux culture are so much indebted, describes four puffs of smoke being made by scouts to warn their distant camp of the presence of enemies. Walker, writing at the turn of the century, does not credit this statement, unlike his usual practice, to any specific Indian informant, all of them being mature participants in pre and very early reservation society. James H. Howard, of blessed memory, in communicating with Raymond De Mallie who edited Walker's material, chides Walker for indulging himself in "'white man's Indian lore'" in reference to certain aspects of the significance of warbonnets.[1] I fail to understand why neither of these good friends took Walker to task also on the "lore" of making smoke.

The warbonnet misconception alluded to above can be conveniently dispensed with right now. Practically everyone, including Indians, believes that each feather in this type of headdress, with or without single or double tail, represents a coup or at least some kind of battle memento. Howard makes

---

[1] James R. Walker, "Lakota Society," Raymond J. De Mallie, ed., University of Nebraska Press, Lincoln (1982), pp. 85-86, 103.

clear that as warbonnets without tails, as is the
usual form, all ordinarily contain the same number
of feathers there can be no individual counting of
exploits or honors. He maintains that the usual
number of eagle feathers employed is 31 and is in
error insofar as a minor detail is concerned. There
are usually 32 feathers around the crown of a
warbonnet if a single golden eagle is used. Twelve
feathers are from the tail and ten from each upper
wing. One "spike" from a wing tip often emanates
from the back of the crown thus making 33 feathers
not counting the downy plumes that are usually
used. The better bonnets require all tail feathers,
the three eagles needed (36 feathers) contributing
to the number of those shot, picked up beneath power
lines after electrocuting themselves by excreting on
them, or run down on horseback or in cars after they
have gorged themselves on carrion. In the old days
among some Northern Plains people they were ritually
strangled by a professional eagle catcher waiting in
a covered, baited pit.

        Someone with a war history like that of
Sitting Bull or the noted chiefs White Bear of the
Kiowas or Plenty Coups of the Crows would need an
awful lot of feathers in the construction of a
bonnet if all exploits were accounted for. Some
Plains people, including favored rich kids, even in
pre-reservation days displayed such regalia as
pretentiously as they could and so evoked the
disdain of the men properly entitled to them.
Warbonnets were in the historic period practically
limited to the Plains and the copycats of the
Plateau, but there is evidence that they were known
to some Eastern Seaboard societies. By the turn of
the century any Indian who wanted to was wearing
one, most of these dandies having never tasted
warfare. It has for more than a century been an
international Indian symbol. Warbonnets are found
among German hobbyists, Florida Seminoles, San Blas
Indians from Panama married to Chickahominies from
Virginia (they were merchant seamen who made their
way to such places as Norfolk), and the Iroquois of
New York and Canada. Indian politicians, including
people far removed from the Plains, still love to
stick warbonnets on White politicians' heads. In
1962 a Crow delegation was received by President

John F. Kennedy, the visitors thwarted in their attempt to crown him with a warbonnet when Commissioner Philleo Nash snatched it from their hands. Some politicians harbor some serious sensitivities in recalling the ludicrous figure of Calvin Coolidge with the warbonnet he sported, a gift from the Pine Ridge Sioux he visited one summer.

"An Indian will never kill an eagle," said the Fort Peck Sioux visitor to my office, this courageous assertion made in behalf of some of his fellow tribesmen who had been charged with selling eagle feathers. A lecturer of sorts, he had told college students that, among other things, the Sioux derived from the Aztecs, peoples as distinct as Albanians are from Laotians. If he believed that perhaps he also believed eagles would cooperatively loosen and drop their feathers when required. Most Indian peoples used eagle feathers with impunity, including arrow fletching, except for some like Creeks and Seminoles who will not wear one unless it has been ritually treated to prevent illness such as scrofula. They are extremely cautious in this respect but I am unaware of anything resembling such concerns among Plains people for whom eagle feathers are so popular. Further, and contrary to the arguments put forth about the sacredness of bald eagles, the feathers of this species of fish-eater are simply not in evidence in any of the extensive collections of regalia and decorative art. Apparently, Indian people shared Ben Franklin's views of the bald eagle, the wild turkey being on the Eastern Seaboard as respected and cherished by Indians as by him. He obviously lost the argument championing the turkey as the national symbol.

It is the feathers and other parts such as talons, and wing bones for whistles, of not the bald eagle but the golden variety that are used. Iroquois and Delawares made a headdress of the whole breast, neck and head. The single photo that I have seen of a Delaware bald eagle headdress of this type is, I am convinced, of an unauthentic 20th century innovation of some Delaware descendants still found in New Jersey. These days some Indians and some hobbyists will use bald eagle feathers, all sorts of instant traditions being employed by way of

184

justification. The celebrated Cheyenne warrior Wooden Leg, whose matter-of-fact observations on mundane events are of great value ethnographically (but whose account of the Custer battle is much less so), delighted in shooting any eagles that came his way, but undoubtedly golden eagles.[2]

In the present chapter's necessarily incomplete review of ethnographic Indian mythology we proceed to a quite different creature of an even more romantic aura than the eagle, the American bison. "We killed the buffalo" is almost as popular a form of self-flagellation expressed by the larger society as "we stole their land." Indian people whose ancestors never saw a buffalo, or who were certainly never dependent on their flesh or their hides, contribute to this extension of the national guilt. The destruction of buffalo actually preceded the era of westward expansion to and through the Plains. I refer to the Woods buffalo, a somewhat larger variety than the better known Plains animal. This herbivore, known throughout the Eastern Seaboard, has generally been forgotten except by some naturalists. These days Iroquois, Cherokees, Creeks, and Seminoles are not quite sure why they have extremely ancient buffalo dances or at least masks reminiscent of those Woodland beasts that their ancestors helped kill off for trade purposes. The Woods buffalo disappeared very soon after European contact. A friend of mine in Florida is convinced that his tribe's buffalo dance is a recent, totally unauthentic import, but few Florida Seminoles seem to realize that their people came from north Florida, Georgia and Alabama, all locales that contained the Woodland herds.

Indian trade, in the popular consciousness, is synonymous with European and American intercourse. Trade, of course, has existed from the beginnings of human society, trade routes being

---

[2] *Thomas B. Marquis, "Wooden Leg, A Warrior Who Fought Custer," University of Nebraska Press, Lincoln (1957), pp. 317-319.*

ancient in America north of Mexico, and from Mexico. Many of our highways, towns and cities owe their origins to established, pre-contact Indian trade routes and centers. "Exploitation," "commercialization," "professional hide hunting" and similar epithets, in reality accusations, are never applied to Indians in relation to the buffalo. One of the favorite techniques of harvesting buffalo, which persisted well beyond the acquisition of the horse, was to drive the herds over cliffs or into canyons or arroyos. Inherently, the practice was extremely wasteful. Archaeologists have found at an eastern Colorado site that of precisely 190 of the animals of the older, larger bison species that were driven down into an arroyo, about 40 were untouched by the hunters. These were trampled and covered by others of the herd and left to die. It is also evident that many of the buffalo not among the last to topple were only partially and very crudely butchered.[3]

Only in the late historic period did the Plains tribes themselves seriously threaten the great herds, but an earlier trade in robes had long been carried on with peoples such as the Pueblos. Even on the Plains the nomadic hunters traded robes for corn with much more sedentary societies like the Mandans and Arikaras. The Cheyennes became noted as middle men in these pursuits. With the appearance of metal tools and implements, weapons like steel lance heads and guns, and cloth and beads, the nomadic tribes became truly commercial, and the sedentary, earth lodge dwellers became semi-sedentary in intensifying the hunting of the buffalo. Their growing populations alone may have spelled the end of the buffalo, but it is difficult, given the lateness of this acculturation period, to separate many elements from the all-pervasive trade with Whites. Agency heads, army officers, missionaries and some traders began urging

---

[3] Joe Ben Wheat, "The Olsen-Chubbuck site: a Paleo-Indian bison kill," Society for American Archaeology, Memoir No. 26 (1972).

conservation measures on the profligate, mounted tribes long prior to the appearance of White hide and tongue hunters. Indian hunters, primarily because of seasonally and domestically imposed roles, could not, of course, approach the slaughter perpetrated by the White "professionals" who operated in crews unencumbered by families.

We can at this point get William F. "Buffalo Bill" Cody out of the way of fact and truth. Buffalo Bill may have been a professional buffalo hunter but that, besides being a showman in later life, is all he was. He never fought Indians, but his press agent Ned Buntline created of him a fearless scout who killed a Cheyenne chief, Yellow Hand, in a hand to hand fight at the Battle of Warbonnet Gorge, and so prevented these Cheyennes from joining their kinsmen who had with the Sioux just wiped out Custer. There was no such Cheyenne chief; there is no such gorge; and there was no such battle. Ripley's "Believe It or Not" repeated this fabrication as late as March of 1986.[4] The fictional chief's name was changed to "Yellowhair" by the individual who submitted this bit of Americana, undoubtedly confusing Yellow Hand with Yellow Hair, the erroneous name for Custer. His name translates as Long Hair for both the Sioux and Cheyennes.

The skin tipi was first constructed in the Woodlands. It was, for example, the Sioux winter shelter in Minnesota. When many tribes or portions of them began drifting toward the Plains they did so as pedestrians, Blackfeet, Crees and Kiowas being among the earliest arrivals. Dogs assisted in the transport of their possessions, including small tents with short poles. With the horses the tipis grew, and with wealthy, that is, horse-rich families, the tipis were enlarged proportionately in size and number, and skin does not last too long in the elements. Estimates and native accounts vary, but it appears that an ordinary dwelling of this

---

4 "Believe It or Not," in the Washington Post, Sunday Comics (March 2, 1986).

type required at least 15 skins. That is a lot of buffalo. No one can consume that much meat or use that much sinew for sewing. Further, that means so many more buffalo have to be killed for robes for personal use and even more for trade. We have little in the way of useful accounts in terms of the logistics for even a young, average family, but we do know that in good times these great beasts were killed on a whim, solely for the kidneys or other delicacies. We also know that some traders had the temerity to charge for a long-barreled rifle as many flat skins as would reach the tip of the bore when the weapon was held vertically with the stock resting on the ground.

The agent James McLaughlin arranged for the last buffalo hunt of any scope. This slaughter occurred in the month of June of 1882 when a herd that he estimated at 50,000 was discovered at the west end of what became the separate Standing Rock Reservation in the Dakotas. With no thought of involving the rest of the Sioux of the then unfragmented Great Sioux Reservation, McLaughlin permitted his charges to organize in an orderly, ceremonial manner, a grand hunt. Most of these people had not seen buffalo since the mid 1870's; some of the younger people not at all, this herd having inexplicably escaped both Indian and White hunters. Five thousand animals were killed by some 600 persons, among them some agency employees and military personnel. Although McLaughlin got more live calves than he requested there was no effort made on the part of chiefs, BIA or military officers or anyone else to corral or otherwise preserve any portion of the herd. There is no information about the fate of the remainder, if the figure of 50,000 is acceptable.[5] I very strongly suspect that the herd was nowhere near the size given and that it was virtually destroyed.

Before entirely leaving the buffalo and eagle

---

[5] James McLaughlin, "My Friend the Indian," Superior Publishing Company, Seattle (1970).

mythology we turn to the famous but really very minor chief whose name was corrupted to Seattle. An architect who misread my intentions in pursuing this book offered that I "surely can find nothing wrong with Seattle's speech." Actually, both a "speech" and a "letter" are involved, and there is everything wrong with these so often quoted pieces of romanticism beginning with the fact that they are purely fictional. It is painful, but I suppose obligatory, to quote one of the more common versions of the purported letter which I think is even more popular than the speech:

> *The Great Chief in Washington sends word that he wishes to buy our land ... But we will consider your offer, for we know if we do not ... the white man may come with guns and take our lands ... How can you buy or sell the sky--the warmth of the land? The idea is strange to us. Yet we do not own the freshness of the air or the sparkle of the water ... Every part of this earth is sacred to my people. ... When the buffaloes are all slaughtered, the wild horses all tamed, the secret corners of the forest heavy with the scent of many men, and the views of the ripe hills blotted by talking wires, where is the thicket? Gone. Where is the eagle? Gone.*[6]

This is allegedly the 1855 letter that this Duwamish fisherman Indian from western Washington, who never saw a buffalo or a wild horse but who was surrounded by eagles, wrote to President Franklin Pierce. The speech attributed to Seattle, in similar vein but with no mention of fauna, he supposedly made to Governor Isaac Stevens of treaty-making fame. I was persuaded many years ago that no Indian, and surely

---

[6] *Quoted in "Letters to the Editors,"* Washington Star and Daily News *(May 28, 1973).*

not a Duwamish, spoke or wrote this pretty nonsense, but we are all indebted to Jerry L. Clark for taking the trouble to research the matter. Clark, of the National Archives and Records Administration, says specifically of the oration (but in actuality concerning either of these Seattle laments) that it "has surfaced in today's world and has been used to justify and fortify current attitudes regarding the treatment of the first Americans and the natural environment in the United States." Clark believes that a Dr. Henry A. Smith, who treated the chief, probably concocted the speech. Regarding the letter there is not a trace. The researcher concludes: "The historical record suggests that the compliant and passive individual named Seattle is not recognizable in the image of the defiant and angry man whose words reverberate in our time."[7] Meanwhile, the speech and the letter are read and frequently memorized by thousands including avid Europeans. The speech itself is on display for all to see in the capital city as part of the Smithsonian's "Nation of Nations" exhibit.

The father of the good friend who registered shock upon discovering the Seminole apartment complex exchanged blood with a Seminole, the two being scratched with a needle. The Seminoles are among the Southeastern tribes who scratch on ceremonial occasions and who not long ago punished children in this fashion, the mother's brother usually being called upon to perform this duty. The Seminole "blood brother" apparently suffered no ill effects but the Fort Lauderdale businessman very nearly lost his arm from the resulting infection. Many years ago a Sioux couple was visited by a White couple they had not seen in a long time. The men being particularly close and desiring to be even closer it was decided to seek the services of one of the oldest and most traditional shamans on the

---

[7] *Jerry L. Clark, "Thus Spoke Chief Seattle: The Story of an Undocumented Speech," in* Our Heritage in Documents, *National Archives, Washington (Spring 1985), pp. 58-65.*

reservation to forge a truly unbreakable bond. The "Eagle Doctor," whose personal power derived from that particular bird, was braided, spoke little English and was renowned as a healer. I attended some of his shamanistic ceremonies always, as is traditional, held in totally darkened cabins. The Eagle Doctor, employing a pipe, prayed over and with the two friends, cut each of them on the arm and bound their limbs together. I was not present, but the following day the proceedings were related to me in some detail and I was later provided with a photograph of the highlight of the ceremony. This I cherish, not only in memory of the two Sioux participants but also as one of the finest examples possible of the strength of instant tradition. The institution of blood brotherhood, not to be confused with other forms of ceremonial blood letting, is well known in the Old World, including Australia. It is foreign to the Americas; but even aged conjurors go to the movies or in some other manner learn of such ceremonies that seem to lend themselves so beautifully to Indian tradition.

Harry Tegnaeus, in his fascinating ethnography on this subject, gives short shrift to any such rites among American Indians. He says of Indians that "we would suspect that many of the ideas with reference to the blood-pact derived from elsewhere and must sometimes be looked upon as white man's folklore about Indians."[8] To me Tegnaeus is being too cautious. If any specific accounts are valid, such as that he cites for Coast Pomos of California, such could not in my view remain isolated. Blood brotherhood in kinship-oriented societies is the sort of thing that spreads like wildfire. Indian people create kinship bonds by adoption, something that could be very easily accomplished by, for example, Seminoles and Iroquois within their matrilineal clan systems but who do not

---

[8] Harry Tegnaeus, "Blood-Brothers: an ethno-sociological study of the institutions of blood-brotherhood with special reference to Africa," Philosophical Library, Inc., New York (1952), p. 42.

now do so. The Sioux, however, still have a strong adoption complex and without benefit of a clan system.

Friends, and strangers, constantly take me to task for puritanism. They assert that tipis for Mohawks, totem poles for Seminoles, treaties for those who don't have them and blood brothers for anyone can all be of inestimable value to individual Indians and whole tribal societies. A very engaging Norwegian anthropologist, who has worked extensively with Micmacs of Nova Scotia, had little patience with my attitudes regarding instant tradition and other related aspects of Indian mythology. In our private discussion he staunchly maintained that the recent acquisition by young Micmacs of many of the items of the conventional or pan-Indian inventory, which are strongly Plains in nature, has been of real value in healing and enhancing their self-image. I have no basic quarrel with him. But if junk and artificiality are of worth how much more so would be the authentic coupled with a genuine knowledge of origin and function?

We arrive at one of the pillars of American folklore. Indian people are not particularly interested in Sacajawea but to the rest of American society she is a heroine possessed of ability and sagacity nothing less than superhuman. This obscure young Shoshone woman, with her small child, would have achieved the stature of an American madonna had it not been for the presence of a brutal French husband. The Bird Woman, as her Hidatsa name translates, was a Northern Shoshone who had been captured in her early teens by the Hidatsas and then sold to her husband. She is universally credited with guiding the Lewis and Clark Expedition westward through the Plains and Plateau country to the Pacific. That is patently absurd. Not a soul anywhere, including the most seasoned warrior-hunter or trader, could possibly have done so. What this woman was able to do, and thus possibly saved the expedition, was arrange for the purchase of much needed horses from her own people. Undoubtedly, we will all be besieged till the end of time with representations of the lady in fringed dress, and bearing her infant son on her back, pointing with

192

outstretched arm and finger to the great ocean. If she pointed Lewis and Clark anywhere she probably did so with her lower lip and chin, a widespread Indian trait.

I played cowboys and Indians, sometimes right on the sidewalks of the Bronx, and always insisted on being one of the Indians. In contrast with the international image fed by cheap novels, movies and innumerable cartoons, puns and jokes there has never been a battle between cowboys and Indians and little real trouble of any sort. In fact, cattlemen and their employees, the cowboys, not only fed Indians they often hired them and intermarried with them. This is easily explained. The great domestic herds of the Plains and the Southwest did not come into existence until the buffalo were essentially gone and the tribes had been placed on the reservation dole. It was the cowboys, therefore, who drove the herds to reservations to form a very large part of that dole. Some men, until agency officials put a stop to the practice, would stick arrows into the cattle in the same way that they had hunted the buffalo. Numerous Indian people are descended from cowboys, particularly Mexicans, and some Blacks, to say nothing of Indian cowboys. On Pine Ridge Reservation a locale usually known as Spanish Creek was so named for the Mexican cowboy-Sioux wife families who settled there.

On occasion Indians rustled cattle (on Lower Brule Reservation they left arrows protruding from live cows with which they were expected to develop a herd), begged cattlemen for meat or charged them in terms of so many head for crossing their reservations. There were some memorable multiple murders involving cowboys and Indians. The Ghost Dance troubles of 1890-91 occurred in western South Dakota after all of the Plains tribes had been reduced to reservation status and were eating meat, when it was available, usually provided by commercial herds. Two Sticks, a Mnikonju Sioux, brooded for three years over the killing of his relatives at Wounded Knee. Enlisting his son known by the same name and three others, Two Sticks had his revenge when the four young men shot three White cowhands, including a boy, and their cook in a bunkhouse at the western edge of Pine Ridge. The young Two Sticks was killed by Indian police; the other three were exonerated on the basis of their age and because it was established that the older man was the instigator. The drawings of this incident by the excellent Sioux ethnographic artist, Bad Heart Bull, are particularly attractive.[9] Two Sticks was hanged at Deadwood, South Dakota, in 1894, the event being memorialized in some Sioux calendars (see following plate).

Less than two weeks after the Wounded Knee debacle, the three Culbertson brothers, ranchers who can be called cowboys, killed a man by the name of Few Tails and severely wounded his wife Clown Woman. They also fired on another Sioux and his wife and children. They wounded the woman and an infant died of starvation and exposure while the family fled. These people were returning from an authorized hunting trip west of Pine Ridge. The attack was totally unprovoked. Just prior to this atrocity a young Brule Sioux, Plenty Horses, gunned down Lieutenant Edward W. Casey without warning at the conclusion of an amicable palaver. The officer was liked by the Sioux chiefs and beloved of the Northern Cheyenne scouts under his command. The Culbertsons and Plenty Horses were tried and exonerated on the basis of the state of war that prevailed at the time.[10] Nonsense; these were all, including the murders instigated by Two Sticks, despicable acts perpetrated absent anything resembling battle conditions.

Turning to a much lighter note, a preconception very often heard and read, I devote a

---

[9] "A Pictographic History of the Oglala Sioux," Helen H. Blish, ed., University of Nebraska Press, Lincoln (1967).

[10] Useful accounts of the Culbertson and Plenty Horses affairs are found in Robert M. Utley, "The Last Days of the Sioux Nation," Yale University Press, New Haven and London (1963).

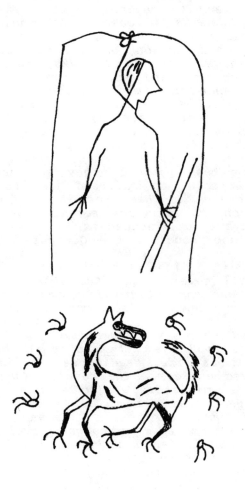

Above: Two Sticks was hanged. Below: Rabid Dog prayed. Drawn by the author from a photocopy of the Wounded Bear calendar (less than actual size).

195

few lines to the Indian steel or "high iron" workers, principally Canadian Mohawks. This phenomenon owes its beginnings to a small crew of Caughnawaga Mohawks of Quebec who found employment early in this century on a modest steel bridge that was under construction on their reserve. Soon afterward large crews of Mohawks, including their St. Regis cousins and still other Iroquois, made their appearance in numbers quite disproportionate to their respective tribal populations. They have become famous for their work on internationally known skyscrapers. Although the Indian crews have a strong penchant for travelling immense distances in pursuing their profession, necessarily leaving their families for long periods, they and other Mohawks who were attracted to railroad jobs formed a very visible enclave in New York City, including a Protestant church in which services were conducted in their beautiful language. This was within an Italian neighborhood in the Gowanus Canal area in Brooklyn.

I will never forget the story related to me by a Mohawk who conducted Indian shows and made some crafts to supplement his income. One evening he found at his apartment door a most agitated Italian who insisted that only an Indian could remove the spell of the evil eye (il malocchio) that had been inflicted on his wife, traditional Italian conjuring having proved useless. The bemused Mohawk provided him with a miniature false face, one of the artifacts he carved for sale. Within a week his very grateful neighbor returned to announce that his wife was fully cured and bought several of these miniatures, one for each member of his family. Some Mohawks may be known for efficacious amulets, and many are known for excellent basketry and beadwork, but the whole tribe, at least the male division, is regarded to be comprised of individuals who have no fear of height. It's obviously genetic, says the general public who then applies the attribute to all Indians. If genetic then whose genes are responsible? It is inconceivable that any Iroquois is free of European ancestry. Many who prefer to speak their tribal language, including Mohawk, have not a hint of an Indian phenotype. Mohawks do fall to their deaths from dizzying heights. What they share in common with all other high iron workers is their disdain for belts or other safety devices. Why these men are not required by law to be secured while working is to me absolutely incomprehensible.

"They're just bucks; that's all they are, just bucks." So said the mixed blood high school student, who is now a professional Indian with a federal program office, about the full bloods in his school. He also called the girls "squaws" and so did the full blood boys. They still do, but the license is, of course, reserved to Indians. Squaw simply means woman in Narragansett. Many of the Indian terms that have made their way into the English language, like powwow meaning a shaman or a ceremonial gathering, are derived from Algonquian languages of southern New England.[11] If Indian people of any level of acculturation are going to persist in the use of terms like "squaw," "buck," "brave" and the more recent "skins", they can hardly expect anything much different from the rest of American society. While being coached by several Western Shoshone women in a card game I think now quite traditional in that society, I was told that it simply was called "Squaw Game." It took at least a minute for the players to agree that the proper translation in English was "Fives," each player being dealt that many cards. In 1969 I wrote the following memorandum to the Commissioner:

> A Washington Post article titled
> Higher Education, Finally, Among the
> Navajos, by Colman McCarthy, Monday,
> August 11, p. A-10, employs the term
> "squaw" in reference to Navajo women
> generally and in one instance to old
> women. The same article deplores the
> bad manners of some tourists and the

---

[11] An excellent source for these Algonquian-English terms is the "Handbook of American Indians North of Mexico," Frederick Webb Hodge, ed., Bureau of American Ethnology, Bulletin 30, Washington, Government Printing Office (1907).

*contempt they sometimes display toward
Indians. The blind spot here is
rather obvious ...*

*As a Bureau employee, friend and
colleague of many Indians, and the
husband of a member of the Minnesota
Chippewa Tribe, I resent the use of
the term "squaw" and I am very
surprised to find it in a Washington
news article. I realize that this is
not the first time "squaw" has been
employed by news media, but in so far
as at least Washington papers are
concerned, might not it be the last?*

*The memo was well received by the BIA chiefs and the
newspaper forthwith published a complaining letter
to the editor signed by the Acting Commissioner.
While discussing this incident with an Irish scholar
he asked: "Has The Post smartened up yet?" I
replied that The Post had certainly not. When
Interior Secretary James Watt failed to bag an elk
while on a hunting trip to Fort Hall Reservation in
Idaho he was obliged to dance with the women. The
Post, in the text of an article and in the caption
of a photo depicting Watt sporting a head kerchief
and shawl like the Shoshone women, referred to them
as squaws.*

    *One of my pet peeves concerns what both
Whites and Indians say about Indian languages. If
language is humankind's highest accomplishment, and
of course it is, then it deserves the highest
respect. Indian languages have been relegated to a
position that is not much above the gibberish of
Tarzan movies or the speech of the Lone Ranger's
"faithful Indian companion" Tonto (which, by the
way, means "stupid" in Spanish and nothing in any
Indian language). Popular views are often similar
to those of the Australian dignitary who years ago
was being interviewed on a television talk show. As
if Aborigines are of interest to most Australians or
that they are knowledgeable about them, he was asked
if they had a language. I experienced real pain in
hearing him reply that they did not have a genuine
language but only some unconnected sounds. There*

are many Australian aboriginal languages. Every one of them has a structure infinitely more complex than English. The Down Under visitor's attitude is analagous to that of the grandmother of a mixed blood Flathead woman then married to a Turtle Mountain Metis. She, in her husband's presence, related that her grandmother considered "Chippewa" to be a "real language, not like Flathead." Evidently, the old lady considered the Metis jargon, because it contains such strong French elements, to be intrinsically superior to Flathead, a Salishan language. The couple was impressed when informed that Chippewa or Ojibwa in itself, and Flathead, and every other language on earth except for some trade jargons are indeed full languages; and that most of them make English look easy.

Indian speech, in popular terminology, is "dialect" not language, this form of ignorance not differing from that of Italian Americans who will at least give lip service to the merits of studying official Italian but exhibit contempt for the local "dialects" of their grandparents. Despite all the nativism that has been espoused by the BIA since the IRA days and particularly as of the sixties, and despite the Indian preference policy, that agency can still be counted on to do things that belie any true appreciation of tradition. A straight-faced and typical example appears in a slick 1984 BIA publication. Concerning the bilingual approach to learning, it is stated of an Eskimo area in Alaska that: "Under this bilingual concept, students in the program are being taught in _tribal dialects_ with short periods each day devoted to the study of English, a foreign _language_ to most of them (emphases mine)".[12] I will refrain from comment on such irresponsible education philosophies and methods from which, fortunately, our immigrant ancestors were spared.

There is much other evidence of the lack of

---

12 "American Indians," Bureau of Indian Affairs, Department of the Interior, Washington (1984), p. 16.

respect, often enough unconsciously expressed, for Indian languages. Most annoying to me, and so acceptable to the general society and many Indians, are the old practices of hyphenating Indian words and translating personal names. It is especially ironic that the Oklahoma Cherokees, in establishing their tribal cultural and tourist center, named it "Tsa-La-Gi," supposedly the tribe's own name. Tsalagi, from whence we derive Chalakee and later Cherokee, is actually the Creek name for these people, possibly referring to their mountainous location. Sequoyah, the Cherokee intellectual, invented a complex syllabary (not an alphabet) that was adopted by the entire tribe. For them to hyphenate any term in their language is truly self-denigrating. Curiously, no one seems to write "Cher-o-kee."

The people who, absent any intellectual curiousity, simply shrug off the meanings of their own names, given or familial, nevertheless insist that an Indian name must be translatable into English. All names have or had meaning, at least to someone, even if they are "baby names" for kids or pets. The riders on commuter buses who ask what Tecumseh means (Meteor) and Geronimo (simply Jerome in Spanish and I don't know what it means) would register reactions ranging through pride, amusement and shock if just their surnames were translated into frontier style English. People known to me personally would answer to Joe Eats Dog, Tony Drinks Water, Louis Left Hand, Louis Good Day, Tom Found In the Well, Joe High Mountain and Steve Grows Plenty. Sounds like a bunch of Blackfeet or Assiniboines? They are all Italian Americans and what might have become my own name appears last. In the case of many tribes the individual or personal names of heads of family, including women, were translated (or untranslated such as among Comanches) and became surnames. Some of the translations are the results of the efforts of intelligent interpreters; many others are not. Some are merely jokes and some, as with every single Florida Seminole male of the last century, are nicknames like Billie, Tommie and Willie or, in the fuller sense, Charlie Osceola or Sam Huff. Among the Oklahoma Creeks and Seminoles the surname Harjo is as common as Smith in the rest of America. This is the result of a curious rendition. _Hadjo_ (there is no "r" in Muskogee) is very frequently the last adjective in a formal male Creek or Seminole personal name. Although these people usually say that it means "drunk" or "crazy" it really connotes power or strength. Ignorant Whites created a surname of this adjective and no Creek or Seminole stopped them.

In numerous instances truly prestigious names, when translated, either lost their meaning or became pejorative or ludicrous. Hawk Louse (a slightly fictional but authentic name that now embraces a large family) derives from the honorable concept that the insect accompanying the bird flies at least as high as the bird itself. The descendants of Medicine Bottle are proud of their ancestor although the name itself has disappeared. They seemingly fully accept the English version of this Mdewakanton Santee Sioux leader's personal name. The translation is a disaster. The name in its original form is Jhanjhan Wakan and the meaning is Holy Light. _Jhanjhan_ is something clear or light itself, and in time became the Sioux term for a glass bottle. It is hardly worth the space to explain that most of the "medicine" names found among Indian people are frontier translations for "sacred," "holy," or "mysterious" in a religious sense. The readers of these lines, if they have not already done so, might find it an intellectual or at least amusing exercise to translate their own and some ancestor's names. The reward might come in the form of a Red Cloud (very impressive but Scarlet Sky is a much better rendition) or a Meteor; but also possible is a Moose Dung (a Red Lake Chippewa chief who signed an 1863 treaty), or a Ties His Penis Into a Knot (someone about whose other attributes we know nothing but whose death is memorialized in a Sioux calendar) or a Rabid Dog, a Sioux who apparently had a great religious experience in the 1830's (see plate on p. 195).

In 1960 I was invited to participate in the annual conference of the Catholic missionaries, mostly Jesuits, serving in the Dakotas. I was specifically asked to address the group on aspects of traditional Sioux religion. This was the very

201

early stages of Catholic efforts to understand that
Indian spiritual concepts and practices are
something more than "superstition," that is, that
there was some sort of "religion" associated with
what they vaguely knew, and feared, to be still
popular shamanistic activities. Accordingly, I
arrived with some props including a catlinite pipe,
some of the more common root and dried flower
medicines (that are also "medicine") in use, and the
materials to construct the kind of altar, always on
the floor, that would be considered representative
of shamanism. I was careful to include in my talk
mention of the highly individualistic nature of
shamanism as compared to a priesthood.

A lengthy introduction by the superior of the
host mission contained so many errors and
preconceptions that I was obliged, with respectful
apologies, to correct them before referring to my
notes. I began with some statements contrasting the
religion of the audience of priests and brothers and
the dual religion of many of their parishioners. In
no more than three or four minutes it became evident
that something was very wrong. The listeners,
extremely attentive, were almost to a man obviously
very perplexed. When I paused to request assistance
one of the good fathers said that he thought he was
speaking for everyone in asking me to distinguish
between "proselytizing" and "non-proselytizing"
religions. And these were supposed to be scholars
all. I did explain; and I also very abruptly
altered the tone of that particular address.

The religious figures among tribal peoples do
not as a rule proselytize. Judaism, in this
respect, remains a tribal religion although on some
rare occasions during what is now ancient history
some missionary activity was engaged in by Jews. In
brief, a rabbi in Old Russia, assuming he was given
permission (which is ridiculous), did not go around
trying to convert the Christians, but the local
Orthodox priests would have loved to convert him and
his whole congregation--if the Jews required no
coaxing, that is. Russians were much more
interested in converting people like Aleuts. With
the exception of such revitalization or messianic
movements as preached by Handsome Lake to the New

202

York and Canadian Iroquois after the American
Revolution, the Ghost Dance of the Plains, and the
Peyote religion which is essentially a twentieth
century phenomenon, Indians did not proselytize. In
fact, even when they did, their efforts were
directed only to Indians with priority given to
their fellow tribesmen. With the Plains Ghost Dance
the Messiah was not expected to appear as anyone but
an Indian, tribe unspecified, and only for the
benefit of Indians. The Whites were expected to
disappear while simultaneously the buffalo and other
game would reappear along with dead Indians.

Indians do not produce priests in the
European sense, individuals who were themselves the
products of a body of religious knowledge and
philosophy learned through such institutions as
seminaries, and who were charged with maintaining
the religious orthodoxy of the society. Very much
in contrast with the now ancient film image, which
has been fully ingested by many young Indians,
Indian people did not construct scenes in which the
tribal medicine man whispered into the ear of, or
publicly exhorted, the tribal chief about some
troublesome Whites. The misconception is so old and
so strong among Whites who have no reference but the
history of European clerical influence, I am
surprised that deliberate efforts were not made to
secure the signatures of religious figures on
treaties. Shamans did and still do all sorts of
things like cure the sick, foretell calamities or
good tidings, and cast spells or cast them out, but
they did not, again in violation of one of the more
sacred Hollywood images, conduct any weddings.
Instant tradition, however, has gone so far among
some Indian people that they are now being married
by shamans. Among these are the same shamans who
publicly support militant politicians by praying
over them, tying charms to their hair, and
accompanying them, while displaying pipes, on their
television interviews or in conferences or
demonstrations. This is very much like the role of
a bishop-advisor in relation to a European monarch
or a warring feudal lord. It is hardly
characteristic of Indian society.

The most renowned Indian today is not any one

of the historic leaders but a man called Black Elk. He was not a priest although sometimes referred to as such, but he has given rise, including on campuses, to a cult--the Black Elk or Sacred Hoop cult. Black Elk, an Oglala Sioux (what else?), as a young man fought the U.S. troops during the Ghost Dance hostilities on Pine Ridge Reservation. At the extraordinarily tender age of nine he received an equally extraordinarily detailed religious vision, called his "great vision," promising Sioux solidarity and independence. His vision is repeated in Neihardt's very popular book, replete with some fascinating native line drawings, that made him a cult figure when the publication was unearthed during the sixties.[13] It also made the sacred hoop to which he often alluded a symbol for Indian unity and militancy everywhere, and a symbol for White students who proclaim their adherence to the religion of Black Elk. The Neihardt publication is carried around by some young Indians, and more so by some Whites, like Mao's "Little Red Book." The second book about Black Elk, by Brown, seems not to be as well known.[14] Neither should be read by anyone who is a stranger to Sioux ethnohistory. Neither makes any mention of Black Elk's given Christian name, Nicholas.

Black Elk was respected by Indians and Whites alike. He was one of an impressive number of truly traditional Teton Sioux shamans until his death in 1950 at a very late age. I never met "Nick" Black Elk but I knew, even prior to first reaching South Dakota four years after he died, that he was a long-time Catholic catechist and an officer in Catholic lay organizations. In neither the Neihardt nor Brown books is there the slightest hint that

---

[13] John G. Neihardt, "Black Elk Speaks," William Morrow and Co., New York (1932); second publication by the University of Nebraska Press, Lincoln (1961).

[14] Joseph Epes Brown, "The Sacred Pipe," University of Oklahoma Press, Norman (1953).

in a manner reminiscent of the last and early twentieth centuries when the agents, sometimes under the title "Major," operated like petty tyrants and in violation of every protection contained in this country's Constitution and Bill of Rights. They often administered in the most personalized terms, their benevolence (and there was plenty of that) evident in as public a manner as their viciousness, things like the jailing of dissidents or traditional healers being commonplace. These same agents were sought by Indian people for a great variety of reasons and their successors are still; but fortunately on a much reduced level, partly because they are Indians themselves. I was present when an old Sioux couple would not be dissuaded from seeing a very busy Superintendent. Through an interpreter the old folks explained that he was their only resort in securing the return home of their errant, off-reservation son. He was needed to chop firewood. The poor, harassed official demurring, the father finally shot his outstretched finger at his "Father" declaring in English, "You got the power." There was a time when the son would have been extradited (he was not too far off-reservation) and forced to provide the needed fuel; and this is precisely what the parents expected.

Indians, in terms of their forming relatively insignificant, exotic ethnic and racial entities dependent on an overwhelmingly large, dominant society, are to my knowledge the first such peoples anywhere to be placed on a continuing dole. Loss of land and economy, warfare, confinement and any other factors that can with ease be added to the more tragic experiences of Indian-American relations cannot, in my view, equal the damage done by the dole system under whatever guise. I am not referring merely to rations, which fortunately many tribes escaped, but every form of give-away practiced by federal agencies. Added to this are the gifts in cash and kind distributed by Indian-interest groups, churches, some state and county organizations (like Florida with its "Seminole Indian" auto tags that only require a token payment), and the handouts from uncounted individual members of the larger society.

An unauthorized "treaty council" delegation
of three full bloods who had traveled by car more
than two thousand miles to Washington was broke on
arrival. Our office could offer little more than
coffee and sympathy. However, in a day or two they
picked up money from the BIA Social Services shop,
Travelers Aid and, no surprise to anyone, Senator
Ted Kennedy. These people were not misrepresenting
themselves in their eyes and did not journey to the
capital city for a handout. This kind of scene is
typical of what has long since become Indian demand
and expectation. I must be forgiven for adding that
I found this particular group absolutely delightful,
but their attitude not much different from that of
the truly impoverished man who said in my presence
to his adolescent son, "When the Whiteman wants to
give you something you just take it; that's what I
always do." A close friend who was well employed as
a maintenance man at a BIA school displayed to me an
ordinary wrench that he brought home at lunchtime.
"This is the way I get back some of what they owe
me," he said, meaning for the historic loss of
lands. Given the combination of these rationales
and the antiquity of the dole system no real effort
is needed to understand the depth and the hostility
of Indian dependence. It flourishes in some
extremely subtle yet basic forms. When I naively
asked a friend and co-worker why all of the churches
of the major or national denominations were termed
"missions" he, an Indian and a practicing
Episcopalian, said he could only answer for his
church. He patiently explained that some fellow
members of his congregation periodically brought up
the matter of applying for full church status but
they had always been defeated resoundingly. Without
mission status the church would be required to be
self-supporting. But on that reservation and on
many other reservations, and in communities in
Oklahoma, I am personally aware of very local, truly
native Christian congregations that built their own
churches, often poor structures, are totally
self-supporting, and usually outdo the missions in
fervor and attendance. They are also distinguished
in employing the tribal language and exclusively
native clergy.

In Indian communities real difficulty is
exhibited in distinguishing between special Indian

210

programs and poor peoples programs. Aid to
Dependent Children (ADC) and Old Age Assistance are
among those services often regarded to be extensions
of the reservation system with its now very old BIA
welfare or much newer tribal grants. It should be
emphasized that on most reservations categorical
assistance, especially ADC, constitutes the economic
base, contrary to what Indian cattlemen, farmers and
other entrepreneurs want us all to believe.
Misspending the ADC or old age check is commonplace,
with the latter all too often not by the recipients
and with the former the result is that many kids do
indeed go hungry. There are fortunately, or
unfortunately, traditional kinship obligations.
They can, as has been said, be disfunctional in the
contemporary Indian world.

        I know of no anecdote or incident more
illustrative of the quality of Indian dependence
than the following concerning the commodities or
surplus foods program. This aspect of the dole, now
so much of a reservation fixture, is in the eyes of
many the legitimate child of the old ration system
and, naturally, treaty-based. On Pine Ridge I was
visited on a wintry morning by two men, state
officials, exhibiting grim visages. I still don't
know why they were sicced on me, but that aside they
were investigating the administration of the surplus
foods program. They explained that they could not
find the tribal official in charge, and that every
effort made to communicate with him over a long
period had failed. They had for the same period
received no accounting for these federal foodstuffs
that are handled by the states. One gentleman said,
"We're about ready to throw in the towel," meaning
that they were considering a recommendation that the
program be extinguished on that particular
reservation. In their company, I was able to
quickly locate the man responsible. He was an aged
mixed blood who was in reality conscientious but
not, however, given to submitting written reports or
accounts. He also had little assistance. I left
the state people with him and went about my business.
The following day they assured me that they were
satisfied with the accountability. The distribution
of powdered milk, cornmeal, peanut butter and so
forth would not, therefore, be affected.

Meanwhile, the "moccasin telegraph" being what it was and is, the word had gone out that the program was in jeopardy. Days later, at a crowded district meeting (unemployed Indians are notorious for lengthy and frequent meetings), the matter was quickly brought to the floor, those present being unaware that despite the initial threat all was well. An unimpeachable full blood approaching middle-age, a member of the tribal council and an accomplished traditional singer and dancer who also assisted his shaman father-in-law, was among those most agitated. He arose to ask in English: "What does it mean? Won't we be Indians anymore?"

Numerous Indians and many other Americans of every conceivable socioeconomic level remain convinced of the continuing neglect of Indians by the federal government. This alleged neglect proceeds to the persistent belief in "atrocities," very contemporary atrocities. Very recently I had to explain to an Arab friend that the Wounded Knee tragedy of 1890 has absolutely no connection with the current Navajo-Hopi land dispute, that Indians are not starving in concentration camps, and that they are free to live anywhere. He, a relative newcomer to this country and a Palestinian refugee, is hardly to be blamed for his errors in consideration of the garbage spewed by such fonts of information as the Washington Post. Several years ago that newspaper published an interview with Russell Means, a lionized Sioux militant, detailing his assertions concerning the mass sterilization of Indian women. This oft repeated charge evidently emanates from the actual sterilization in IHS hospitals of some women who had misunderstood or had changed their minds, or perhaps had been strongly persuaded to undergo the surgery, whatever the circumstances a serious matter. On a purely personal basis I telephoned the reporter, who is given to some rotten journalese on ethnic subjects, and asked him if he knew anything about exploding tribal populations and whether he had discussed these monstrous allegations with the IHS. In amused tones he responded negatively to both questions. More maddening is that the Indian Health Service, headquartered in the Washington metropolitan area, did not utter a word in explanation, rebuttal or defense.

The intrepid Paul Harvey, with a radio audience of millions, almost caused me to cut myself shaving during his morning broadcast of July 26, 1985. Speaking of the worsening situation in South Africa, Harvey accused the American public of "selective indignation" to the effect that many more have died in the Mideast and in Northern Ireland than in South Africa, and that Blacks in that country have a much higher standard of living than found on "any Indian reservation." I am being kind to Harvey in stooping to respond that Blacks in that tortured land are, unlike Indians, denied practically every freedom including freedom of expression, their "townships" make most reservations look attractive physically, and Indian incomes would appear staggering to most Blacks. The South African Blacks are also denied guns and are practically devoid of them while Indians, like all other Americans, can if they wish arm themselves to the teeth.

All other often unavoidable historic factors aside, it was the suppression, actual or intended, of Indian culture that formed the prime example of the extent of the institutionalization of Indian dependency, and the usually total acceptance of the power of the dominant society. In these United States nobody has the right to deliberately or consciously deny to anyone the freedom of cultural expression. That is, however, precisely what was done with many Indian societies, the practice extending well into this century. As late as the year preceding the Indian Citizenship Act, Commissioner Charles H. Burke delivered an announcement to all reservation Indians concerning the cultural, including religious, activities regarded by him to be distasteful or actually dangerous. This single page missive, titled A MESSAGE (in Gothic letters) TO ALL INDIANS, is dated February 24, 1923.[1] It is accompanied by a memorandum of February 14 to the Agency Superintendents. I have often cautioned that it is

---

[1] Bureau of Indian Affairs, File No. 10429-22-063, Part 1, Washington.

impossible to avoid the direct or indirect influence of the Teton or Western Sioux in assessing the growth of federal Indian policy. The cited memo provides a perfect example of this phenomenon, the Commissioner explaining that the message is the result of the complaints and recommendations delivered during a conference held with missionaries and others, including Indians, in the Sioux country. That memo, more than all other material included in the official BIA file on the subject of Indian dancing, is distinguished by its misinformation and plain, ordinary ignorance. The very first condemnation refers to the "ituranpi" as a form of "gambling and lottery." The _otuhanpi_ or "give-away," employing a better Sioux orthography, has no relation whatsoever to gambling. It is a means of honoring the living or the deceased, from a graduating senior or a returned serviceman to a memorial observance, by distributing often large quantities of goods and cash. The goods may include the finest artifacts to the furniture and pots and pans, the latter excesses usually being the expressions of a bereaved family. As many Indian observers have lamented, the give-away, or "redistribution of wealth" as it is known anthropologically (a vapid concept), today often involves recipients who have neither the means nor the discipline to reciprocate.

Burke's message to all Indians included the rest of the Plains people, and such diverse societies as Pueblos and Chippewas, Klamaths and Paiutes, and Tlingits of Alaska (who hold "potlatches," very expensive and elaborate give-aways notorious for conspicuous consumption). Many of these societies in 1923 did not know who and where the Sioux were. This bureaucrat turned religious and cultural proselyte also listed among the evils in the message itself dancing for the entertainment of Whites (many bleeding hearts would agree with Burke in this, and then take trips around the world to be entertained by other tribal peoples), dancing to the neglect of stock and gardens, the torturing of bodies (undoubtedly an allusion to the Sun Dance), and the handling of poisonous snakes. The last must have referred to the Hopi Snake Dance, an ancient and harmless religious ceremony. The message's concluding paragraphs state:

> I could issue an order against these useless and harmful performances, but I would much rather have you give them up of your own free will and, therefore, I ask you now in this letter to do so. I urge you to come to an understanding and an agreement with your Superintendent to hold no gatherings in the months when the seed-time, cultivation of crops and the harvest need your attention, and at other times to meet for only a short period and to have no drugs, intoxicants, or gambling, and no dancing that the Superintendent does not approve.
>
> If at the end of one year the reports which I receive show that you are doing as requested, I shall be very glad for I will know that you are making progress in other and more important ways, but if the reports show that you reject this plea, then some other course will have to be taken.

Moving beyond the chutzpa, the ethnocentrism and the unconstitutionality of Burke's message—and the not so subtle threat—other material in the file and still other factors deserve attention here. Burke's directives were generally ignored (but the schools continued to punish Indians for speaking their own languages). On the Plains, dancing and give-aways remained so strong that I do not think even the encouragements of the IRA proponents had any significant effect. The Navajos and the Pueblos were surely untouched, and the eastern Oklahoma traditionalists had always displayed a classic indifference to any such federal pronouncements. The New York Iroquois traditional people could not have cared less. Burke ended up apologizing to the Pueblos and others, saying that he really had not meant people like them. What is much more pertinent

are the letters of support sent to Burke by full
bloods with assurances that they were innocent of
such transgressions but there were bad Indians
everywhere. Some of these people were the parents
and grandparents of professional Indian types who
are regarded to be conservators of tradition; and
dance and sing too. The poor letter writers were
displaying, in addition to whatever else may have
motivated them, their terror of any alteration or
dimunition of the federal-Indian relationship that
might be brought on by their relatives bowing and
weaving to the accompaniment of drum and song. Of
course, we do not know how much of this support
might have been solicited by agency personnel or the
clergy. We do know that not a single tribe, or
individual member of any level of acculturation, or
any non-Indian, issued a formal challenge in court.

The Oglala tribal council secretary looked up
from her desk and asked with some sarcasm: "You
mean now we can do just anything we want?" What
remained unsaid and thinly disguised by her tone was
her apprehension that if the response were positive
her whole tribe's special position would be
lessened. The subject, this being the summer of
1960, was whether self-torture, entirely voluntary,
could be reintroduced into the Sun Dance. The
response, positive, was provided by myself to her
and everyone else in the bulging outer office. I
reminded all present that as of the new climate
engendered by the IRA all official interference with
traditional practices had ceased.

What had prompted the lady's question was the
appearance about two days earlier of a huge, loudly
assertive individual of a strictly Sioux phenotype
but bearing a strictly German surname, who announced
that he was to fulfill a vow to be "pierced" during
the dance. This man who was from another Teton
Sioux tribe had spent many years in California and
was barely known on Pine Ridge Reservation.
However, an accommodating Sun Dance committee and
the hired shaman-director attached a hide rope to
the sacred cottonwood center pole. Then they sat
down to wait and see who would be arrested first.
Piercing of the flesh, a basic feature of the old
Sun Dance, had not been associated with that

216

ceremony on any Sioux reservation since 1883. That
was two years after the official federal banning of
the Sun Dance, again the result of White fear and
perceptions of Sioux culture. Another, somewhat
practical, consideration was that such gatherings
involved thousands, entirely too many Indians in one
place, many of them veterans of the 1876-77 war.
The ban was only half-heartedly extended or not at
all to such others as the Cheyennes and Arapahoes,
and the Utes and Northern Shoshones, who formed much
smaller tribes and who rarely saw in their Sun
Dances any form of torture besides thirst, hunger
and exhaustion.

        By the end of the day before the ceremony a
lot of people, including the shaman who was to
pierce the visitor, became nervous enough to ask the
Agency Superintendent for permission to revive this
rite. I don't know what he said to them but they
came away apparently satisfied. I do know that the
agency boss was even more nervous than they. He
telephoned me to convey that he wanted an official
witness, besides himself, to this barbarism. As the
first song began he made remarks about "these
people" having to understand that "they need to
conform." I tried to reassure him by relating that
my wife and I had witnessed very deep piercing of
the shoulders at a Turtle Mountain Plains Ojibwa
ceremony two months previous, adding that the only
ones who had ever bothered this very small full
blood element were some highly offended, traditional
Catholic Metis. Several years later I learned from
the excellent man, a totally acculturated Cherokee
who for a long time headed the BIA Law and Order
office, that the Superintendent had in a perfect
panic telephoned him at home in the wee hours of the
morning of the piercing. He was still laughing and
related that he had laughed over the phone at the
Superintendent, telling him that in such matters
Indians "could do as they damned pleased."

        The big Sioux, one of only several dancers,
had only to back away from the center pole for the
tiny pin, attached to the rope and barely inserted
beneath the skin of one breast, to practically fall
out of its own weight. But neither the Father nor
the Grandfather had anyone shackled, and the Father

217

in fact was busy snapping photos. The following year, again alone, the dancer was very deeply pierced in one breast and considerable effort was needed to break free. This, in 1961, marked the true beginning of the reintroduction of piercing. By the late 1960's more Sioux (and Whites and other Indians or people who said they were) than in the pre and early reservation days were swinging from Sun Dance poles. Although apparently lessening of late, for a time the ability to display the resulting ceremonial scars was the supreme affirmation of Indianness in general and Siouxishness in particular. A similar phenomenon is found in powwowism throughout the country, the attempts to emulate the Sioux often resulting in gaudy but sterile pan-Indian shams. In this new nativism context, deserving of special emphasis is that despite the history sketched above Indian people assert that without the continuation of their peculiar political status they will lose their traditions and identity. It is particularly disturbing to hear these same assertions made by paper tribes that have little or nothing in the way of authentic tradition, but do indeed have a "government to government" relationship, and often without a viable reservation-based community. Maybe they think that Congress will revive the old culture for them and simultaneously make the reservation bloom.

"Back to the rez!" has become a slogan for many young Indian people, including those who have been decently employed, who decide to return to whatever aspects of the dole or whatever psychological supports that are to be found. Others, of course, simply want a vacation from the urban climate. Many were never prepared to leave the reservations and never will be as long as present reservation conditions prevail. There are still others who journey great distances to return to reservations to receive valuable benefits. A close friend once provided transportation for me from Chicago to South Dakota. In addition to myself and the other sardines in his car was a young, very pregnant woman who had been well established in the Chicago area. She was returning to Rosebud Reservation, also our driver's home, to have her baby in the IHS hospital absolutely free of any cost. A colleague in the BIA central office, when told about this, retorted, "They're always trying to take the reservation with them," actually referring to Indians who demand such services in the cities in which they reside.

In my estimation many tribes, surely most of those of the Plains, would have been quickly reduced to a pariah existence, and would have quickly lost their identity and populations, if reservations and federal protection had not been made available to them. With many other tribal groups and whole culture areas, these observations I do not think apply on the basis of aboriginal and historic socioeconomic factors. The Great Basin peoples, small, scattered hunter-gatherer groups, were not greatly in need of reservations. They were, in fact, adapting to ranch work and the life of mining settlements, in family groups, prior to reservations being created for them, mostly by Executive Order in this century. There is little available in the literature regarding Basin acculturation, but I am much impressed with the numbers of now very aged Paiutes and Western Shoshones who never lived on a reservation but remain very tribal in identity. Their English is usually colloquial, and they have retained their own languages. I have seen older Northern Paiutes scoff when young, nativistic relatives demanded interpreters for them at public meetings. It has been emphasized that the Oklahoma tribes have by no means disappeared along with their reservation status and almost all their land.

Reservations were a mistake in most of California. Some of these "rancherias" have never been occupied to any meaningful extent. I am convinced that the establishment of reservations for the Florida Seminoles was a grave error, and equally convinced that it is very fortunate that the Spaniards, Mexicans and Americans successively recognized the land titles of the Pueblos of the Rio Grande, Zuni, and Hopi. If I find it fortunate that such diverse entities as the Iroquois, Plateau tribes, and Southwest peoples like Apaches and Navajos, and Pimas and Papagos, were provided lands, protection and attention I also remain convinced

that the reservation system almost everywhere is
bankrupt. Some reservations are no longer places
fit for anyone to live; raising children on them is
unthinkable. Indian people evidently agree. In
most tribal situations half or more of the
membership has left the reservation. There are,
however, some exceptions. Only very few of the
members of the Seminole Tribe of Florida do not
reside in their compact reservation settlements
where the offspring of and participants in serial
marriages see one another on a daily basis--a
situation repeated in numerous Indian communities.

    "You know how hard it is <u>on the outside</u>.
They just can't live and they have to pay for
<u>everything</u>." The gentle old lady was speaking of
her children who had tried life in California. She
extended her remarks while kindly cooking for me,
and emitted a cry of grief when I told her what I
paid for rent in suburban Maryland. Her attitude is
to be compared with that of her cousin, a little
older and perhaps even more traditional, who sadly
but firmly preached to her numerous grandchildren to
leave as quickly as possible to escape what she
considered a dangerous atmosphere. Old people from
societies as distant culturally and geographically
as the Sioux are from the Florida Seminoles and both
from San Carlos Apaches seem almost unanimous in
saying that things on their respective reservations
are truly bad. They have become terrified of the
young, the same young who regard themselves to be
the protectors of the old culture and the old
people. A colleague extremely familiar with the
last-named reservation society related detailed
accounts of such situations as old Apache folks with
their purchases of groceries having to be escorted
home from the stores by police or trusted
relatives. (With the neighboring White Mountain
Apaches things are evidently much healthier in every
respect). All of this kind of behavior was surely
unknown in pre and early reservation days.
Nevertheless, "off the reservation" or "on the
outside" are the kinds of phrases that persist in
being equally terrifying to those who might consider
leaving or have tried with unhappy results.
Simultaneously, and adding to the fear experienced
by Indian people, federal agencies have for some

time been reducing Indian programing. The made-work activities, including thôse that created the proverbial leaf rakers and an army of "aides" in social and educational services, have virtually disappeared.

The Indian Health Service considered limiting hospital care to one-quarter blood and great was the ensuing consternation. Instead of retreating to the old blood quantum criterion, no one seemed to have the courage to propose that those who can afford to pay do so. Policy makers who think along blood quantum lines are apparently unaware of the existence of rich full bloods and destitute individuals on the books as less than one-quarter blood. However, I have seen many, poor, elderly full bloods patiently occupying benches in the hospital while whole families of affluent ranchers who looked and were essentially White were being treated, as Indians, without charge. But even in the most remote areas, where the only hospital facilities are those provided by the IHS, Whites, Blacks and Hispanics, including federal employees, cannot utilize the facilities except in emergencies. This is nonsense. Such hospitals should serve the entire local, rural populace, the poor of any ethnic or racial derivation treated accordingly as they are elsewhere in American society. "Indian" health and sanitation programs should be of a local community service nature in the establishment of such facilities as potable water, clinics and, above all, education and assistance in the basics of disease and trauma prevention.

The forms of paranoia peculiar to the reservation subculture are all related to the pervasive hostile dependency. I have long been convinced that if there must be Indian dependency, and there will be for who knows how long, it would be much healthier and in the long run more productive for as much of that dependency as possible to be transferred to the tribe--assuming the existence of a viable tribal organization and a viable tribe. The tribes say in unison that they can do it themselves, and then scream in even greater unity, no matter how much money they may have, if the federal government is suspected of

*withdrawing or reducing funding. The government
doesn't know how to honestly and humanely identify,
qualify, and appropriately limit its business with
Indians, although unquestionably many politicians
and executives would love to do so. Meanwhile,
those tribes that have assumed by contract the
operation of programs remain secure in the knowledge
that "retrocession" is always an option. This means
that if they go under, like throwing the money in
every direction, Washington will reassume the burden
or in some other way bail them out. As a result of
the confusion and lack of policy direction, the
operations of many tribal and agency offices have
for some time been overlapping. In some instances
the former have outdistanced the latter.*

*Unless and until the federal personnel remove
their patronizing selves from the scene, and the
label "Indian" is removed from all program packages
that are not geared to community needs that are
peculiarly Indian, or peculiarly local, only
retrogression and waste will continue to be
evident. The terms "agency," "Agency Superintentent"
and the like must simply disappear along with the
administered reservation system. It will be noted
that I have not said a word about tribal land and
other physical and natural resources.*

*One of the few Indians with whom I have
discussed this philosophy was the late Carl Thorpe,
the well liked and so well spoken son of the
Potawatomi-Sac and Fox athlete Jim Thorpe of Olympic
fame. Carl not only totally accepted the view
outlined above (and it can be only outlined in this
book), but told me that he had said identical things
to the small task force on policy with which he was
then serving. But what does the BIA periodically
threaten? To abolish the area offices and
strengthen the agencies. I cannot think of a more
perverse approach. What is needed are area or
regional offices staffed with very highly trained,
traveling (meaning not in reservation residence)
specialists available to encourage and assist the
tribes and local communities. What is also needed
is that these people be recruited without such a
damnable obstacle as Indian preference. What would
result, incidently, would be a relatively small*

"Office of Indian Tribal Programing" within the Department of the Interior (who but someone like me has affairs with Indians?). Its principal function would be that of assisting the tribes, within designated development areas, in the "highest and best use" (an old BIA expression) of land, location, timber, water, grass, minerals and human resources like cultural heritage. Federal funding would surely be needed in most tribal situations, but the present budget is swelled by the perpetuation of the BIA school system.

Concerning Bureau education, I will not dwell on this half-dead dinosaur. The states should assume the responsibility for all grade and high school education, whether or not a given enrollment is 100 percent Indian and sociologically full blood at that. Nobody is going to accuse me of insensitivity concerning full blood kids who may be surrounded by non-Indians. My first grade school, where I was too young to appreciate much in the way of such distinctions, was 95 percent Jewish; my second, where I became very much aware, was 90 percent Irish as were the high school and college I attended. As said earlier, most reservation children are in public school systems. For those now in "Indian" schools who might be faced with the changes attendant in "White Bull Day School" (or high school) to "Frederickton Public School," I sincerely believe that the very crisis nature of such changes can be expected to provoke intense interest on the part of many parents and whole communities in education itself. It can be very advantageous to burn a building.

The tribal community colleges, and those with full accreditation, all viewed with great suspicion by myself and other observers of the Indian scene, are properly the business of the tribes. They would be free, as they are presently, to seek funding from any and all possible sources. As to BIA off-reservation boarding schools, including Haskell, abolishment of them is long overdue. There are many who can be expected to deliver heart-rending moans to the effect that such schools cater primarily to those from isolated areas. They know only too well that ' for a long period these schools have

223

*essentially been havens for the victims of often
shocking home situations and for others who have
been in trouble with the law. In Florida a large
number of teen-age boys was remanded to my custody
by county juvenile court judges who were very
familiar with the BIA system. They were always
assured that the boys would be placed in Oklahoma
boarding schools. A White woman employed for some
years with BIA education said: "A lot of Indian
kids would be in jail if it were not for our
schools." None of these rationales will do.
Concerning isolation factors, what happens to the
children of modern, White cowboys, neighbors of
equally isolated Indians, who live nowhere near a
school?*

*There is an immediate, crying need for
omnibus legislation to finally define a tribe, its
membership, and the relationships of such entities
and individuals to the federal government and the
states. No definition of Indianness, including
Alaskan peoples, should in the legal sense extend
beyond that of formal, official enrollment with a
tribe fully recognized by Congress. No tribe
unwilling to construct and maintain such roll, given
whatever assistance is necessary, should be
conducting business as a recognized Indian political
organization if a government to government
relationship persists. (I didn't say "sovereignty"
and I believe the distinction can be made).*

*I hope that such legislation would provide
for the reservation system and the term itself to be
replaced by the establishment of "Indian Tribal
Development Areas." Such areas would be designated
by the Secretary of the Interior, and recognized by
Congress, only given the existence of a viable
tribal community with lands at least sufficient for
decent residential purposes. Such sites, as
discussed previously, could be formed of existing
tribal holdings, and allotments, and available
federal acreage near such holdings that in many
instances should have long since been restored to
the tribes. Lands specifically designated for
inclusion in tribal development areas should remain
inalienable along with all other tribal lands
presently recognized as such. Federal Indian funds*

from whatever agency should be limited, when needed, to contracting with the tribes for programing within such development areas. However, the tribes should be required to use their own funds to support as many social and economic projects as possible, from remedial reading to higher education, from land development to manufacturing and, yes, from tourism to the realistic marketing of crafts--and ethnohistorical studies that I hope are as free as possible of a climate of chauvinism. You can't have all this and per capita payments in the bargain.

The paper tribes, those without significant holdings and needy, tribal communities, should be ignored. Urban Indian organizations should not receive, as my Choctaw friend put it, a dime; there will never be enough money to do a truly proper job with the more isolated, less acculturated, really poor communities. Why the tribal leaders have permitted federal aid to the urbanites is beyond me. And in this connection it cannot be too strongly emphasized that every precaution would have to be taken to prevent established urban Indians from going back to the rez and grabbing every job that might be generated. One of the primary purposes in so defining and so enhancing the local, rural Indian community is to prepare many people for life elsewhere--and elsewhere in most instances means the metropolis. How many other Americans in isolated or economically depressed areas need much the same kind of attention?

Some time after I retired I requested an appointment with the very new and extremely busy Assistant Secretary for Indian Affairs, Ross O. Swimmer. I wanted to air the concept and term Tribal Development Area, as a substitute for reservation, with Mr. Swimmer but was able to meet with him for precisely three minutes; the time limitation was my suggestion given his schedule. His immediate reaction was that the abandonment of the term "reservation" would constitute a treaty violation and would be severely resisted by the tribes. Well, everything is resisted by the tribes but further largesse and support of sovereignty. His own tribe, the Cherokee Nation of Oklahoma as earlier identified, has absolutely nothing left by

way of treaty rights and no reservation status. Mr.
Swimmer, however, has been in the forefront among
Indian leaders in establishing what can readily be
called tribal development areas on existing tribal
lands. What has to be done to overcome the
blinding, overwhelming force inherent in words like
"treaty" and "reservation?"

    I have not forgotten the matter of
jurisdiction. Concerning recognized or assumed
hunting and fishing treaty rights, and tribal civil
and criminal jurisdiction, those exhausting,
counterproductive extensions of the artificiality
known as tribal sovereignty, I have said most of my
piece. It should come as no surprise that I fully
support that omnibus legislation provide, without
qualification, for full state jurisdiction to be
extended to every square foot of Indian lands and
all Indian waters. Many tribes are in a position to
support special police, judicial and rehabilitation
programs in cooperation with the states and their
subdivisions. The states, when they start howling
as some will surely do, ought to be reminded that
they have been providing services for poor Whites
and Hispanics, especially in the Southwest that
contains the larger tribes with resident
memberships, who have never had enough land or
income to pay anything significant in taxes.

    In 1961, when most reservation atmospheres
were quite bad enough given the extent of the loss
of cultural identity and the omnipresence of
virtually every sociopsychological disease, the
anthropologist Bernard James had an article
published that, to my understanding, was not well
received by his peers. About the situation at Lac
Court Oreilles, a northern Wisconsin Chippewa
reservation that I visited just briefly enough to be
appalled, James concluded:

        Policy implications for the
    conduct of American reservations flow
    from the interpretation of the Indian
    subculture I have advanced. I cannot
    explore these here. But if it is
    correct to conclude that native
    cultures have been replaced by reserva-

226

tion subcultures of a "poor-White" type, and an essential functional requirement for their existence, as we know them, is an extreme socio-economic status differential, prescriptions that attempt to perpetuate this "Indian way of life" may be both unwise and inhumane.[2]

Those Indian societies that have retained a healthy, useful body of tradition need no assistance from anyone else in perpetuating such cultural concepts and practices for as long as they so desire. Those very numerous Indian people who have absolutely nothing but a reservation subculture are enduring a pathetic, dangerous existence. It is indeed "unwise and inhumane" for the guilt-ridden romanticists in the dominant society, and Indian tribal and intertribal leadership, to demand the continued subsidization of this existence.

---

[2] *Bernard J. James, "Socio-Psychological Dimensions of Ojibwa Acculturation," in the* American Anthropologist*, Vol. 63, No. 4 (August 1961), p. 744.*

EPILOGUE

For seven days in November 1972, perhaps five hundred Indians, mostly members of the American Indian Movement, occupied the Bureau of Indian Affairs building on Constitution Avenue in Washington. What was announced as a peaceful effort to demonstrate Indian grievances about "broken treaties" and "broken promises" ended in riotous disorder.

William L. Claiborne and Grayson Mitchell began their article of November 9th in the Washington Post *as follows:*

> *Claiming proudly that they have "changed the course of history," the last of hundreds of rebellious American Indians vacated the Bureau of Indian Affairs building last night, leaving behind widespread destruction.*
>
> *"For all practical purposes we have destroyed the BIA," declared Dennis Banks, national field director of the American Indian Movement, and a leader of the "Trail of Broken Treaties" caravan whose members occupied the buildings [sic] for seven days.*

Practically every original painting in the building, the work of Indian artists, was vandalized or stolen, as was a vast quantity of artifacts ranging from Navajo rugs and Pueblo pottery to Eskimo stone carvings. Windows, bookcases and restrooms were smashed to virtual nothingness and many important files were removed or destroyed. The place was a shambles.

With few exceptions, the leaders were urban residents as were most of the occupiers of the building. Most were very young. Many were Canadian Iroquois, and a large contingent was comprised of triracial people from North Carolina. There was not a single tribal chairman, and only one member of a tribal council, in the entire group.

A sergeant of the police precinct that encompassed the BIA headquarters spoke of the "uprising in the Indian building." (Almost a year earlier about 26 militants, who were encouraged by some BIA Indian appointees, staged an ugly incident in the same building and were arrested. The charges were dropped by the U.S. Attorney's office because they were "Indians visiting in a building for Indians"). A friend of mine, shortly after the AIM people left, remarked on the telephone that "at least they have a better right to it than the _mulignand_ (a Neapolitan term for eggplant employed by many Italian Americans in reference to Blacks)."

Some of the leaders obliged news cameramen by posing with commercial archery equipment removed from one of the offices. From the resulting photos it was obvious that they neither knew how to grip the bows nor nock the arrows. These same AIM leaders have on occasion boasted that they surely know how to use guns. At the "inauguration" of one of the national figures, Dennis Banks in fact, this worthy was escorted into the meeting place by flanking guards, each armed with a shotgun to the great delight of the media.

The "tribal leaders," as they were dubbed by local television, were paid 66,700 dollars to get out of town. These funds, earmarked by federal agencies for the relief of poverty-stricken reservation Indians, were turned over to the leadership for that announced purpose by a greatly relieved Nixon administration. The occupiers had exhibited the decency to vacate the building immediately prior to Election Day. The chiefs disappeared after some television interviews, leaving their young, broke, longhaired followers all over the downtown area. Some of these proceeded to wreck the YMCA building where they had been given lodging.

Such irresponsible behavior on the part of politicians, bureaucrats and media manipulators encouraged the more militant Indians, and mindless non-Indian supporters, to take up guns in many places in the country. The 72 day armed occupation of Wounded Knee in 1973 is internationally known but was very poorly reported. Not until after that debacle was it recognized that the site was much more than a "hamlet" occupied by storekeepers. It was the center of a very poor full blood community of about five hundred, among them aged traditionalists who were driven from their homes. These included a venerable officer of the Native American Church, a Southern Ponca married to an Oglala Sioux woman. The news media remained singularly unaware of the old couple's eviction and the death of the gentleman of a heart attack shortly thereafter. The harm done to the susceptible younger Sioux who supported either the constituted tribal government or the militants, some of whom are still engaged in a vendetta, is not so easily weighed.

Those with guns, who have been so successful in further tarnishing the all too often poor local Indian image, have killed cattle, illegally, so that they indeed can have something to eat (at Wounded Knee some White hostages had to show them how to butcher). They have descended on the tribal centers of Minnesota's Red Lake Chippewa Band and the Seminole Nation of Oklahoma, and with the latter in 1983 effectively brought an end to tribal government for three or four years. They have threatened a number of other tribes and communities and are responsible for the destruction of public and private property in upstate New York and elsewhere. Local Indians and Whites, who might be termed vigilantes, have responded in kind. As a consequence an increasingly aroused public, but still comprised primarily of persons and organizations near or within Indian country, is questioning, usually in a climate of anger and ignorance, the continuation of the special position of Indians. This reassessment should not and cannot be made by them or those who think Indians ought to be given guns, or segregated schools, or treaty rights, or sovereignty or any other damaged goods they would demand be denied to the rest of the citizenry.